Studying and working in Germany

A student guide

Peter James
and David Kaufman

Manchester University Press
Manchester and New York

Distributed exclusively in the USA by Palgrave

Published by Manchester University Press
Oxford Road, Manchester M13 9NR, UK
and Room 400, 175 Fifth Avenue, New York, NY 10010, USA
www.manchesteruniversitypress.co.uk

Distributed exclusively in the USA by
Palgrave, 175 Fifth Avenue, New York, NY 10010, USA

Distributed exclusively in Canada by
UBC Press, University of British Columbia, 2029 West Mall,
Vancouver, BC, Canada V6T 1Z2

British Library Cataloguing-in-Publication Data
A catalogue record for this book is available from the British Library

Library of Congress Cataloging-in-Publication Data applied for

ISBN 0 7190 5499 0 *hardback*
      0 7190 5500 8 *paperback*

First published 2002

10 09 08 07 06 05 04 03 02   10 9 8 7 6 5 4 3 2 1

Typeset in Ehrhardt and News Gothic
by Koinonia, Manchester
Printed in Great Britain
by Biddles Ltd, Guildford and King's Lynn

Contents

Acknowledgements

The authors wish to record their thanks to the German Academic Exchange Service, and to Dr Sebastian Fohrbeck in particular, for providing invaluable information on studying and living in Germany. The authors are also grateful to their colleagues in German higher education institutions, as well as to the numerous people in student foreign offices in Germany for their help and cooperation in providing information which was unobtainable elsewhere. They are also indebted to several generations of their own students who wrote placement reports following a stay in Germany and who thus assisted them in updating and expanding their knowledge in the area of German placements generally.

A note on German spelling

In this guide we are following the rules for German orthography which were laid down in the 1998 spelling reform, which seeks to remove anomalies and to make German spelling and punctuation easier to learn. There has been a great deal of controversy regarding the reform and much resistance to it among the population. Despite this, most German publishers have accepted the inevitable and the new rules are now being implemented in nearly all the newspapers (the *Frankfurter Allgemeine Zeitung* reverted to the old orthography in August 2000) and are being taught in German schools. The old spellings may be used in parallel with the old ones, but by the year 2005 they will be regarded as obsolete. Clearly, older people are unlikely to alter the way in which they write, but the generation now growing up will be using only the new system, and so we too are bowing to the inevitable and making use of the new rules in so far as they affect any of the spelling in this guide.

The new rules intend to rationalise spelling, the use of small and capital letters and of *scharfes s (ß)*, which as far as we can see is the only new rule we need to implement here. The reform as it applies to *scharfes s* is probably the most controversial of the changes, since it has a dramatic effect on the way a page of print looks. The rules were always felt to be excessively complex by English students of German (and probably by many other nationalities as well) and it has to be said that the new rule – note the singular – makes it very easy indeed. The only criticism as far as this part of the reform is concerned is that it does not go far enough: one school of thought is that given there were to be changes made, why not simply abolish *scharfes s* altogether, as has been done in Switzerland?

In case you are not aware of the changes as they apply to the use of *scharfes s* we note them here. *Scharfes s* now occurs only after a long vowel. So *Gruß* (greeting) and *schließen* (to close) retain their old spelling, but *daß* > *dass*, *mußte* > *musste*. We have adopted the reformed spelling, so that we write *Schloss* (castle), not *Schloß*. However, where *scharfes s* is part of someone's name, we have retained that spelling, even if it is not preceded by a long vowel.

Introduction

This guide is aimed at all Anglophone students who are going to study or work in Germany. Its purpose is to offer encouragement and assistance to students who are about to embark on a German placement so that they will be able to derive the maximum benefit from their stay in Germany. Consequently, one of its prime aims is to help students from other countries find their way around the German higher education system. While the guide is likely to be of particular use to students of modern languages undertaking a placement at a German university, the information is not restricted to language courses, and practical advice is also offered to any young people who do not intend studying full-time but nevertheless wish to spend a limited period of residence working in Germany, for example, as a language assistant or on a work placement.

The German system is different in various respects, and we are confident that British, American and other students in the English-speaking world will find the practical advice and tips given here valuable. The book aims to help to prepare students for their placement and guide them through the paperwork involved. We offer practical hints to students who might otherwise be intimidated by the thought of having to fend for themselves in an unfamiliar system. Detailed information is also presented on many institutions of higher education in various parts of the Federal Republic.

Chapter 1 provides some background information and looks at the implications of Germany's federal structure, especially for the education system. The second chapter addresses the practicalities of what you need to do before you leave, including matters such as insurance, documentation, accommodation and the like. Chapter 3 offers students assistance with the type of form they will have to complete. In Chapter 4 some guidance is given on the use of the Internet as a tool for the preliminary research of project topics and as a general source of information. Chapter 5 concentrates on registration and enrolment procedures when you arrive at your placement centre. The alternative to full-time study – the question of working in Germany – is dealt with in Chapter 6, and the seventh chapter prepares students for the important issue of leaving Germany and getting ready to return to a study programme at home. The final chapter of the guide provides detailed information on some seventy institutions of higher education across Germany.

In the appendices we include detailed instructions on how to fill in application forms for a place at a German university and for university accommodation, a sample *curriculum vitae*, and a list of useful addresses.

Undertaking a lengthy placement in another country can seem a daunting task. It will, however, be that much easier if you adopt a positive attitude. Those who view the glass as being half full rather than half empty and follow the simple guidelines proposed here will certainly be well on the way to getting the best out of their German placement. With some careful preparation and a common-sense approach, you should have both a profitable and an enjoyable stay.

We hope that this guide will perhaps help current and future generations of students to benefit from a successful and enjoyable placement, and to improve their knowledge and understanding of Germany, its language, people and culture.

1
Background

1.1 Germany's federal structure

Germany has a long tradition of federalism, stretching all the way back to 1871, when the nation state of Germany was first formed. The German term *Föderalismus*, derived from the Latin *foedus*, meaning federation or alliance, implies a type of state organisation in which there is devolution of power from the centre to the constituent parts or regions, in Germany's case the federal states. In political terms this means a decentralised system, where real power-sharing exists, divided between the central government in Berlin and several regional ones.

The Federal Republic's present federalist, or decentralised, structure influences many aspects of present-day German life, not only the political framework. These include the school and higher education systems. The country consists of sixteen federal states (*Bundesländer*, see Figure 1.1). Each federal state, or (*Bundes*)*land*, has its own capital and a degree of autonomy in certain areas, notably in the fields of education, policing, culture (including broadcasting) and health. Since each of these sixteen federal states displays individual differences owing to its own cultural traditions and regional idiosyncrasies, it will be helpful for you to know in which state, or *Land*, you are going to study or work and to find out something about that area.

This guide deals with Germany, since that is the country visited by the majority of students on courses related to German Studies. If you are planning a visit to Austria or German-speaking Switzerland, both of which also have a federal structure, you will find contact addresses in an appendix at the back of the book. Wherever you go, the same principle applies: find out as much as you can about the specific region you are going to visit. Many places are twinned with cities and towns in Germany,

Fig. 1.1 Map of German Länder

and, to a lesser extent, in Austria and Switzerland. This can be an important first step in finding out something about your future destination, its location in a wider context, and the types of industry you will find there. It will be advantageous to make use of any links which already exist.

If you are interested in the business and economic environment of Germany, it is likely to be important to understand the local circumstances which obtain in the particular region or *Bundesland* where your placement will take place. In the business world this might affect, to give just one example, the demand for certain products, and therefore a company's sales and marketing strategy. Students who have to research or write a project may well find that there is a relevant topic in one region which may not be appropriate elsewhere. It would be useful to have that sort of information in advance.

In this respect you will find that the political, economic, social and cultural situation often varies from one federal state to the next, and, in some cases, even within a federal state. Such differences appear to be even more substantial when it comes to comparisons between the north and south of Germany, and certainly between east and west. It is likely that you will still encounter the biggest differences in German life between territories which used to belong to the former GDR (German Democratic Republic – *Deutsche Demokratische Republik, DDR*) and those in the old FRG (Federal Republic of Germany – *Bundesrepublik Deutschland, BRD*). Consequently you cannot accurately make generalisations which are valid for the whole of Germany. Regional variation and local customs play a decisive role and will affect practical considerations for students in German higher education too. To give just one example, semester dates may well vary from one federal state to another, and also from one type of institution to another.

So it is of fundamental importance to understand that Germany is organised along decentralised, federal lines. It pays to be aware of the wider context of your placement centre, including the federal state – and even the region within that state – in which it is situated.

1.2 The education system and the *Länder*

Article 7 of the German Basic Law (*Grundgesetz*) gives the state the responsibility for the organisation and supervision of education. This includes primary and secondary schooling, plus the tertiary sector, including further education and parts of vocational training.

Although the German word *Kindergarten*, and the concept it represents, has been taken over by many countries, it does not formally constitute a part of the German state education system. This means that attending a kindergarten, whilst highly recommended for the benefits it brings, is voluntary and linked to a financial contribution. Despite the fact that in Germany today all children between the ages of three and six (the age at which compulsory schooling starts) have the right to go to a kindergarten, only around 70 per cent do so.

The first four years (age 6–10) of compulsory schooling are spent at primary school (*Grundschule*). An important characteristic of the German school system is the three-tier secondary system, whereby pupils normally attend one of three types of school, based on a combination of the parents' wishes and the teachers' assessment of the pupil during the last two years of primary education. It is also possible to delay the choice of secondary school for two years during an orientation stage (*Orientierungsstufe*), and in most federal states, though not all, pupils can attend a comprehensive school (*Gesamtschule*). Most German secondary school children attend either a *Hauptschule* (age 10–15/16), a *Realschule* (age 10–16) or a *Gymnasium* (age 10–19). Anyone who fails to attain the standard set has to repeat the school year (*sitzenbleiben*), which of course lengthens the time spent at school.

In terms of intellectual level and predicted academic achievement, the *Hauptschule* is at the lowest level, leading simply to the general school leaving certificate (*Hauptschulabschluss*), the *Realschule* leads to its own leaving certificate, the *Realschulabschluss*, sometimes still referred to as the *Mittlere Reife* examination (the approximate equivalent of GCSE in Britain), and the *Gymnasium*, often translated into English as grammar school, leads to the *Abitur* examination, which opens the door to higher education (see 1.2.1). In the 1960s around two thirds of German secondary pupils attended the *Hauptschule*, with less than one fifth going to the *Gymnasium*, but in recent years the situation has changed: nowadays more German pupils attend a *Gymnasium* (around 35 per cent) than a *Hauptschule* (around 25 per cent), with around 40 per cent at the *Realschule*. The above is no more than an outline, in general terms, of the German school system, which can, and does, vary from one *Bundesland* to the next.

Some form of education is compulsory from the age of six until eighteen, but the last two years of this may include education/training via attendance at a part-time vocational school (*Berufsschule*). Vocational training enjoys a long tradition in Germany, stretching back to the thirteenth century. The current dual system (*das duale System*) usually combines an initial on-the-job apprenticeship in a firm with attendance at a vocational school on a day-release basis – normally one or two days per week. This means that a German pupil may not leave school at the age of fifteen or sixteen with few or no qualifications and never attend an educational establishment again. While there have been some recent calls in Germany for reforming this system of vocational training, it has frequently been the object of admiration from abroad.

For those who wish to make up for any academic qualifications they missed at school, including the *Abitur*, a variety of part-time evening classes and full-time colleges of adult and further education colleges exist. This alternative route to higher education is known in German as

Table 1 School holidays for summer 2000 in the German federal states

Baden-Württemberg	27 July–9 September
Bayern	27 July–11 September
Berlin	20 July–2 September
Brandenburg	20 July–2 September
Bremen	13 July–26 August
Hamburg	20 July–30 August
Hessen	23 June–4 August
Mecklenburg-Vorpommern	20 July–30 August
Niedersachsen	13 July–23 August
Nordrhein-Westfalen	29 June–12 August
Rheinland-Pfalz	23 June–4 August
Saarland	22 June–2 August
Sachsen	13 July–23 August
Sachsen-Anhalt	13 July–23 August
Schleswig-Holstein	20 July–2 September
Thüringen	13 July–23 August

Source: *So machen 2000 die Schulkinder in Deutschland Ferien (ADAC München)*

der zweite Bildungsweg – the second education route.

A fundamental feature of German schooling and higher education (HE) is that each *Land* possesses cultural sovereignty (*Kulturhoheit*), making it responsible for its own system; the detailed regulations and curricula are therefore laid down (in tablets of stone usually!) by the education ministries situated in the *Land* capitals, e.g. Stuttgart, Munich, Düsseldorf, etc. Owing to cultural sovereignty in the federal system, each of the sixteen *Länder* fixes its own dates for the school holidays. This applies throughout the year, but is most noticeable in the case of the summer holidays, where staggering the holidays is a deliberate attempt to alleviate congestion on the German motorways. Table 1, which gives the actual summer holiday dates for each federal state for the year 2000, serves to illustrate the point.

1.2.1 Conditions at German universities

The *Abitur*, or *Allgemeine Hochschulreife*, is the school-leaving certificate which entitles a German student to enter higher education. *Anyone* who attains this is entitled to study at a German institution of higher education. A substantial increase in the number of pupils now attending the grammar school (*Gymnasium*), which leads to the *Abitur* and the right to study, has led to serious overcrowding in some German universities. Numbers have gone through the roof: from around 300,000 students (in West Germany) in 1960 the figure shot up to over 1.8 million (in the new united Germany) by 1994, with an estimated figure of close to two million students in the year 2000. While this does not mean that you will automatically be taught in huge groups under a system of mass education – some institutions still have a smaller, more personal atmosphere – you should be prepared for the fact that some German lecture theatres may be extremely crowded. Crowded or not, there are – as yet – no tuition fees in German higher education.

1.2.2 Age profiles

There are various routes leading to higher education (HE). Even German students who have taken the standard route via a nine-year course at a grammar school (*Gymnasium*) are likely to be at least twenty or twenty-one when they start their studies, and it is not particularly unusual in Germany for people to start studying in their mid-twenties, having done an apprenticeship first. Male students might have spent approximately nine months in the army (conscription), or slightly longer if they have opted for the alternative to military service (*Ersatzdienst*), which involves service in the community. It is, however, sometimes possible to postpone national service until after completion of a university course.

The average age at which German students graduate is twenty-eight. Some are over thirty when they leave HE. This means that foreign students studying in Germany should be prepared for the fact that their German counterparts may well be older than they are. To take the example of Great Britain, British undergraduates, most of whom are aged between eighteen and twenty-one or twenty-two, are often surprised to meet German students who are aged twenty-five or twenty-six on average, and in some cases twenty-nine or thirty. Conversely, many German employers are reluctant to accept that British students in their early twenties are actually fully qualified graduates, since this is impossible under the German system.

1.2.3 Aspects of the German university system

One of the founding principles of German university education was that of academic freedom (*die akademische Freiheit*), based on the ideas of

Wilhelm von Humboldt (1767–1835). Humboldt was a philosopher, linguist and educationalist, who believed among other things that people must be free to teach, learn and research as they wish. He believed in combining teaching and research. Humboldt's theories imply freedom for university lecturers to choose how and what they teach and in which areas they engage in research. As far as students are concerned, Humboldt's concept implied a certain freedom to select and structure their own field of study (James 1998: 115).

The German system of HE does not 'spoon-feed' its students in any way. They are encouraged to be independent learners, fending for themselves: they are expected to consult notice boards, put together their own timetable, register for examinations at the correct time (leniency will not be shown if you miss deadlines), and generally take responsibility for their own study programme. Lecturers are not normally as accessible as their British or American counterparts. However, they do have a weekly consultation hour (*Sprechstunde*). This time is usually written up on the door of a lecturer's room. If you need to see a member of staff, it is very important to go at the stated time. It is essential to know this, check the time and be prepared to go along and wait in the queue, sometimes for up to an hour, until the lecturer can see you. In fact you will probably meet and get talking to German students while you are waiting, as they will be waiting too because they are used to the system.

Depending on what you are used to in your own situation, this, and other aspects of the German system, might initially appear somewhat rigid and impersonal. It is worth remembering, however, that part of the experience of living abroad is adapting to another system. Different approaches often have advantages as well as disadvantages, even if the advantages do not become apparent at once. Try to adopt the practice of giving things a fair trial before criticising. Every country has different ways of doing things, and none of them, including your own, has the perfect system.

1.3 Categories of institution in higher education

Although there are many different types of higher education institutions in Germany, this book will deal with the three where you are most likely to be studying: a university (*Universität, Uni*), a *Fachhochschule* (*FH*), which is more like a new university or former polytechnic in the UK, or possibly a teacher training college, a *Pädagogische Hochschule* (*PH*). There are over 300 higher education institutions (HEIs) in Germany. Over 70 per cent of first-year students attend a university.

German universities vary greatly from the oldest, traditional ones, such as Heidelberg (founded in 1386), Leipzig (1409) and Halle-Wittenberg (1694) to the new universities of the 1960s and 1970s such as Bochum (1962), Bremen (1971) and Augsburg (1970). They also vary tremendously in size from the universities of Munich and Cologne, and the Freie Universität Berlin, each with around 60,000 students, to much smaller establishments like Bamberg (*c.* 8,000 students), Magdeburg (*c.* 6,000) and Greifswald (*c.* 5,000).

1.3.1 Recent developments

In the 1960s and 1970s there was a period of expansion in West German higher education. This was a time when many new HEIs were established, and a higher education law (*Hochschulrahmengesetz*) was passed in 1976, which spells out, for example, that citizens of other EU member states have the same rights as citizens of the FRG to study at German universities, provided they have the necessary linguistic knowledge. Each of the federal states then adapted its own legislation to fit in with the framework law. Since the 1977 decision to open up HE (*Öffnungs-beschluss*), the number of students in Germany has just about doubled. There has also been a marked increase in the number of women studying (the situation nowadays is a fifty-fifty split between male and female students), as well as an increase in the number of students from working class families (*Arbeiterfamilien*) (Bode 1996: 297).

The aim of opening up HE to more young people was certainly attained, but it was, in the view of some, gained at the expense of quality (*Masse statt Klasse*) because the huge expansion in student numbers in the university sector was not matched by a corresponding increase in funding and staffing. Partly as a result of this, German university courses are now among the longest in Europe (see above). This means that a system of limited access (*Numerus Clausus* – NC) to some courses is in operation, especially, for example, to those which depend on laboratory places.

The central office which deals with all admissions in Germany (*Zentralstelle für die Vergabe von Studienplätzen*, *ZVS*) tries to regulate the allocation of places, partly on the basis, in the case of NC subjects, of *Abitur* results and the amount of time potential students have been waiting. In a relatively recent attempt to reduce the length of time German students take to acquire their qualifications – thirteen semesters (i.e. six and a half years) on average – the number of semesters a degree course should last is now fixed (*Regelstudienzeit*). However, although more HEIs are now trying to enforce these recommended periods of study by demanding fees from students who exceed the limit, others – notably the more traditional universities – still view the new recommendations merely as guidelines. The old German image of the eternal student (*der ewige Student*), while gradually disappearing, is not quite dead!

The courses at a German university lead to the award of *Staatsexamen* for students in traditional disciplines where the state lays down the required standards. On the other hand, courses at a Fachhochschule tend to be shorter, of a more vocational nature, and lead to the award of a state-recognised diploma (*Diplom*). There is a move afoot to try to increase the proportion of students (around 28 per cent currently) following courses at an FH, but many German students still opt for the greater prestige value, as they see it, attached to university status. In addition there are, of course, a number of other higher education establishments in Germany, such as colleges of art and music, theological colleges, technical and comprehensive universities, sports colleges and other institutions, all of which are more specialised.

A new development at German universities – of particular interest to non-linguists – has been a move towards more international recognition of qualifications. Over a hundred Bachelor's and Master's degrees are currently offered at German universities, many of which are taught in English, across a wide range of disciplines from business to engineering. These include both Bachelor and Master of Business Administration (BBA and MBA), taught in both German and English – and, in some cases, in other languages too. This has come about as a result of the realisation that German degrees, e.g. *Diplomingenieur* and the like, were not well recognised abroad. The development is a major bonus for the internationalisation of German higher education. There are approximately one hundred such courses already and more on the way. The German Academic Exchange Service (DAAD) has details of such courses, and many others besides (*www.daad.de/london*).

1.4 Nature of courses

Once you are in your placement centre, you should ask where you can get hold of a *Vorlesungsverzeichnis*. This is an invaluable paperback publication which contains a list (*Verzeichnis*) of all the lectures (*Vorlesungen*, sometimes also called *Veranstaltungen*) on offer. This publication is sometimes free or there might be a small charge, depending on the institution you are attending, but it is a 'must'. Students of the German language should enrol for the classes in German as a Foreign Language

(*Deutsch als Fremdsprache*). Such classes are usually run by the Academic Foreign Office (*Akademisches Auslandsamt* – AAA), which deals with foreign students and is an essential point of contact for you.

The *Auslandsamt* normally offers an essential introductory/orientation course for foreign students, as well as a great deal of useful information on registering for email and computer use, sports facilities, cultural events and subsidised visits. Make sure you find out about cheap weekend trips to Berlin and the like. Many such excursions (*Ausflüge*) are both educational and enjoyable, and because they are subsidised, offer an excellent opportunity which would otherwise cost considerably more. You must keep in close touch with the *Auslandsamt*, read notices on a regular basis and ask your friends among German students to keep you informed about events on the social calendar of which you might not be aware. Remember: you will have to fend for yourself, develop personal initiative and not be slow in coming forward in Germany!

If a special course of any kind has been arranged for you by your home institution, or even if it is simply a question of a small group following a German for foreigners course, you really *must* make every effort to attend all sessions and do any related work, including a language proficiency test/examination. Absenteeism and/or lack of commitment goes down very badly with German lecturers and administrators, and this is understandable, where special courses have been offered. Special programmes are unusual in the German system. Try to remember that, whether you think it fair or not, your behaviour in your placement centre will influence the foreign institution's impression not just of you personally but also of your home institution. Furthermore, it may well affect the provision and treatment received by next year's group of students.

Once you are registered (*immatrikuliert*) at a German HEI (higher education institution) you are allowed to attend lectures in any discipline. This contrasts with some countries where you might be registered in just one department, which may not necessarily entitle you to attend lectures in other departments across the same university. If you are a student of modern languages, it would be especially beneficial to listen to lectures in German, and to practise taking notes, in any subject area, and this should not normally be a problem in Germany. This is a valuable exercise in itself and a useful way of extending your passive vocabulary; it is also recommended as a way of meeting other students.

1.5 Types of qualification

Clearly there are many different types of qualification available from German HEIs, most of which will not concern you directly, unless you are taking part in a dual or triple qualification scheme. Since you will, however, come across some of them on application forms, it is worthwhile understanding just a few of the basic terms.

In Germany, for example, there are two stages of study for a German student: the initial part of the course, stage one, is the *Grundstudium*, usually covering the first four semesters at university, and between two and four semesters at an FH, ending with an intermediate examination (*Zwischenprüfung*). Stage two is the main part of the course (*Hauptstudium*), which ends with a final examination (*Staatsexamen*). In subjects such as medicine, veterinary science and dentistry the course of study will also end with a state recognised examination (*Staatsprüfung*).

Studies at a *Fachhochschule* usually lead to a *Diplomprüfung*. If you complete a dual or triple qualification involving a placement at an FH you could be awarded a *Diplom* attached to the subject, e.g. *Diplomdolmetscher(in)* or *Diplomübersetzer(in)* if you take a course in interpreting or translating, or *Diplombetriebswirt(in)* for business studies.

What will be compulsory for many students, particularly those who require credit points from their home institution, is the collection of a *Schein*, or certificate, to prove attendance and completion of homework and/or an examination in a given number of courses. For students from Europe the European Credit Transfer System (ECTS) operates. This can give you credit for courses attended and assignments/examinations taken, so check carefully with your home institution before you leave concerning what credits you need to collect.

On arrival in Germany you should make it clear early on to any German lecturers whose classes you attend that you will require credit points or a *Schein* and a mark (*Note*) for attendance and/or work submitted. Ask what homework (*Hausarbeit*) or test (*Klausurarbeit*) you need to do in order to get a mark. Do not forget that if you are on a four-to-six-month placement in a German-speaking country, results of tests taken and *Scheine* may not be available until the end of the semester or later – which might be after you have left. Approach your lecturers in good time and ask them when you will be able to obtain marks or arrange for them to be forwarded. The advice is: plan a little and think ahead.

The mark system used at German HEIs ranges from 1 to 6, with 1 being the best. Marks from 1 to 4 are pass marks, with 5 and 6 denoting failure. A mark of 1 is very good (*sehr gut*), 2 is good (*gut*), 3 is satisfactory (*befriedigend*), 4 is a borderline pass (*ausreichend*), 5 is unsatisfactory (*mangelhaft*) and 6 is the worst mark, inadequate (*ungenügend*). The full range of marks in-between is used, using decimal points, e.g. 1.7 (written as 1,7 in German) or 2,3. In some institutions any mark below 4,5 is considered a fail.

1.6 The educational experience

The educational experience you undergo on placement will clearly be different from what you are used to, as you will be operating in a different environment. This is a valuable experience in itself. Many students profit considerably in terms of personal development from a placement abroad. For instance, it can be an eye-opener to realise that the way things are done in your own country is not always perfect. The way some things work in another culture or country may be better or worse in your view. It may also be neither, but simply different, which can be an important lesson to learn. Everyone is entitled to his or her opinion, but opinions differ, and sometimes it is advisable to wait just a little before jumping in too soon with an observation which might be ill-judged. You may not have understood the full picture and the reasons why a different approach from the one you are used to has been taken to something in Germany. Please do not travel abroad expecting everything to be the same as it is at home. You must display a certain degree of flexibility and be ready to adapt: when in Rome ...

Not only does the German system of HE differ from that of other countries, remember that it varies slightly from region to region. You are entering another culture and it is up to you to find out how that culture functions and why, rather than trying to change it or extol the virtues of your own system. You may find yourself in a relatively small FH or PH (or even a small university) with a friendly, personal atmosphere. Equally, you could be attending overcrowded lectures at a large German university, delivered by a German professor, who has to use a microphone to be heard, on a stage at the front of a massive auditorium. Such a situation is of course, initially, likely to make you feel more like a statistic than an individual used to being given personal attention. However, given that this is the way things are, you might as well take advantage of the situation and do your utmost to meet people and make friends in any of the groups in which you work.

Part of the educational experience is certainly the registration proce-dure (see 5.1), during which you will need to collect lots of paper, including receipts (*Quittungen*), documents (*Unterlagen*) and certificates (*Scheine*). Never throw any of this ammunition away in the paper war (*Papierkrieg*) of German bureaucracy, since you often need to show one bit of paper in order to get another, which may be absolutely vital in the enrolment/registration (*Einschreibung/Anmeldung*) procedure (*sich einschreiben/sich anmelden* = to register). You may also need it in order to sign up for events organised by the academic foreign office (*Auslandsamt*). Remember, however, that the majority of the paperwork involved in the registration process can be taken care of in easy stages in the first two or three weeks.

1.6.1 Lectures

As we have seen, in Germany students are responsible for putting together their own timetables and usually decide themselves when to take their final examinations. This is another reason why courses often last longer than in other countries, although there has been a trend recently towards shortening study programmes, partly on financial grounds. It is certainly the case that you will need to act independently. We cannot stress enough that the German system will not spoon-feed you!

Many lectures (*Vorlesungen* or *Veranstaltungen*) are fairly formal and crowded affairs, normally lasting ninety minutes. Some may be held in a big lecture hall (*Aula*) with the lecturer standing on the stage at the front with a microphone. There is a German convention associated with what is called the 'academic quarter' (*das akademische Viertel*) which means that lectures usually begin a quarter of an hour after the advertised time and finish earlier too. So a lecture advertised in the *Vorlesungsverzeichnis* as 10.00 until 12.00 will actually start at 10.15 and finish at 11.45, thus lasting ninety minutes. Nevertheless it pays to arrive in good time if you want to get a seat in what may be an overcrowded lecture hall.

To give just one example of the German system: a foreign language lecture might contain a group of approximately eighty or ninety students who have been asked to prepare a written translation. The students will probably be asked to correct their own work during the session and are unlikely to get their homework marked on an individual basis or receive very much personal attention or feedback. Small group work would certainly be a big exception in Germany. Even seminar groups, though smaller than lectures, may contain forty or fifty students in some institutions.

Given the large numbers of students at most institutions, it is normally not easy to be seen by lecturers on an individual basis, unless you make a definite appointment or go along to their *Sprechstunde*. You must understand that in the German system lecturers are unlikely to be available at other times. It is important to realise that a tutoring or guidance system along the lines of the British or American model does not usually exist in Germany.

1.6.2 Using the library

The library system at a German HEI will probably be different from what you are used to at home. It is not easy to generalise, since the library systems in operation vary not only from one federal state to another but also from one library to another. However you might find that it is not possible to browse through the library shelves in some HEIs. You are often required to know exactly which book or article you are looking for and will be asked to complete a requisition slip with precise details of title and author which then has to be handed in at the issue desk. In such a system you have to return later the same day or possibly the next day in order to collect the requested item. The same system may well apply if you need to consult something on microfiche or reference material from the stack. You will almost certainly have to familiarise yourself with the library catalogues. Just as with anything else in a different culture/country, you should not expect things to work in exactly the same way as they do at home.

2
Practical advice before you leave

2.1 Speaking to others

Clearly, it is always sensible to get advice from people who have been to the place you are about to visit. Make the most of any connections you may still have from school, pen-friends, other contacts abroad or German nationals living locally. Remember the advice about finding out as much as possible not just about the country but also the part you are going to visit.

Most students should be able to arrange meetings with older students in their home institutions who have been to the placement centre already. This is obviously a source of vital information regarding tips and 'do's and don'ts.' Make a list of all the 'nitty-gritty' practical questions you have on what to take (and what not), how to travel, arrange insurance, etc. You should also speak to any German exchange students presently attending your university, who will, in most cases, be from the foreign universities to which you are going. Start off by asking about differences they have noticed between the systems in the two countries. This is a wonderful opportunity to find out details of the placement centre to which you will be going, from a peer's point of view.

Many students say after their placement that they enjoyed it, but that it took them a couple of months to settle in. If you find out as much as you can about your centre before you set off and make some preparations, you will probably be able to cut down on the period of settling in and adapting to your new environment. Students on modern language courses who go on two placements often say that they settled into their second placement more quickly than their first. This is of course understandable, but the way to make sure you do not 'lose' too much time settling in on your first placement is to follow the advice

given here concerning preparation and collecting information before
you leave home.

2.2 Selecting a centre

Students whose study programmes contain an element of economics or
business studies might find it useful to contact their local Chamber of
Commerce or various government offices, for example, in Great Britain
the Department of Trade and Industry. Such organisations can sometimes
provide valuable addresses and contact numbers, as well as background
information on the German business environment and the general political
and economic scene.

For the vast majority of students going on placement the home
institution will almost certainly have established linked institutions abroad,
in which case it is likely that you will simply be allocated a placement
centre. On the other hand it is possible that you may be offered a choice
of one of several placement centres, or that you are organising your
residence in Germany yourself. Some students wish to go to an area they
already know from an earlier contact such as perhaps a school exchange
or a visit to a pen-friend. However, it is often preferable to get to know
a different region, since obviously this will enhance your knowledge of
the country.

2.3 Accommodation

If money were no object, there would be no great problem in seeking
accommodation for a short stay in Germany, but finding something for
several months which suits the student purse is more tricky. Student
accommodation in flats or houses on the open market can be hard to
come by, and it can be expensive too, although it might be possible (but
not easy) to organise a 'swap' with a German student coming to your
university at the time when you will be in Germany. The logistics of this
can of course be difficult, but such arrangements do work well. In such
cases it can be of great benefit, especially for language students, to be
living in shared private accommodation with German students. Having
to search and find something suitable and not prohibitively expensive on
the open market when you arrive in Germany is extremely difficult and
therefore normally not recommended.

Given that you are a student, your best bet is to try to obtain a place

in a student hall of residence (*Studentenwohnheim*). If it is possible for
your home institution to help you to organise this, you would be well
advised to go for that option. Rent for student halls in Germany does not
include any food, but they are reasonably priced for the student budget,
and it is normally a useful way of getting to know local students and
participating in student social life. Another advantage is that many halls,
though not all, are close to the place of study. Some German halls of
residence have a student bar (with 'student prices') in them. This is
clearly an ideal place to socialise, meet new people and speak German.
Any inhibitions about speaking a foreign language have a tendency to
disappear gradually in direct proportion to the amount of alcohol
consumed, though we are not recommending that you become an
alcoholic! One method of gaining all the above-mentioned advantages,
while possibly drinking slightly less, is to do what some of our students
have done and enter your name on the rota for working behind the bar.
This is an even better way of making new friends and speaking the
language.

If you are going to stay in hall, it is not worth lugging bulky bedding
with you to Germany. Some halls provide bedding, but even if it is not
provided, you can buy a pillow (*Kissen*), pillowcase (*Kissenüberzug*) and
featherbed/duvet (*Federbett*) cheaply on the spot at a German department store such as Horten or Kaufhaus. Take a sleeping-bag with you if
you are in any doubt. Kitchen utensils can also be acquired relatively
cheaply in Germany. Remember that plugs for any electrical equipment
you might take will be different. British three-pin plugs will certainly
not fit the German two-pin sockets, so an international adapter would be
useful, unless you simply change any plugs when you arrive.

Whatever accommodation you have organised, be prepared for the
possibility that you might need temporary accommodation for the first
few days, since you should not simply expect something to be ready for
you to move into immediately when you arrive. This will certainly not
be the case if you arrive towards the end of the month. In Germany
accommodation of any sort, including rooms in student halls of residence, is normally available from the first day (or occasionally, by way of
exception, from the fifteenth) of the month. Remember that, if you are
planning to arrive for the beginning of the winter semester, 3 October is
a public holiday throughout Germany, commemorating the date of
German Unity in 1990 (*Tag der deutschen Einheit*).

There are around 750 youth hostels in Germany, which are generally
clean and well run, as well as being the cheapest option if you need
'emergency' accommodation for a few days when you first arrive, which

may well be the case. For a student under the age of 27 a room in a German youth hostel will cost approximately DM 30–40 per night. Take an international youth hostel card with you and before you leave check the address and telephone number of the nearest one from our University and Towns section in Chapter eight. Do _not_ leave things to the last minute, arrive to find you have either no accommodation or a room that you cannot move into until the following week and then, because you are dragging a lot of heavy luggage around with you, go to the first hotel you come to in the city centre after leaving the railway station. It will be expensive!

Actually, a useful tip, if you do arrive at a main rail station in Germany and have to telephone a youth hostel or make arrangements of whatever sort while trying to keep an eye on a lot of luggage, is to look for the signs to the luggage lockers (_Schließfächer_), where for just a small charge – you normally insert a DM 2 coin – you will be able to store your luggage safely.

If you are going to stay in a student hall, you will probably be required to pay two months' rent when you arrive – one month's rent (_Miete_) in advance, and a deposit (_Kaution_), the equivalent of one month's rent, which is returned to you when you leave, providing you have not broken or damaged anything. Incidentally, it is your responsibility to warn people when you will be leaving and make sure you get your deposit back before you leave. This is normally a straightforward procedure when you are on the spot, but more complicated if you try to do this after you have left the country.

2.4 Financial arrangements

It is a good idea to make sure that you have some of the local currency with you when you arrive. Open a current account (_ein laufendes Konto_) at a bank straight away, so that you can arrange to have any payments you need to make, such as an accommodation deposit, via a bank transfer (_eine Überweisung_). This is the usual way of carrying out financial transactions in Germany. For regular (monthly) payments such as rent you can set up a standing order (_Dauerauftrag_). In Germany salaries, rents, etc., are normally paid on a monthly basis.

You might find that there are still a few situations in Germany in which credit cards are not accepted as readily as in the USA and the UK, for example in some smaller hotels and restaurants. As you are likely to need change straight away for bus/tram tickets, etc., you should go to the bureau de change at the railway station or airport to get some coins. As a general rule of thumb, it is sensible to take some local currency with you, as well as some travellers' cheques – although bank charges for cashing them vary – plus some of your own currency which could be kept as a back-up to be changed only in an emergency. The Eurocheque system has now been phased out, but you can use your Switch card or equivalent to access cash machines in Germany, and you can, of course, arrange to have money transferred from a bank in your own country, once you have settled in to your placement centre and opened a local bank account. Euro notes and coins will be introduced in January 2002, so opening a Euro account will also become a possibility.

Even though there are no longer local education authority grants in Great Britain, for British students it is still worth getting in touch with your LEA to ask about finance. You may find that you are entitled to claim for one return journey to your placement centre, where the placement is a compulsory part of your course. If you normally receive an educational bursary as a full-time student in your country, you may be eligible for an additional grant for a stay abroad.

If your home institution is in Europe and informs you that you are entitled to receive a SOCRATES (ERASMUS) grant, remember that the amount of money is normally determined in Brussels and that your own institution may have little or no control over how much is paid and when it is paid. Unfortunately the recent trend has been towards a substantial reduction in the amount of money available, so do not rely on receiving any such money – view it as a possible bonus, if it materialises at all.

It is likely that you will need proof of what financial support you have when you arrive in Germany. This could take the form of a letter from your university, or even from your parents, simply to confirm that you will have the required financial means to support yourself while studying abroad. This is something else which ought to be taken care of before you leave.

2.5 Health and general insurance

2.5.1 Personal insurance

You must take out insurance against personal injury, and theft, loss or damage to luggage. It should be straightforward to find an insurer in your home country who will provide the required service via a relatively inexpensive overall package. Many insurance companies offer reduced rates to students and there are now student advisory services in some countries which specialise in appropriate levels of protection for students for a full year with very reasonable premiums. Property such as personal computers can often be included nowadays at little extra cost.

The best offers will probably come from firms which are specialised in dealing with students, and details are likely to be available from your own students' union or society. Enquire well in advance about what is available and make certain that you have sufficient cover. Accidents do happen, and it is no use putting your head in the sand and thinking it cannot happen to you, then realising that it can when it is too late. Remember that most insurance companies require you to notify them (and they charge extra premiums) of what they regard as specialist and potentially dangerous activities such as skiing. It pays to read your policy carefully, and, if you are going to go in for any high-risk sports or pastimes, get yourself properly insured first, because insurance policies vary and they definitely do *not* cover anything and everything.

2.5.2 Medical insurance

All citizens of the European Union (EU) are entitled to medical treatment in another member state, providing they have the E111 insurance form. There may be slight variations, according to country and work status. Visiting a doctor and obtaining free medical attention is normally a straightforward procedure in Germany, as long as you have the right form.

In the UK the E111 form is obtainable from a post office. If you come from anywhere outside Europe, it is essential that you familiarise yourself, well in advance, with the regulations concerning health insurance. This can be done via the nearest German Embassy (*Botschaft*) or DAAD. If you consider visiting Austria, there are different regulations which can be obtained from the Austrian Academic Exchange Service (ÖAD) or Austrian embassies (see appendix for addresses). Ask in your home institution too. If you are an American, Canadian or Australian citizen, you should find out, in good time, how you obtain insurance cover in Germany from your country.

As soon as you arrive in your placement centre, you must go to the local sickness insurance office – in Germany this is called *die Allgemeine Ortskrankenkasse* (AOK) – where you must show your E111 form, or equivalent, and get an exemption certificate (*Befreiungsschein*). This form entitles you to free medical treatment in Germany. You must be certain that you have the relevant documentation and take it with you. As long as you have this, you can avoid having to pay a very high fee while abroad to insure yourself against ill health. It is quite possible that you will still be offered health insurance packages in Germany at reduced, though still pretty expensive, student rates. There is no need to take these, as long as you have covered yourself before leaving home and have the documentation to prove it.

It is worth noting when going to the AOK, or any other German office for that matter, that their opening hours generally may vary from what you are used to. Many offices in Germany open only in the mornings from approximately 08.00 until 12.00. Those that do open in the afternoon normally do so on a restricted basis, e.g. from 13.00 till 15.00 or 14.00 till 16.00. The working day in Germany starts and finishes at least sixty to ninety minutes earlier than in some countries. Most schools begin at 08.00 and it is quite usual for manual workers to start work at 07.00 and office staff to start at 07.30. You will find that it will not be much use getting up at 11.00 and strolling down to an office which closes at 11.30!

2.6 **Documentation required**

You will of course need a valid passport – North American students will probably need a residence permit visa stamped in their passport – and health insurance (e.g. the E111 form or its equivalent).

You will have to complete an application form for the relevant HEI. For Germany applications are normally required by 15 July at the very latest for entry in October for the winter semester (WS) and by 15 January for entry in March/April for the summer semester (SS). Please make sure that you comply with the deadlines. Requirements may vary slightly, but you will probably need copies of your school-leaving certificates – the equivalent of the German *Abitur*.

If you are applying for a place in a hall of residence, you will need to complete a separate application form. It is a good idea to take some form of written confirmation of financial support for your stay (see 2.4). Confirmation that you are enrolled/registered as a full-time student at your home institution should be taken with you, and you are also recommended to obtain an international student card from your own students' union at home, which could be useful when you first arrive in Germany. Remember to take documents proving that you have personal, travel and luggage insurance (see above).

2.7 **Things to take with you**

Apart from the documents mentioned above (passport/visa, health insurance, copies of examination certificates, proof of financial support, international student and youth hostel cards, etc.), it is worthwhile pausing to think about what else you need. For instance, you should take with you a supply of any medication you take on a regular basis, in case you run out or cannot obtain exactly the same thing abroad. A few passport photos will come in handy for any forms you have to complete on arrival – and there will be some, as registration (see 3.1 below) is a serious business in the German-speaking countries. You have been warned!

Take photocopies of all documents, including your passport, and keep them separate from the originals. If you should lose any important documents, the copies will be an enormous help to you when you apply to replace them.

It might be useful to take a couple of small presents, for example a packet of English tea, or some speciality from your own country or region, which usually goes down well if you are invited to someone's home. In that situation, taking flowers or a small present is the normal practice in Germany. It is also nice to have something with you, as a small 'thank you' for a friend, or someone who has been particularly helpful, when you are leaving.

2.7.1 Mobile phones

If, as nowadays is likely, you use a mobile phone (*ein Handy* as it is called in German), then you might as well take it along with you for your period of residence. You must, however, make sure that you have the entitlement to use it abroad, and this is likely to depend on the type of contract you have. If you pay rental to a mobile phone company, you will find that, provided you have been with them for a given number of months, you will simply have to contact their service centre in order to have your mobile activated for use in Europe. If you are on a 'pay as you go' tariff, then you may be able to make use of it abroad, but it might be cheaper for you simply to find the most favourable 'pay as you go' deal in Germany.

2.8 **Travel arrangements**

As far as travel arrangements to your destination are concerned, investigate all the special offers. There is a range of student reductions and cheaper flights now available (special prices for young people under 26) to many European airports, as well as reduced fare deals by rail or coach. Many of the cheap flights nowadays are no more expensive than rail travel, although some bus fares (in Europe) may be – though not necessarily – the cheapest option for someone on a tight budget. There are also several ferry services. For example, if you are going anywhere in northern Germany from northern Britain, the Hull-Rotterdam ferry, followed by a three-hour train journey through Holland might be worth considering. Alternatively, a flight to Amsterdam or Brussels and a train to the Düsseldorf/Cologne area is often convenient.

Generally speaking, train travel in Germany is a reasonably punctual, clean and pleasant experience. Wherever you are travelling from, it is a good idea to find out about the many special offers and student discounts. There is no shortage of cheaper fares. However, make sure you have the latest information, as such travel offers are frequently amended and updated.

When travelling in Europe please remember the time difference: Germany is on Central European Time (*Mitteleuropäische Zeit – MEZ*), one hour ahead of the United Kingdom and six hours ahead of US east coast time. Make sure that you do *not* arrive at a weekend or late in the evening when everywhere will be closed. Even if you have to get up very early or travel through the night, it is essential that you arrive at your destination during office hours – in the morning if possible – so that you can get the all-important paper work done, collect your hall key, etc. Do not arrive at 9 pm on a Friday evening and expect a reception committee. Nowhere will be open and the porter (*Hausmeister*) in the hall of residence will have gone home!

Once you are settled in to your placement centre, you must find out about the numerous special offers on the German rail network, such as the *Bahncard*, greatly reduced weekend travel for students and the like. Keep asking – you could be missing out on some terrific offers. Public transport in Germany is of a generally high standard. The German Travel Service can provide details of timetables. These are also available from the Internet (see 4.2).

Even if you have a car, it might be advisable to leave it at home, especially if you are not used to driving on the German *Autobahn*. With the exception of certain stretches where restrictions now apply, there is still no national speed limit on German motorways, and it shows! Drivers used to driving on the left should be particularly careful. If you do intend driving, you are entitled to drive on your own licence for up to one year, but no longer. A certified, i.e. an officially approved, German translation, is required in some federal states, and an international driving licence, obtained from a national automobile association in your own country, is recommended.

A safer and healthier alternative to driving might be to buy a second-hand bicycle when you are in Germany. It is possible to acquire one cheaply at many German HEIs (look at the notice boards in the *Mensa*), and even to sell it for more or less the same price again when you leave. Many students have found this means of transport very handy, especially in predominantly flat areas such as Oldenburg.

With so many cheap travel offers there is no need to hitchhike. It is not only unnecessary, but also illegal for you to try and hitch and illegal for a driver to offer you a lift in many regions of Germany. Since it is extremely dangerous, hitchhiking is to be avoided at all costs. For this reason many HEIs in Germany run a safe and sensible organisation called the *Mitfahrzentrale*, whereby several students can arrange to be given a lift, in return for a small charge to cover petrol costs, by someone whose name has been provided under the scheme and who is driving to your destination. These arrangements are made in advance at the HEI. If you do take part in the *Mitfahrzentrale* scheme, make sure that it is a genuine one and that you travel with other students.

2.9 Students with little previous knowledge of German

If you are a student with little knowledge of German, the Goethe Institutes throughout the world provide German language courses and certificates which are accepted as proof of proficiency. It is in any case advisable for anyone contemplating a placement in a German-speaking country to take a basic German course. This will add to the enjoyment of your stay and help you to find your way around more easily. If you have taken a basic German language course before you go, you should at least be able to follow signs and get about when you arrive. This will make you feel more confident, help you a little in shops and almost certainly increase your overall enjoyment of the placement. Even if you can manage only a few phrases at first, the mere fact that you have made the effort is likely to go down well with the local inhabitants.

You may have met, either in Germany or your own country, a number of Germans who speak virtually perfect English – there are plenty of them around. Nevertheless, not everyone in Germany speaks fluent English, whatever you might have heard. Often you find that it is pre-cisely when you most need an interpreter that you are faced with one of the German population who knows either very little English or none at all. It will certainly give you a psychological boost to complete a basic 'survival kit' course in the German language before you go. Simply having made the effort, and not assuming that 'they' will speak English, will be well received by your hosts.

3
Completing the forms

3.1 Application to study

You will need to complete an application form (*Bewerbungsblatt* or *Antrag auf Zulassung zum Studium*) to apply for a place to study at a German university. This has to be done well in advance. You will normally need to make an application (*einen Antrag stellen*) and send in the completed form to arrive by 15 July at the very latest for a *Wintersemester* start in September/October and by 15 January for a *Sommersemester* start in March/April. Since the application forms sometimes appear complicated, completing them can be a daunting task, although there has been a recent move – well overdue in some cases – to shorten and simplify the forms. Nowadays, the forms for some institutions can be downloaded from the Internet.

You will probably be faced with an application form, when applying for a place to study at a German university, which has really been designed for German students. Consequently some of the information asked for may not apply to you as a foreign student. An example of a typical form is provided in the appendices. You will normally require a passport-size photograph to be attached to your form. It is useful to take some spare photos with you, as there will be other forms to complete, once you are in your destination, which will almost certainly require a photo too.

The first thing to indicate will probably be which semester and year you are applying for. Then you fill in details of your name (surname first normally), as it appears on your passport/identification papers, and term-time and home address – make sure you give the address at which you can be contacted most quickly, e.g. home address over the summer, plus any telephone, email or fax numbers where you could be reached quickly. You are often asked to indicate the main subject (*Hauptfach*) that you wish to study. As a languages student, this will normally be German as a foreign language, so write in *Deutsch als Fremdsprache*. That should suffice.

If you are not a languages student and wish to study another subject, e.g. economics (*Wirtschaftswissenschaften* or *Volkswirtschaftslehre*, VWL) or business studies (*Betriebswirtschaftslehre*, BWL) then enter that. It should not be necessary to apply for alternative courses of study, even though these are asked for on the form (this is an example of something which is really aimed at local students), especially if your home institution has a regular exchange scheme with the university abroad. You may be asked for a correspondence address, but there is no need to complete this, unless it is different from the home address you have provided. There may be a space on the form for the final qualification you are aiming for (*angestrebter Studienabschluss*), but this will probably not apply to you if you are on a one-semester exchange. If you are aiming to gain a German qualification (this will probably not apply to most foreign students), then you will need to indicate which one.

The foreign HEI will require copies – do *not* send the originals – of your certificates which gained you entrance to your home institution, e.g. A levels in Great Britain. You will be asked if you have attended a preparatory course (*Studienkolleg*), usually for foreign students; again, this will probably not be the case. You may need to fill in the name of your current home institution and/or state for how many semesters you have been studying so far. On most application forms there are questions for foreign students regarding their knowledge of German. If you are studying German as a full-time student, then you should make this clear, and you may be asked for proof of proficiency (*Nachweis*) in the form of either your university/college marks or any examinations passed, or certificates obtained, e.g. from the Goethe Institute.

A very important aspect is how you intend to finance your period of study. This is purely because the authorities in Germany do not want to find themselves in the position of enrolling foreign students who do not have the financial means to support themselves. If you are in receipt of any kind of grant (*Stipendium*), you must give details. It is a good idea to take with you a letter from your parents or someone else, stating that you will have sufficient funds during your placement, but when completing the form it is usually enough to make it clear that you can support yourself financially. As a rough guide, it is estimated that a current student in Germany needs at least DM 1,400 per month to live, including accommodation costs. You must be certain that you will have enough money and will not be relying on applying for funding from Germany (which you will *not* get).

You might be asked if you have the right of asylum (*Asylrecht*), which we assume is unlikely to be the case with most people. Indicate on the form that you are part of an official exchange programme (e.g. SOCRATES in Europe), if that is the case, and state when you intend to arrive in your placement centre. Your application should be accompanied by a passport-size photograph and a *curriculum vitae* (*Lebenslauf*) in German. This can sometimes be filled in on the application form, or it might be preferable to submit it separately. A German assistant or *Lektor* can perhaps help you with this; a brief CV (one side of A4) is normally sufficient. See Appendix III.

Not all the questions included in a lengthy form will be relevant to you as a foreign student. For example, there may be nothing to complete regarding other German universities you have attended, and if you are asked for special reasons for selecting the foreign HEI, it would be enough simply to enter *Austauschprogramm* (exchange programme). With any application it is essential to read everything through again before signing and dating it and also getting an official stamp from your home HEI. At the end of the form, where you sign the application, there is usually a note to the effect that in signing you are giving an assurance that, to the best of your knowledge, all the information you have given is correct. If any of the information given, including details of certificates and qualifications enclosed, is misleading or inaccurate, your application will not be processed. See Appendix 1 for a form and detailed instructions for filling it in.

3.2 Applying for a place in a hall of residence

A separate application is required for those who wish to apply for a place in a student hall of residence in Germany. Some people on placement may wish to seek alternative accommodation on the open market, but remember that this is extremely overcrowded in most university towns and often not within the financial means of the average student. Some German institutions may offer a *Servicepaket*. This is a special accommodation package which might offer special facilities, e.g. a room with Internet connections, meal tickets (*Mensamarken*), travel tickets (*Semesterticket*), etc. Such a package is usually more expensive of course, since it offers additional benefits, and needs to be given particular scrutiny. With or without the *Servicepaket*, a place in hall undoubtedly has a number of advantages for students (see 2.3).

The application forms for halls are normally fairly straightforward to complete. Some halls may ask you to decide between a single or shared room. Although your first inclination might be to opt for a single room, if available, some German halls offer what they call a double room (*Doppelzimmer*), which is in fact like two separate single rooms which share a toilet and shower. Some sort of double room or shared apartment arrangement in hall is sometimes cheaper and has the added advantage that you are more likely to meet other students, thereby getting plenty of practice in spoken German.

You will first of all be asked to indicate what sort of room you would prefer, although there is no guarantee that you will get your first choice. Most institutions will provide information on the various halls of residence on offer, so you can opt for a particular hall if your home institution does not already have an arrangement with one. Many places nowadays will ask if you are a smoker (*Raucher*) or non-smoker (*Nichtraucher*). Incidentally, you could find that certain parts of the HEI where you are going to study may be restricted to non-smokers, so keep an eye out for the signs.

There is often a set date when your written agreement or contract (*Vertrag*) will begin – usually the first day of the appropriate month in Germany. If you are asked whether you have already lived in hall, as on the sample form, this really applies only to Germany, but you could say that you have lived in hall in your own country, if that is the case. 'Shared' accommodation in hall is sometimes the best option (see above), even though you may not think so initially. Again you will have to fill in your surname, first names (all of them if you have more than one), male/female (*männlich/weiblich*), nationality, home and current addresses with contact numbers – email, telephone, fax, as applicable – as on the sample.

Some HEIs might require details of your parents' professions (*Beruf*) and net incomes (*Nettoeinkommen*) in DM per month, as well as any dependent brothers and sisters in your family. German students are normally asked to state the amount of money – again the equivalent in the local currency per month – they have at their disposal, and from what source (*Herkunft*), e.g. parents (*Eltern*), own income (*eigene Einkünfte*), a German grant (*Bafög*), or any other grants (*Stipendien*). This is because they want to know that you can support yourself during your placement and also because some German HEIs allocate the limited places in hall according to social criteria. Some institutions may ask you to fill in something on your background, including interests and hobbies, residence abroad (*Auslandsaufenthalte*), foreign languages spoken, etc. (see sample form). You might have already provided much of this material already in the form of a *curriculum vitae*/résumé (*Lebenslauf*). See Appendix 1 for a typical form and detailed instructions on how to fill it in.

4
Using the Internet as a research tool prior to departure for Germany

Students should nowadays be able to access the Internet at their university computer facilities almost at will, and many have access at home. We have, however, found there to be a certain technophobia, not to say Luddism, among some elements, which can have a rather negative effect on any attempt to access information. Even among people happy and prepared to make use of computers, we have found a tendency to blunder about asking the wrong questions, and with this in mind we give here some guidance on the use of the Internet. We also indicate the URLs of useful sites, but in some cases we will suggest that you use a key word or phrase to write into a search engine, if we believe that this will lead to an instant 'hit'. Well, we have just used the acronym 'URL', and the Internet jargon words 'site', 'address', 'search engine', and 'hit'. If you know what they all mean, you can probably skip the whole of this chapter, and if you don't know what they mean – just don't tell anybody, read this, and in a few minutes you will be as big an Internet expert as any of your more knowledgeable friends. There follows a short glossary of the terms we will be using:

Address	Place where *site* is based; the address will usually look something like this: *http://www.something.something*.
Address box	Long, narrow rectangle near the top of the screen, where you can write in *addresses*, which will usually have the prefix *http://www*.
Click on	Use mouse button to highlight *link*.
Favourites	These are *Microsoft's* name for the bookmarks with which you can keep an address book of useful sites to which you can return at the click of a mouse.
Hit	Finding of a *site* which is relevant to the question you have put to a *search engine*.

Home page   The first page, the welcome page, of any *site*.

http   The *Hypertext Transfer Protocol* is simply the start of any internet address, and sounds as if it has walked out of a piece of science fiction, which in a way it has.

Link   Every time you look at an article or a list of *hits* on the Internet, certain words will be picked out in blue. These are called *links*. *Click on* them to be taken to the linked *site*.

Screen   The contents of your computer screen at any given moment.

Scrolling   Moving up and down the screen, using the mouse and the right side-bar, or the cursor buttons on your keyboard.

Search engine Data base which contains vast amounts of information, which you can access by writing *addresses* into the *Address* box or by writing key words or phrases into the *Find this* or *Search* box.

Site   Place at which information is stored.

URL   Uniform Resource Locator, which locates the thing you are looking for.

www   *World Wide Web.*

Once you know which university you will be attending, you can use the web site, whose URL is included in this guide beneath each university address, to acquaint yourself with the university and area – the web sites of most universities have links to the town where they are based. (See 4.1.1 if you do not know how to input a web site address.) If you have time, just go through all the links which look interesting (see also 4.3 for the *Meine Stadt* web site, which takes a very thorough look at many towns in the FRG and which almost certainly will include the town where you will be studying).

The *AStA* sites (see 7.1.4), especially, have various useful messages, such as what meals are on offer at the *Mensa* this week, or when the next protest is to take place – that vital information which every student needs to know in order to function. Some of the institutions give very clear and detailed information about themselves, with excellent links to points of local interest, while others seem to wish to remain discreet and impenetrable. However, you should find sufficient information within this guide to help you to form a picture of the institution you are to visit and to see you through your first days and weeks there.

4.1 **Projects**

If you are going to be writing an extended essay or working on a project during your stay, you would be well advised to make a start before you leave your home university. Your library is, of course, one primary source of information about the country, but you will be able to find many specialised sites on the Internet, which may help you to find an angle for your topic.

4.1.1 Accessing newspapers and their archives as primary sources

Before you do anything, you should read a few articles on the theme of your project, and it has to be said that however good your library might be, finding linked topics in the printed versions of newspapers or news magazines is very time-consuming, whereas with the Internet you can make use of newspaper archive databases, many of which give you free use. All the main newspapers, whether broadsheets or tabloids, have web sites with access to their latest editions (with the strange exception of the *Frankfurter Allgemeine Zeitung*, which, at this juncture, still only lists article titles and expects you to buy the paper!).

We are going to assume that you can log on to the Internet. If this is not the case, then ask someone for help. Our experience is that for most people the problems start *after* logging on.

Using the prefix for websites (http://www) type into the address box http://www.welt.de/ which is the address of the newspaper *Die Welt*. Now click on 'Go' or 'Go to' to the right of the box (or hit the return key on your keyboard) and this will take you straight to *Die Welt*. This newspaper has an excellent archive going back several years, and if you want to do something on ecology, for example, then typing *Umwelt* into the archive slot at the top right of your screen will give you more than 2000 references. This may be rather more than you have bargained for, but you will see on the right of your screen the words *Archiv* and *Einfache Suche*; the latter will allow you to specify how far back into the past you wish to go, say six months, and this will produce a (reduced) list of articles where the word occurred during that period.

Try the same procedure by typing in *http://sueddeutsche.de*. This will take you to the homepage of *Süddeutsche Zeitung*, which offers a thirty-day archive. The following address will take you to various newspaper archives:

http://www.grass-gis.de/bibliotheken/zeitungsarchive.html

Stern, Spiegel, and *focus* have sites at:

http://www.stern.de/
http://www.spiegel.de
http://www.focus.de

respectively.

If you type http://www.schramka.de/links/zeitung.htm into your address box, this will provide you with a vast list of regional and national newspapers. We have included the name of the local newspaper(s) for each of the towns mentioned in this guide – but the above URL lists the majority of newspapers published in Germany.

When you find a site you think you will be returning to frequently, make yourself a 'favourite' by clicking on 'Favourites' at the top middle of your screen, then click on 'Add' in the box which has opened on the left of your screen and *Create* your link in *New Folder* – call it *Zeitungen.*

These newspaper sites should help you in your preliminary research, when you are deciding on the tack which you wish to pursue. Problems caused by mistyping, etc., can easily be rectified by going to the *Find this* or *Search* box in the upper middle part of your screen. For example, at the time of writing, typing *Zeitungsarchive* into this box produced a list in which this was the second 'hit'. If it is not the second 'hit', scroll down the list of sites: you will be certain to find it quickly.

The *Search* box is an excellent tool in any search engine: in it you can write a key word or phrase, which with only a little luck will lead you to much relevant information. Try typing *Zeitungen* into the *Search* box, and you will find most of the sites mentioned above very quickly indeed.

Clearly, these instructions are intended to be a rudimentary guide to accessing information, but they really are sufficient for you to find anything you need. In our opinion, experimenting with search engines will soon make you more than competent.

4.1.2 Politics

http://www.grass-gis.de/bibliotheken/bundesaemter.html Try this address if you are a politics student or are simply interested in the way the Federal Republic works.

It gives you links to all the Federal institutions of Germany: government offices, ministries, *Bundesbank*, all the Federal agencies, the *Bundesarchiv*, texts of German laws, sites for each of the *Länder*, from where you can obtain a great deal of information about the region where you will based. Some of the sites offer free brochures and booklets which you can order online and which will be sent to you within a fortnight. If we go back to our *Umwelt* project (the environment is not a topic we would necessarily encourage, but in our experience it is one of the most popular choices, and there is a vast amount of information available), then a visit to the *Umweltministerium*, whether the Federal one or one of its regional counterparts, will give you access to more than enough information for you to start planning your topic – in German – well in advance. The *Bayerisches Staatsministerium für Landesentwicklung und Umweltfragen* (Bavarian State Ministry for Regional Development and Environmental Issues) will send you brochures relating to all sorts of pollution and procedures to combat it, at the click of a mouse, and you will find that many of the others will do so as well. The full address needs to be typed, since typing *Bundesämter* into a search engine will not get you straight to this site.

http://www.bpb.de/ This is the site for the *Bundeszentrale für politische Bildung* (Federal Central Office for Political Education) which gives you access to the archive of *Das Parlament*'s supplement (*Beilage*), with its very wide-ranging themes, to discussion groups, and much historical and current affairs material.

http://www.pz-net.de/ At this site you can get a free subscription to *PZ* (*Die Politische Zeitschrift*), which provides articles on current affairs.

http://mainz-online.de/internet/links/parteien.html This address will take you to a list of the mainstream parties in the FRG.

4.1.3 Economics

http://www.ifo.de/orcl/dbssi/main.htm If you need economic information this is the address of the *Institut für Wirtschaftsforschung* (Institute of Economic research) in Munich, or http://www.uni-kiel.de:8080/ IfW/ which is the address of the *Institut fur Weltwirtschaft* (Institute of International Economics) at the University of Kiel, both of which offer enormous amounts of information and links.

http://www.handelsblatt.com/ The *Handelsblatt* is a newspaper with general economic information.

http://194.64.225.24/WirtschaftsWoche/Wiwo_CDA/0,1702,304,00. html *Wirtschaftswoche*, which has daily updated business and economic news. Typing *Wirtschaftswoche* into a search box will give you an instant 'hit' for this address.

4.1.4 Culture, literature and *Germanistik* (Germanic Studies)

http://www.phil.uni-erlangen.de/~p2gerlw/ressourc/suchen.html If you
are studying for a more traditional degree, with elements of literature or
philosophy, then sites such as the University of Erlangen's resource
centre are excellent. If you type *Germanistik im Internet* into your search
engine, you should get an instant 'hit'. The resources here are very wide-
ranging: links to institutes and institutions, to many aspects of German –
texts, materials aimed specifically at students taking German as a foreign
language, dictionaries, databases. The site has so many links that if you
follow each little trail you will be likely to find information about most
aspects of German culture. It will even take you to a site which will find
German postal codes for you.

4.1.5 Language

http://www.uncg.edu/~lixlpurc/german.html If you feel that you need
to do some extra work on your German before you leave your home
country, or you are at the end of your term or semester and you want to
learn some more about Germany, try Professor Lixl-Purcell's language
and civilisation site at the University of Carolina, which provides links to
much background material and many language exercises for students of
German. Typing 'German Internet Trails' into a search engine should
get you a direct 'hit'.

http://www.duden.de/ The *Duden Verlag* site which, among other
things, allows you to check that you are producing German which has
the new orthography (see note on German spelling, p. x) and which lists
all the new spellings.

http://www.ids-mannheim.de/ Here you can access all sorts of information about the German language and, again, about the spelling reform.

4.1.6 Generally useful sites about Germany

http://www.statistik-bund.de/ If you are writing something which
requires statistics, then take a look at this site which will bring you to a
set of data covering many aspects of German life and *Landeskunde* –
geography, population, prices, environment, elections, etc. This is
excellent material for you to add to presentations and projects, and there
are free brochures and booklets on offer.

http://goethe.de/ For various general resources about Germany, try
this site which will take you to the home page of the Goethe Institut. This

provides links to its branches worldwide, to information about the courses it runs, materials for students of German, bibliographies, a link called *Deutschland von A bis Z*, which should help to inspire you with topics for any project work you might have to perform, and altogether to much background information.

http://members.aol.com/artefact/daf-links.html This is an astonishingly good site which has more than 350 links provided by someone called Hartmut Schoenherr, who must have worked exceedingly hard to produce this information. His site is another which is probably sufficient by itself to lead you to any information you might need, and it is aimed specifically at learners and teachers of German. Links take you to search engines, dictionaries and encyclopaedias, newspapers, magazines, media, geography, politics, society, environment, history, culture, German, German as a foreign language, economics, law, science, technology, medicine, education, etc. If you are stuck for a topic for an extended essay/project, you really should be able to get some ideas here.

4.2 Travel arrangements

4 2.1 Rail

http://www.bahn.de/ If you are going to make a rail journey, and you want to know how to get from A to B, then the *Deutsche Bundesbahn* has a clever site where you can input the name of the town from which you will be travelling, destination, date you wish to travel, and the time of day, and you will be given a choice of trains, connections, whatever you might need. This could well be a faster process than going to the station and could save you money if you were thinking of going to a travel agent's in Germany, where an enquiry of this nature now tends to attract a charge. If you are planning an itinerary while you are still at home, incidentally, this is probably a much more reliable source of information than that obtainable from, for example, any British railway enquiry service – simply because it is very difficult for people who do not speak German to interpret the German timetable.

4.2.2 Air

http://flug.de/ Here you will find cheap or student flights, and air timetables.

http://www.lufthansa.com/ This provides information on flight availability, promotions, etc.

4.3 Finding out information about towns

http://www.meinestadt.de/ This gives you access to information on
14,000 German towns, so that you really should be able to find out about
any town you are likely to visit. There are links to local media, general
information about industry and business, sport, art, culture and anything
you might wish to enquire about.

4.4 Search engines

We tend to favour Google, but Lycos, Ask Jeeves, Yahoo are also good.
The *Deutsche Meta-Suchmaschine* interrogates many other German and
international search engines. You can find it by going to the Schoenherr site
mentioned above: his very first set of addresses will take to you not only to
this one, but to a plethora of others. We can only wish you good hunting.

5
Practical advice for when you are in Germany

5.1 Registration and enrolment procedures

Your first port of call in trying to find your way through what might at first seem like the labyrinth of registration procedure is the student Foreign Office (*Auslandsamt*) at the HEI you are attending. You should have been in touch before your arrival and should pay regular visits there during your placement. There is often an introductory one-week or two-week orientation course for foreign students immediately preceding the start of the semester, which you should make every effort to attend.

After that you will have to take your health insurance document to the local AOK office (see 2.5.2), since you will need the exemption certificate (*Befreiungsschein*) when enrolling on your course. You must then return to the *Auslandsamt* where you will get notification of admission/ acceptance as a student (*Zulassungsbescheid, Zulassung zum Studium*), as soon as the question of proficiency in the German language has been clarified. You will normally have to take the DSH (*Deutsche Sprachprüfung für den Hochschulzugang*). This is nothing to worry about, simply a standard language test for any foreign student, so exemption from it is possible only in special cases.

Next, the *Auslandsamt* will give you a registration number (*Matrikelnummer*). *Immatrikuliert* (*angemeldet/ eingeschrieben* are also used), means 'registered'. The registration form tells you when and where you must register. This will be at another important office, the *Studentensekretariat*, sometimes called the *Immatrikulationsamt*. Since the procedures vary slightly from institution to institution, ask at the *Auslandsamt* which documents you have to take with you for your official registration. These will almost certainly include your *Zulassungsbescheid* (acceptance certificate), your health certificate, and probably proof of being a student at your home institution, plus proof of being able to support yourself financially during your stay (see 2.4).

Foreign students having to go through all the paperwork of official registration sometimes feel as if they are just running from one office to the next, which is probably precisely what they *are* doing. Tedious though this may seem, it is nevertheless essential to complete the registration procedure properly. The staff in the *Auslandsamt* are there to help you, so there is no need to be embarrassed because you are having to go back there yet again; they will not expect you to apologise: it is their job to give you information and offer assistance, and most of them will. So, always be patient, friendly and polite, keep smiling, but keep asking.

If the German paper war (*Papierkrieg*) does start to get you down, perhaps you can console yourself by thinking of two points: first, if you get yourself organised, you can complete all the formalities in the first two or three weeks of your stay, and second, most of us are not aware of what registration procedures foreigners have to go through in our own country. It is often much more than you would imagine – talk to foreign students at your home institution and see how they react to the bureaucracy there.

As there are as yet no tuition fees at HEIs in Germany, the only money you will be asked to pay is a so-called *Sozialgebühr*, a 'social contribution'. This might be requested via the students' union (*Asta*) or the accommodation office (*Studentenwerk*). This fee usually amounts to around DM 60–90 per semester – it can vary. Paying this entitles you to a student identity card or pass (*Studentenausweis*), which means you are registered as a student and are allowed to use all the university facilities, e.g. library, sports and computer facilities. You will receive a course record book (*Studienbuch*), where you can record which lectures you have been attending. That will help you to obtain any certificates (*Scheine*) you require or to register for any examinations you wish to take there.

The student pass enables you to claim other student reductions for local cultural events, cheap food tickets in the student canteen (*Mensa*), discount fares and the like. In many university towns and cities you can get a *Semesterticket*, for a fee of around DM 100–150, allowing you to use any means of public transport without further charge for a whole semester. This is normally excellent value for money and therefore something which any student on a placement visit to Germany will recommend to future students. All registration is valid for one semester only.

Finally, let's recapitulate and outline the trail you might have to follow at a typical institution:

1. Arrival (at a convenient time). NB 3 October is a public holiday in Germany!
2. Go to your accommodation, having already announced your ETA and arranged to meet caretaker/landlord to collect keys, pay your deposit, drop off suitcases; alternatively go to youth hostel if accommodation is not yet available. Recover from journey.
3. It is now probably the next day. Go to the AOK and obtain a certificate in exchange for your medical insurance certificate, such as the E111 for EU citizens.
4. While you are doing this errand, it might be a good idea to find yourself a conveniently situated bank and open an account (see 5.3) since you will almost certainly be paying your rent by direct debit, and you will need an account number straight away.
5. By now it will probably be too late to go to the *Auslandsamt*, so this might be the time to find your way around the town, and anyway you might need to buy a few things for your room. So take some time out to look around the shops.
6. This is probably the following day. Make an early trip to the *Auslandsamt* taking with you the AOK certificate, and your proof of acceptance as a student (*Zulassung*), which will have been sent to your home address.
7. You will then be provided with further *Bescheinigungen*, with which you will be able to obtain various concessions. At some institutions, once you have registered as a student, you will, a few days later, receive your student identity card (*Studentenausweis*) and a *Semesterticket*.
8. You then have to register with the residents' office (*Einwohnermeldeamt*) and, if, as is likely, you are staying for more than three months, also with the aliens' office (*Ausländerbehörde*).

Regardless of which German office you are visiting, always go armed with all your documentation, including your passport and any bits of paper you have been collecting, and you shouldn't go far wrong.

5.2 Finding a doctor

You are legally obliged to have health insurance in Germany. The health system is of a high standard, but expensive. In order to avoid very high charges, should you require medical treatment abroad, please follow the advice given on health and insurance in 2.5. It is no use saying 'I'm never ill.' You must find out well in advance what documentation you need to acquire and take with you from your home country and/or institution before you leave. Otherwise you will be asked to pay something in the order of DM 800 for health insurance for one semester – and that is a reduced student rate!

For European holidaymakers or people on a short visit to Germany, it is sufficient to keep the E111 form close by them, but foreign students spending several months there must take their health cover form to the local sickness benefit office (*AOK – Allgemeine Ortskrankenkasse*) as soon as they arrive. This office is not allowed to recommend a doctor; if you should need a doctor while you are in Germany, you will be given a brochure which includes the names of all the doctors in the area. The essential form for you to obtain is the *Befreiungsschein*, or exemption certificate, which confirms that you are exempt from the normal charges when you register for your course.

Remember the advice regarding taking with you a good supply of any medication you are likely to need whilst you are away. If you do suffer from any condition for which you might possibly need to see a doctor while abroad, it might be worth looking up a few terms in a German dictionary before you go, or speaking to a German contact who could help you with one or two items of vocabulary, in case you have to explain something about your condition or illness when in Germany. Should you have to visit a doctor for some other reason, always let him/her know if you are taking some other medication already, since some medicines may react badly to others.

5.3 Opening a bank account

If you are spending a few months in the Federal Republic, you will need to open a bank account at one of the major banks, e.g. the Deutsche Bank, Commerzbank, Dresdener Bank, or possibly open one at a savings bank (*Sparkasse*) or a post office (*Postbank*). You can open a current account (*ein laufendes Konto* or *ein Girokonto*), from which you can follow the standard German practice of transferring money (*eine Überweisung*) from your bank to someone else's to cover any payments you have to make. If there are payments recurring on a regular basis, e.g. your monthly rent, you can set up a standing order (*Dauerauftrag*). A fixed amount can then be deducted automatically from your account on a fixed date each month. If you have a recurring bill to pay which varies in the precise amount, you can organise a direct debit (*Lastschrift*). You will be able to check any transactions on your bank statement (*Kontoauszug*).

Banks, savings banks and post office banks offer approximately the same service in Germany. As a rule, banks open from 09.00 until 16.00 and on Thursdays they normally remain open until around 17.30 or 18.30. Some smaller branches shut at lunch time from about 13.00 to 14.30.

5.4 Settling in and making contacts

Adapting socially and culturally to your new environment is a crucial part of your placement. You should try to join a sports or social club, choir, drama group – whatever interests you, in order to immerse yourself in local life. Ideally you should be the only representative of your country within the group that you join. You should make every attempt to get to know the country where you are studying and its people (*Land und Leute kennenlernen*). This knowledge will not only be valuable in itself, but also will help you to make new friends and give you a vital opportunity to acquire new language registers in German. It will also be an enjoyable counterbalance to academic work and make your stay generally more pleasant.

Some people might be a little homesick at first on placement. This is not always the case, but it can happen, especially if you are away from home for the first time. If it is taking you a little longer to settle down than you expected, then this is the point when you should join a society, if you have not done so already, and attend meetings or parties arranged by your subject/departmental club (*Fachschaft*).

Even if, like most of us, you have to force yourself to overcome any natural shyness, you must throw yourself into the way of life in Germany. Join in the things the Germans do and you will almost certainly feel the benefit at once. You will make friends, meet more people, speak more German and probably find out new things about the German people and their customs.

Many people are naturally a little diffident or shy, especially in a strange situation abroad. This is quite normal, but you will have to give yourself a little push in making those all-important contacts, and take the initiative in introducing yourself. It is a little like walking into an echo chamber: if you whisper 'hello', the echo you get back will also be a whisper, whereas if you speak in a clear and friendly manner, you will receive an enthusiastic and friendly response. Learn the German phrase: *Wie man in den Wald hineinruft, so schallt es heraus*. The expression incorporates the idea of 'others will treat you the same way you treat them'. In

other words: you get out only what you are prepared to put in. Life is
what you make it, and the same applies to your German placement!
Someone has to make the first move, so it might as well be you. After all,
even a short conversation in German is helpful for your language skills.

Incidentally, sometimes cultural differences or inadvertent misuse of
language can lead to misunderstandings. It is therefore important to be
ready to smile and apologise if you get the impression that you have said
something which is being received in a way you have not expected, even
if you cannot see what 'faux pas' you have made. Please remember that
a great deal of time and effort has gone into establishing exchange links
with partner institutions that can be destroyed at a stroke if students
behave inconsiderately. Try not to react badly to regulations which may,
at first sight, appear illogical. There may be a good reason for them,
which may become apparent only later.

A study or work placement abroad should teach you to take a broader
view, so that you do not to go in for the kind of silly and indeed xenophobic generalisations you might have heard at home such as 'the Germans
have no sense of humour'. They have a *different* sense of humour, as do
other nations, and the occasion when a joke seems appropriate definitely
differs from one culture to another. A foreign visitor to your country will
probably find your sense of humour strange too – especially at first.

5.5 Telephoning

Most public telephone kiosks in Germany are now for use with a card
(*Telefonkarte*), although coins (*Münzen*) can sometimes still be used too.
You can buy a telephone card, usually for either twelve or fifty marks at
any post office. Check the times for reduced rate calls for both within
Germany and abroad, as it can make quite a difference to the charges.
There are plenty of public telephone boxes from which you can dial
abroad, marked *Ausland*, and you can also ring home from a post office.

Remember that you need the international dialling code, e.g. to dial a
London number (0208 or 0207) from Germany, you need to dial 00
(international code), 44 (country code for the UK) plus 208 or 207 (area
code for either outer or inner London, omitting that first 0), or for
Liverpool 0044 151 (area code for Liverpool) plus the individual number.
To obtain San Francisco in the USA, dial 00, followed by 1 (country code
for the USA) plus 415 (area code for San Francisco) plus the number.
Similarly, dialling Wagga Wagga in Australia would entail using 00, then
61 (country code), 2 (area code) plus the number. For the sake of the

people you are calling, please do not forget the time difference, as they might be slightly less enthusiastic about hearing from you if they have just been woken from a deep sleep in the middle of the night. For dialling to Germany from abroad and also dialling within Germany see also beginning of chapter 7. If you have to ring someone in the evening, it would not normally be thought appropriate to call after 22.00, as some Germans have gone to bed by that time, given that the working day begins early.

5.6 **Radio and television**

Listening to the radio and watching television while you are in Germany will both improve your comprehension and increase your passive vocabulary, as well as enhance your knowledge of various cultural matters relating to the country and its different customs: *andere Länder, andere Sitten*. It might even give you ideas for a project topic, if you need them.

At the same time you must yourself make a real effort *not* to go searching for newspapers and satellite television programmes in English: in fact you should forbid yourself to do so. Your residence in Germany is a chance to immerse yourself in the language and culture of the country for an extended period, and therefore to become really fluent in spoken and written German. Do not waste a golden opportunity. Regular reading of a German daily newspaper, plus radio and television, will bring real benefit over a period of time, not just linguistically but also in terms of cultural and background knowledge of the country (*Landeskunde*).

5.7 **Everyone wants to learn English**

Whether your main discipline is modern languages or not, it would be a missed opportunity if you did not improve your spoken and written German while on placement. The best approach is obviously to read a German newspaper every day, to follow our advice in 5.4, and to mix with as many Germans as possible. Unfortunately, you will almost certainly come across a number of German speakers who will want to practise their English on you because English is the first foreign language at nearly all German schools and a working knowledge of American or British English is also now essential for most, if not all, German businesspeople. Therefore you will meet Germans who have spent some time in an English-speaking country and will want to speak English rather than German. We recommend that you insist, politely but firmly, that you wish to speak only German. You should say, with a smile, '*Bitte sprechen Sie Deutsch. In Deutschland nur Deutsch bitte*'.

At the same time, you should avoid too much contact with other native speakers of English even if your intention is to use German as your *lingua franca*. So try not to look up all those American or English people you met on the way to Germany. Though attempts to speak German with other native speakers of English are laudable, this does not usually work very well, since there is a tendency to learn other people's mistakes, and in cases of doubt you need a German friend to correct you. For this reason alone it is much better to make your friendships with German native speakers.

5.8 Earning some pocket money

Although you should normally avoid speaking English, one chance to turn the fact of being a native speaker of English to your advantage is if you want to earn a little money by offering English classes (see 6.5). As the importance of English as a world language continues to grow, and it is the first foreign language – second to French only in schools in the areas bordering France – in most parts of Germany, many parents are very keen for their children to have private lessons (*Nachhilfeunterricht*). Many German students require English, and since many businesspeople in German-speaking countries also require a working knowledge of British or American English, adult conversation classes are usually in demand. It is worth putting an advertisement on the student notice board (*das schwarze Brett*) or in the local newspaper, using the magic words 'native speaker'. The work is well paid. Ask locally first what the 'going rate' is and make sure that any English classes that you offer are conducted on an official basis, in return for payment, with a clear start and finish time. The rest of the time you should of course speak German. Do not allow yourself to become the person whom a few Germans always address in English whenever they see you.

Other forms of part-time work, though not easy to find, may be available from the local job centre (*Arbeitsamt*), especially when you are available at short notice. If you want to earn some extra money, keep asking as many local contacts as possible. Such work is not necessarily so hard to come by, and if you feel the need to augment your allowance or loan, it is worth persevering. For further details concerning working in Germany see chapter 6.

5.9 Personal safety

It is obviously in your own interests to take normal safety precautions and use some common sense when you are in Germany, particularly when you first arrive, as any mishaps early on in your stay are likely, of course, to colour your impression of your placement centre. If you would not normally leave your purse or wallet lying around unattended in your own country (and we assume you would not!), then do not do so while on placement in Germany. If you do that, or something similar, it is no use complaining loudly when something gets stolen and telling everyone that Germany is an awful country and that all Germans must be dishonest. It could just as easily have happened at home, and it will happen, if you are careless.

Similarly, if you would not usually walk home alone through dark isolated side streets or take a short cut across the fields in your own country, then do not do so in Germany either, as you would be asking for trouble. Some German cities run a special taxi service for women, where the taxi drivers are women (*Frauentaxis*). There is often a *Frauenbeauftragte* (women's officer) at the German HEI who will be happy to offer assistance, should it be necessary, with matters specifically relevant to women (see also 8.2.5).

6
Working in Germany

6.1 Work placements

Since reunification there has been widespread unemployment in the Federal Republic. The problem is that the full employment enjoyed by the former GDR had been promoted largely by a policy which allowed several individuals to do the work of one; this rather Utopian system could not continue after the Fall of the Wall. Economic reality brought a rapid loss of jobs in the eastern part of the country and with it all the social and political repercussions and upheavals associated with decreasing employment levels. In western Germany, which prior to 1990 had very high employment figures, various other economic factors have had a deleterious effect on the number of jobs available, and the whole country has experienced levels of unemployment unprecedented since the 1930s. In 1996 the number of unemployed crossed the 4,000,000 mark. By 1998 the distribution of unemployed was to the order of about 3,000,000 in the west of the country and about 1,3 million in the east.[1]

So you can see that for foreign nationals wishing to take up employment, even temporary and relatively low paid industrial and business work placements are not easy to procure. Some British HE institutions do have links with firms and are able to organise jobs for their business studies students, for example, but if you are attempting to organise a placement for yourself, then almost certainly you will need to have personal contacts and be able to take advantage of any links your family or friends might have at their disposal.

One area where you might be lucky, however, is information technology

---

1 *Statistisches Bundesamt Deutschland* (Federal Statistical Office) and *Bundesanstalt für Arbeit* (Federal Institute for Employment).

(IT). Here there is such a dearth of expertise in Germany that the government is trying to encourage foreign nationals with specialist knowledge to enter the country.[2] So if you happen to be doing a course which has given you such a specialism, or if you have already worked in the IT sector at home, a work placement in this sector might well be available.

6.2 Seeking work via the university

For students seeking temporary or part-time work, the *Asta* (*Allgemeiner Studentenausschuss*, or to be more politically correct *Allgemeiner Student-Innenausschuss*,[3] loosely equivalent to the students' union in the UK) is a good first port of call. It used to be the case that the *AStA* had a department which acted as an employment agency. Nowadays, you are more likely to find that you will simply be given information as to where you are most likely to find the right contacts. At some institutions it is the *Studentenwerk* which will point you in the right direction. The thing to do – and this is always a useful way of getting yourself into a position where you have to speak German – is go to the AStA or the *Studentenwerk* and ask. If there is no direct help available there, then they will certainly be able to tell you where you should look.

You can also keep an eye on the notice board (*das Schwarze Brett*) in

2 In March 2000, the Federal Chancellor, Gerhard Schröder, announced a programme intended to increase the numbers of students in the field of IT to 35,000–40,000 per year. In addition, because the shortage could not be remedied in the short term, the Federal Government also announced an emergency programme under which large numbers of IT specialists from non-EU countries would be given 'Green Cards', permitting them to work in the FRG for up to five years. The *Bundesvereinigung der Deutschen Arbeitgeberverbände* (German Employers' Federation) welcomed this move, but there was a negative reaction from xenophobic elements in the CDU/CSU, and Jürgen Rüttgers, the (unsuccessful) CDU candidate for the prime-ministership of North-Rhine-Westphalia in the 2000 regional elections, alienated and insulted both indigenous and foreign residents of the state when he spoke of Germany's needing 'Kinder statt Inder' (children rather than Indians).

3 This rather strange-looking word formation was invented in the latter part of the twentieth century in order to put a stop to the linguistic disadvantaging of women in the use of masculine nouns to embrace both sexes in the plural. This was perceived, quite rightly, to be inherently sexist, since the feminine form *Studentin*, or *Lehrerin*, or any feminine noun derived from a masculine was subsumed by its masculine counterpart in the plural. The *-Innen* form, with its strange medial capital letter has become absorbed into and accepted by the language and is to be seen in many written contexts, both in the quality press and in many modern texts.

the department where you are studying. In the English seminars especially you are likely to find requests for private tuition in English (see 6.5) and in the *Mensa* you are also likely to find there are offers of casual work on the notice boards.

6.3 Employment agencies

Try the *AStA* in Berlin, for example, and you might be directed to an organisation with the acronym *TUSMA*, which stands for *Telefonieren und Studenten Machen Alles* (Ring and students will do everything). This organisation places students seeking short-term employment for up to seven days, which is ideal if you want a little casual work to help out with your finances without any long-term commitment. Other towns will have other agencies, and all work in tandem with the *Arbeitsämter* (job centres).

Wherever the *AStA* suggests you apply to for a job, you will need to take various documents with you for filling in the application form. You will need:

- your passport (and if you are from outside the European Union you will need to have a residence and/or work permit (*Aufenthaltserlaubnis/ Arbeitserlaubnis*));
- your *Immatrikulationsbescheinigung* (student registration document, to prove that you are a *bona fide* student);
- a *Lohnsteuerkarte* (income-tax card), obtainable from the local *Lohn-steuerkartenstelle* (the income-tax card issuing office, probably to be found at the local *Rathaus* (town hall)), to which the *AStA* will direct you;
- two passport photographs;
- evidence from the AOK (see 2.5.2) that you have health insurance (you should have registered there during the first few days of your stay) – probably a so-called *Chipkarte* (smart card);
- a *Sozialversicherungsausweis* (Social Security Identity Card), usually also obtainable from the AOK;
- your bank account number.

As was pointed out in section 1.6, it is vital that you take full documentation with you whenever you approach any authority, otherwise you will simply be sent away and asked to come back with the right documents.

6.4 **Teaching assistantships**

Contracts for teaching assistantships are usually given for a complete academic year. This means that they are suitable for students doing a single honours course in German or one in which German is the major component. Those pursuing studies in two languages, where there is the expectation that such students will spend half a year in each of two countries, are therefore unlikely to be successful in any application for this type of post.

There are very great benefits to be gained from working as a teaching assistant for English in a German school: professional, financial, linguistic, and cultural.

For students considering teaching as a career (or even for those who are not, but want to experience different types of occupation), this presents an opportunity to find out what life is like at the front of the classroom. As a teaching assistant you will be expected to give conversation classes, to transmit cultural awareness of your native country, to interact with young people, some of whom may be only two or three years younger than yourself, to operate side by side with experienced teachers, and to take part in the life of the school to which you are assigned; you may well discover that you have a vocation to be a teacher.

The life of an assistant in a German school will not be burdened with administrative responsibilities, and an assistantship offers an excellent opportunity to gain some insight into aspects of German life you might not otherwise discover.

There are, of course, also financial advantages to working as an assistant. Living as a student abroad is going to be a little more expensive than living at home – even when the rates of exchange are very favourable (for Britons at least) – and if you are in the middle of a four-year course, most of which you are having to finance by means of loans or parental contributions, the prospect of a paid year is likely to be very attractive. Although the assistant's salary is not huge, it will certainly cover your accommodation, living, and travelling expenses, and can usually be augmented by giving *Nachhilfestunden* (private tuition) in English.

The assistant will normally give about twelve hours a week of lessons, much of which will involve as much use of English as possible. This rather contradicts our earlier comments, but twelve hours' English teaching is only a fraction of your waking (or indeed working) week, and you will find that the close contact with a school filled with German native speakers will more than compensate you for any enforced use of English – in addition to which you will be in Germany for a whole

academic year. Certainly the linguistic benefits are as great as those
accruing from residence as a student at a university, and if you are a little
shy or are slightly lacking in confidence in yourself, then working as a
teacher and being put into a position where you are called upon to be
authoritative about your language and culture may very well help you to
overcome your inhibitions.

From a cultural standpoint, working in a school will provide you with
an opportunity to examine aspects of German society and life which
might not be so obvious in a university environment. You are likely to
learn much about the concerns of young people, about their family life,
their festivals, their holidays, the way in which schools prepare children
for life, but also about teachers, civil service conditions, and hierarchical
structures which will be different from those in your native country.

If you are thinking of applying for an assistantship, and your
university department has no history of expecting its students to do so,
then British students need to contact the Central Bureau for Educational
Visits and Exchanges in order to obtain the necessary forms. US students,
especially those who wish to become teachers of German, can approach
the US Student Programs Division of the Institute of International
Education, where they will obtain a brochure entitled *Fulbright and
Related Grants for Graduate Study and Research Abroad.* See Appendix V
for addresses.

If you do decide to take this route and are accepted, you will take part
in briefings and receive advice before you go, but you can help yourself
a great deal in the months prior to your departure by collecting as much
varied material about your native country as you can: things which will
not take up too much room in your luggage such as newspaper articles
on general issues, advertisements, pictures, music discs or cassettes,
anything which will help to convey an authentic idea of the nation you
represent. The school to which you are sent is likely to have resources
and a teacher-adviser to whom you will be assigned, but for all contin-
gencies you might obtain a copy of an excellent resource, Friederike
Klippel's *Keep Talking* (see bibliography), which is filled with ideas for
keeping a class going, and is an ideal resource (even for experienced
teachers) since making people talk, who might not always be in the mood
to do so, is one of the most difficult tasks even an experienced teacher
can be presented with – and assistants are, inevitably, inexperienced.

Once you know the name of your school, you might also get in touch
with the current assistant there, who will be able to give you some hints
about what you can expect. If the school has had assistants over a long
period, then it is also likely that there will be an existing arrangement for

accommodation, so that you will simply be able to take over a room or flat from your predecessor. In the unlikely event that there is no such tradition and you are expected to make your own arrangements, then you will receive advice from the organisation through which you have obtained your post.

6.4.1 A reminder: finances and insurance

As you will be paid in arrears, you should also be sure that you take with you or have access to sufficient money to pay for things like a deposit on your room or flat and to cover living expenses for the first few weeks. You will need to open a bank account so that your salary can be paid into it and so that you can pay your rent by standing order (see 2.4). You should also make sure you have insurance cover (see 2.5).

6.5 **Private tuition**

There is a long tradition of private tutoring by the young and unqualified in Germany. So older schoolchildren are often enlisted to help younger pupils with subjects where they are experiencing difficulty. As a native speaker of English you should find it easy to obtain one-to-one and relatively well-paid work to help out with your finances. If you are working in a school, the work will probably be offered to you. If you are studying at a university, you will be able to consult notice boards in English departments, advertise in free newspapers, or simply contact schools in your town and say that you are available for *Nachhilfeunterricht*.

6.6 **Vacation work**

You are likely to have a period of residence in the countries of the languages you are studying as an integral part of your studies, in the third year of a four year course, for example. But you may also want to spend some of your vacation time abroad at an earlier point in your course, or as part of a Gap year before you go to university (see 6.7). If you have the opportunity to spend some time in a German ambience, and you have the inclination, even if the work is menial, it will provide you with some extra foundation and extra confidence before you go on your 'official' visit.

As we have pointed out, skilled work is difficult to find, but if you are prepared to work as an au-pair, or in a hotel or a restaurant, then you will have a good chance of obtaining something. It has been the experience of our students, over years and even recently in the somewhat more depressed work climate, that bar and hotel work have been relatively easy to obtain. Of course, it is not well paid, but on the other hand, the object is to widen linguistic experience rather than to make a fortune – although that would be pleasant as well.

6.6.1 Work as an au pair

Au pairing, once restricted to females, is an area now open to males. Applying for this work is a gamble: we hear of young people who are treated like one of the family, given plenty of free time, supported, even taken on holiday, but also it can happen that the au pairs are exploited as cheap labour. On the other hand, whatever the conditions, a period spent in the bosom of a German family can help you to increase your command of the language enormously in a relatively short time, and it is certainly our experience that students with fairly weak German have made major progress in the course of one summer vacation working as an au pair.

If you are interested in earning your keep and a little pocket money in return for looking after young children and doing some housework, and at the same time taking part in an as it were involuntary immersion course in German, this really is not a bad idea. Incidentally, it is normally part of the contract between the employer and the au pair that time should be given so that there is the opportunity to take part in a formal language course. See Appendix V for the addresses of some agencies.

6.6.2 Hotel and catering

As we have said, it is relatively easy to obtain work in the catering and tourist industries. If you want this type of work, then try the *Zentralstelle für Arbeitsvermittlung* (see Appendix V for address), or if there is a town where you would particularly like to work, write to *das Arbeitsamt der Stadt X* (job centre of town + name). You should be able to find the address of a local job centre from the German telephone directories, which are usually available in large central libraries either as books, or on a CD-ROM, and, of course, you will also find them on the Internet at *http://www. telefonbuch.de/*. There you can simply type the word *Arbeitsamt* in the slot marked *Name*, and the name of the town that interests you in the slot marked *Ort*, hit the start button, and the address will appear.

You could also try to find hotel work in the tourist areas of Austria and German-speaking Switzerland, but be warned: the versions of the language that you will hear in those countries will not necessarily bear any close resemblance to what you have been studying. On the contrary, if you watch an Austrian or Swiss programme on a German television channel, you will find that it is very likely to be subtitled – for its audience of native German speakers.

6.6.3 Voluntary work

There are various organisations via which you might well be able to find rewarding, though unpaid, work. Usually you will have to finance your travel arrangements, but you will be given board and lodgings in return for a 30–35 hour week.

There are several organisations in Germany which offer placements for volunteers, and if you have the inclination to take part in one of their schemes, then on the one hand you will act in the knowledge that you are contributing to the good of others, and on the other you will be making your CV that much more attractive to the potential employer. You will be perceived as having acquired skills which are much sought after: initiative, the ability to work in a team and to pursue and achieve goals. In addition, you will have demonstrated your commitment to language learning and internationalism. Organisations to approach are:

Internationale Begegnung in Gemeinschaftsdiensten e.V. (International Collaboration in Community Services). This is an organisation which was founded in 1965 to promote peace and understanding between peoples by encouraging young people from all over the world to work together on useful social, environmental, or renovation projects.

The IJGD (*Internationale Jugendgemeinschaftsdienste* – International Young People's Community Services), which has similar goals to those of the IBG.

Finally, there is *the Vereinigung Junger Freiwilliger e.V.* (Association of Young Volunteers), which runs 30–40 work camps every year in the eastern part of Germany.

See Appendix V for a list of addresses.

6.7 **Gap year**

There are arguments for and against taking a Gap year. Taking time out adds a further year to the period during which you are being educated and thus delays your entry into the job market; it takes you away from studying for a year, so that you might get out of the habit and find it difficult to readjust to the discipline of academic life; there is the danger that you might opt to do something which turns out to be not what you expected and you drop out, losing a year. You need to examine your own personality to see if this is likely to happen to you.

If, on the other hand, taking a Gap year means that you gain experience in the field you are intending to enter, for example, if you were going to study chemistry and were able to get a work placement as a laboratory assistant, clearly the work would be relevant, and you would be 'keeping your hand in'. For language students, the opportunity to take a year out in a country whose language they are to study is similarly extremely worthwhile: students who have worked as au pairs, or have done some sort of work in their target country, are at a great advantage when they start a language course in HE: they have been busy honing their comprehension and productive skills, building up their active and passive vocabulary – 'keeping their hand in' almost without having to think about it.

You could try any of the addresses mentioned in the vacation work section of Appendix V, and if you are considering voluntary work, you might need to look for several placements since work camps are usually intended to last two or three months. You could also consider taking up a training place as a team leader if you feel that that would suit you – certainly the evidence that you have been able to develop leadership skills will not harm the look of your CV. The organisations will provide you with information about all aspects of their work when you contact them. If you should be interested you should obtain a copy of *The Gap Year Guidebook*, which is published by the Peridot Press (see bibliography).

It is not our intention to persuade anyone to take a Gap year, but it is an option which you might think about if you feel that you can afford the time and it will not cause you any financial hardship.

7
Leaving Germany and returning home

There are a number of important practical steps to take with regard to leaving your placement centre and returning home. This is an aspect of the placement abroad which is sometimes overlooked. Following a few simple guidelines might save time later and possibly reduce the time it takes you to settle back into your study pattern at home. In some cases the time is quite short between settling into your home environment again and getting yourself fully prepared for what might be your final examinations.

7.1 Academic records

Your home institution will most likely require you to submit certificates (*Scheine*, see 1.5) from your German HEI to prove which classes you attended and which examinations and/or assignments you took. You should have found out before you left home what sort of attendance and examination certificates you were going to need, and how many. Your home institution may require its students to have attended a certain minimum number of classes or to provide a minimum number of marks, which gain credit points from the placement abroad and count towards the final qualification at home.

Remember that such certificates and marks do not simply materialise out of thin air: you will have to inform your German lecturers in good time that you require a *Schein* or *Note*, make arrangements to do the appropriate work (*Hausarbeit*), or take the appropriate test (*Klausur*) or examination (*Prüfung*), and then arrange to collect your certificates to take home with you. If you are spending one semester only in Germany, check well in advance when all this can be done. If there really is no way of obtaining evidence of attendance and marks before your departure, leave a forwarding address on a stamped addressed envelope. The best approach is to give your permanent home address. Doing this should save you valuable time when you are back home. If you can, it is, of course, always preferable to sort such things out while you are still on the spot. People who have received any form of grant or award, e.g. a SOCRATES grant, could be required to repay it if they are unable to provide written evidence of marks obtained.

Many universities now ask their students on placement to complete a report form. This may take the form of giving detailed information concerning your centre, accommodation, etc., which will offer future students the sort of help you were given before embarking on your placement. It may also require you to have parts of the form completed by the German staff who taught you. If this is the case, do not leave things until the last moment, as staff in Germany are by no means always available. The best time to catch them is during their consultation hour, or *Sprechstunde* (see 1.2.3).

7.2 Leaving your accommodation

7.2.1 Hall of residence

You will need to give some notice of your intended date of departure. So you should speak to the *Hausmeister* and arrange for your room to be inspected, in order to have your deposit returned. It usually involves much more hassle if you forget and then try to get your money refunded after you have arrived home. Often you can avoid the whole process, providing of course that there are no damages to pay for, by simply not paying the final month's rent, which will be the equivalent of the deposit you had to pay originally. Find out just before you are planning to leave exactly what the situation is.

In Germany a room in hall often has to be reserved and paid for up to the end of the semester, which could mean from the beginning of September until the end of February (winter semester), or the beginning of March or April until the end of August (summer semester). Even if you arrive in mid-September, you will still have to pay for the whole month. Similarly, if you leave before the end of the month, you normally have to pay a full month's rent. Should your German placement be during the summer semester, it is well worth considering staying on until the end of July or August, as you will have accommodation already, which you will almost certainly have to pay for anyway during those months. It might be possible to get some part-time or temporary work in Germany over the summer (see 6.6), and anyway the longer you spend there the more your knowledge of the language and country is likely to improve.

As with everything else, do your best not to create a bad impression while you are there and try to leave on good terms. Any inconsiderate behaviour on your part or damages left behind could adversely affect the reception that future students from your institution will receive. It has been known, in isolated cases, for German university authorities to refuse to take any more students from town X, or even country Y, simply because two or three students from that particular town or country caused serious trouble on just one occasion. Such reactions are fortunately rare and are obviously both illogical and unfair. Nevertheless, if such a situation does occur, the staff at your home university or college cannot force a German HEI to take their students next year. In any case, even if nothing untoward has happened, it is important that you let people know that you are leaving, and when, and tie up any loose ends before you go, including closing your bank account. Even if you anticipate returning to Germany, your return may not be as soon as you anticipate, by which time your account will probably be regarded as 'dead'. However, be sure that all transactions have been completed before you close your account.

7.2.2 Private accommodation

In a minority of cases students might have been living in a house or flat obtained in the private market. If so, it is likely that you will have more formalities to complete before you leave. You will, for instance, have to go through the agreed inventory with your landlord or representative before you leave. Make sure you are aware of the agreed period of notice (*Kündigungsfrist*) and keep to it. Any services such as electricity, gas, water and telephone will need to have been checked/metered, so that the corresponding bills can be received and paid in good time. If your private accommodation has been a success, it might be a good idea to ask if it would be available for future students from your HEI and pass on the address to them, thus saving them the time and trouble of a long search.

Depending on your individual situation, it may be necessary to give some consideration to what accommodation arrangements you are going to make for the next academic year back home. Perhaps you can get in touch with someone back at your home HEI: there might be deadlines for applying for accommodation for next semester, especially if the number of students in your home town/country has increased. You will know your own situation best, but do give the matter some thought.

7.3 German books or material for future use

Thinking ahead to what for many students will be the approaching final year of study, you might try to obtain your final year reading lists. Obviously any German books or texts will be easier to get while you are still in Germany, or there may be a new version of a useful reference work or dictionary you wish to purchase before you leave. Such books will not only be more readily available but also cheaper in Germany than in your home country. Should you be interested in media/film, the same applies to videos and other material. You may want to consider taking out a student subscription to a German newspaper, which could be sent across to your home, as a good way of keeping in touch with German life and current affairs. An alternative might be to make a private arrangement with a German friend – perhaps a keen Anglophile – to exchange materials.

Try to sort out any material you have collected during your stay, so that you do not fill up your suitcase with unwanted papers. At the same time, a quick sort might make you aware of something you wanted to buy before leaving. It will also be a chance to take stock and remind you of any key points you want to include in any report on your placement. A frank evaluation of any courses you attended at the German HEI and a breakdown of vital up-to-date information concerning sporting and computer facilities, shops, places to visit – and places to avoid – helpful contacts at the *Auslandsamt*, etc., will be invaluable to both your placements tutor and future students attending your centre.

7.4 Settling back in

As your German placement draws to a close, you should be sure to make a checklist of tasks to carry out before you leave so that you tie up all the loose ends, and you must prepare properly for your return home to your study programme. You are going to find that time is short as you enter your final year, and you will want to settle in as quickly as possible.

It sometimes happens that students who have coped very well with adapting to life in Germany and thoroughly enjoyed their time there find that it takes them longer than expected to settle back into their home environment again. Many have happy memories of their placement and people they met abroad, only to arrive home to find that their former student friends have now moved on and the home campus has changed so that they may feel slightly disorientated.

This could be the right time to recall how you felt during the first few days or weeks of your time abroad and try to offer help to any foreign students arriving at your home institution. You are in a unique position to do this. Offer a friendly word of encouragement, show any German students how to join a student sports or social club, take them to the student refectory, a cheap café, a local cinema or the theatre. Doing this will actually not only help your foreign visitors to adapt to a new situation but also it will assist you to settle down again more quickly than might otherwise have been the case.

As your final year of study progresses, you may well be asked to give the benefit of your experience of the German system to those students who are being prepared for their placement in the following year. Any advice you can give will be most welcome. Those about to set out on their 'journey into the unknown' will be just as apprehensive and anxious as you were, so try not to emphasise the one negative experience you had in six or twelve months which will have stuck in your mind. Try instead to give a rounded, balanced picture of your placement overall and try to offer reassurance on precisely the points you were concerned about before you left home. If you managed reasonably well financially while you were away (and many students report that they were no worse off living as a student in Germany), then mention that by way of encouragement. A few hints on the 'nitty-gritty' matters of everyday life or tips regarding cheap trips to Berlin or wherever, stressing the positive aspects of your placement, will provide help and encouragement to students who may be slightly daunted by what lies ahead of them.

8
German institutions of higher education and their locations

In choosing the following institutions, we have tried to look at a fair spread of German universities and *Fachhochschulen*, as well as the teacher training colleges, so that every federal state is represented. There are simply too many HEIs to include them all, and therefore it should not be assumed that the exclusion of a particular HEI means that it is not recommended. In each case we have tried to provide any relevant information available on a number of important aspects, such as details for contacting the institution, its accommodation office (*Studentenwerk*), foreign office, vacation courses, the addresses of a youth hostel, the tourist office, sickness benefits office (*AOK*) and the Chamber of Commerce, as well as brief information on the town, local industry and any twinning arrangements with Great Britain and the USA. The relevance of these is explained further below.

When telephone numbers are given, this includes the local dialling code, e.g. 0911 for Nuremberg. If dialling from outside Germany, the country codes prefix needs to be used – e.g. 0049 from the UK – after which the first 0 of the local code is omitted; in the case of Nuremberg you would therefore dial 0049 911, plus the local number. This system applies the other way round too, so that if you were ringing Manchester (code 0161) from Germany, you would dial 0044 (for Great Britain) 161, omitting the 0 (for a fuller explanation see 5.5). Wherever available, fax and email numbers have been included. Although we have made every effort to give accurate and up-to-date information, we have found that at one or two institutions numbers are sometimes changed (apparently) in an arbitrary way.

In some cases institutions which have a lot to recommend them in all other respects lacked just one or two aspects of the provision on our criteria and this accounts for any information gap.

Since a large group of full-time students who spend either a semester or a full year abroad on placement still come from modern languages departments or related university-wide language courses, a major criterion for selection was the language provision and whether the German HEI has a German and/or English department.

The support structure offered by the particular HEI was a further selection criterion. We felt it was also important to look at the full range of facilities offered, so that we tried to ascertain, for example, whether there is a representative with specific responsibility for women, a student foreign office (*Auslandsamt*), and representation for disabled students. We also checked on student computer facilities, the addresses of the Chamber of Commerce, for those interested in local business and industry, and the local health office for registering under the sickness insurance scheme. A thumbnail sketch is given of the town in which the HEI is situated and any local industry is indicated for students who may be researching a project during their stay.

Each entry begins with information on a town, followed by the institutions within that town. There are three sections: universities, *Fachhochschulen* and *Pädagogische Hochschulen* (teacher training colleges).

8.1 Towns: key to the headings

The information here gives you the addresses and contact numbers of important sources of information in and for the town.

8.1.1 *Verkehrsverein* (Tourist office)

Once you know where you are going to be studying in Germany, you should write to the *Verkehrsverein*, the tourist office of the town, requesting an information pack. You will be sent a map of the town and brochures on places of interest. This serves the purpose of encouraging you to write a letter in German, which is good practice anyway, and providing you with material which will help you to orient yourself before you leave your home country. You can also use the Internet to find things out about the town (see 4.3), and you will find publications such as *The Rough Guide to Germany* (see McLachlan 1998) also a great help for your pre-visit preparation.

8.1.2 *Jugendherbergen* (Youth hostels)

If you think you are going to arrive at your destination unavoidably at an inconvenient time (see 2.8 for advice), then you should try and book yourself into the local youth hostel for the night. Prices for such accommodation are relatively low and will certainly be better suited to the student pocket than a hotel. While it is impossible to generalise, you can probably count on most *Jugendherbergen* (youth hostels) or *Jugendgästehäuser* (young people's guesthouses) in Germany to be clean and nowadays to be very much like hotels anyway.

Even if you are not going to need a youth hostel in the town where you will be studying, it is probably a sensible idea to join the Youth Hostels Association in your home country. Membership costs only £12 per year in the UK and gives you access to hostels throughout the world. While you are in Germany you are certainly going to want to travel and youth hostels are the cheapest source of clean accommodation, unless you have friends with whom you can stay in every single place you want to visit. See Appendix V for the addresses of UK and US headquarters of Youth Hostels Associations.

8.1.3 *Industrie- und Handelskammern* (Chambers of Industry and Commerce)

Many students are expected to work on projects or extended essays during their period of residence, and often the topic will be about local business or industry. We are therefore providing addresses and contact numbers for *Industrie- und Handelskammern* which are excellent sources of information. Incidentally, the *IHK*s of Germany have their own web site at *www.ihk.de/* where you will find extensive regional and national links.

8.1.4 *AOK*

You need to visit the *Allgemeine Ortskrankenkasse* with your E111 or equivalent within your first few days in Germany (see 2.5.2). We have therefore included the address of the nearest branch to your institution.

8.1.5 Local newspapers

We give the name of at least one local newspaper, together with its URL, so that you can read up on whatever is going on in the area you will be visiting before you leave your home country. At the time of writing, just one or two of the towns have newspapers which are not online, so that there you will have to wait until you arrive to find out what the local publication is like.

8.1.6 Town, area and industry

Under this heading are included short notes and general remarks:

The derivation of the town's name is explained. This is just in case you are interested in words, which, if you are a language student, you might be. So if, for example, you have always wondered why the English for *Braunschweig* is Brunswick, then you will be given some inkling of the reason. You will find that the names of most towns have to do with their being near water, or on hills, or in valleys – all rather obvious in fact, except that in many cases the words for 'water' or 'river' are not recognisable as such because they have been lost from modern German or come from other languages.

This is followed by notes on the town's size, importance, state (whether bombed during World War II; if bombed, whether restored), any reasons for fame.

The approximate size of the population is given, as is also the number of students attending HE institutions in the town.

The geographical position of the town is indicated: the *Land* in which it is situated, the river it is on, neighbouring towns, closest mountain ranges. We give the English version of the *Land* name. Some names are the same in both languages, such as Baden-Württemberg, Berlin, Brandenburg, Bremen, Hamburg, Saarland and Schleswig-Holstein. Some of the other *Länder* have similar, but not identical names, while one or two others look quite different from their English counterparts:

Bayern: Bavaria
Hessen: Hesse
Niedersachsen: Lower Saxony
Nordrhein-Westfalen: North Rhine-Westphalia
Rheinland-Pfalz: Rhineland-Palatinate
Sachsen: Saxony
Sachsen-Anhalt: Saxony-Anhalt
Mecklenburg-Vorpommern: Mecklenburg-West Pomerania
Thüringen: Thuringia

We point out a few of the most famous sights on offer (some of the towns are very small, so that we may have found only one or two places of interest). These really are meant simply as examples, and your letter to the *Verkehrsverein,* or your visit to the town's Internet site, will provide you with all the information about sightseeing that you might need.

Under 'Culture' we indicate whether the town has museums, theatres, etc.; most do have a wide range of cultural interest: again, you will be able to discover more detail for yourself.

We list the major industries of each town. If you are a business student and have a project to write, you might want to target an industry or company before you leave for Germany. You might consult the Internet, the Yellow Pages for Germany, as well as business directories for Germany, which should be available at central libraries in your home country.

8.1.7 Twinning

Where there is a twinning arrangement between a German town and a British or American counterpart, we have indicated this. If such an arrangement exists between either your home or university town and the town you are visiting in Germany, go to your town hall to find out whether there are any benefits arising from the relationship which you might be able to exploit.

8.2 **Institutions: key to the headings**

The information here is intended to provide you with sufficient details to make contact with appropriate offices and officials at the institution you are to visit.

8.2.1 Universities

The top section indicates the name of the university, which will look either like this:

> *Universität* + name of town, e.g. *Universität Hannover*

or like this:

> Name of person from whom the university has its title + university + town, e.g. *Ruprecht-Karls-Universität Heidelberg*

This is followed by the institution's address, telephone and fax number, and its URL, the *http://* code which gives you its web site (see part 4).

All the other rubrics contain address, telephone and fax numbers, and email address (where they are available).

8.2.2 *Akademisches Auslandsamt*

This is the equivalent of the International Office at a British institution. This is usually your first contact point at a German university, and you will almost certainly already have been in touch with a representative of this office when you first sent off your application form. The people working in this part of the university have often lived abroad themselves, have dealt with many different nationalities, and have understanding of the problems encountered by students when they first enter a new system. You should introduce yourself upon arrival, and if there is anything you do not understand, you will be sure to find help.

The *Auslandsamt* often runs courses in German as a Foreign Language (*Deutsch als Fremdsprache*) at various levels, and if you have been studying the language for a relatively short time, you may find that an intermediate level course will complement your studies in other departments of the university. If you are intending to start German from scratch, you will not be able to do so at a German university. If you wish to take a beginner's course in German, then you should do so at your home institution, or you could go to a Goethe Institut where excellent fast-track immersion courses are available (see 4.1.6).

The *Auslandsamt* is altogether an important source of information for you. You will find that trips, often subsidised, are put on for foreign students (to Berlin, to other major cities, to cultural events in general – theatre and concert visits are organised, for example) so that you should read the notice boards frequently, since clearly, demand for these trips is high, the number of seats available is limited and first comers will be served first. We frequently hear of students missing out on very tempting trips because they failed to watch out for offers advertised on notice boards. Look out for international evenings, at which you will have the opportunity to meet not only German nationals but also people from many other cultures, and the *lingua franca* will be German. You will find that there is a great deal on offer, and – obviously – it is up to you how you exploit it.

8.2.3 *Studentenwerk*

As far as you – a foreign student temporarily in Germany – are concerned, the *Studentenwerk* is roughly the equivalent of the Accommodation Office at a British university. This is not its only function; on the contrary, among its other tasks are economic, social, cultural and health issues, where these relate to student support. But you are likely to come across it mainly as the agent via which you obtain university accommodation, and it is to the *Studentenwerk* that you will be sending application forms if you wish to go into a hall of residence (*Studentenwohnheim/ StudentInnenwohnheim*). It is advisable to send in these applications fairly early and you will have to be patient with the speed of response. Although communication from the *Studentenwerk* can be a bit sparse, it is our experience that the paperwork has invariably been done before students arrive and that there is always a room awaiting them if they have adhered to the procedures indicated to them.

8.2.4 AStA

The *AStA*, which is an acronym standing for *Allgemeiner Studentenaus-schuss* or *Allgemeiner StudentInnenausschuss* – literally: 'General Students' Committee' – is more or less the equivalent of the Students' Union in Great Britain. We have used *AStA* as the name of the rubric we use, but there is some variation in the nomenclature, so that you may find that at some universities the *AStA* has an equivalent called the *Student(Inn)-enrat* (student council, acronym *StuRa*), *Studentenschaft* (student body), *Student(Inn)envertretung* (student representative body). Whatever the name, it is a committee elected by the students and represents them and their interests. It acts as a mediator between the students and the university administration, deals with students' problems and organises social activities. The *AStA* tends to be run by young people. If you have any talent that you think might be useful to them and would like to offer voluntary help, make yourself known to them.

8.2.5 *Frauenbeauftragte* (Women's Officer)

The *Frauenbeauftragte* is the equivalent of the Women's Officer at a British institution. There are very often various women's representatives at departmental and faculty level at most institutions, but we have, where possible, given the name of the institutional representative, who will normally be based in the *Frauenbüro* (Women's Office). There is a tendency at some institutions for the *Frauenbeauftragte* to change from year to year, so that wherever possible we have tried to give contact numbers at the *Frauenbüro*.

While we would hope that women students will not need to call on the *Frauenbeauftragte* because of problems arising from harassment, for example, we are pleased to be able to point out that, although some universities have not yet got round to having women's representatives, such places are in the minority, as you will see from the institutional descriptions.

The *Frauenbeauftragte* will also be able to put you in touch with women's groups should you wish to be involved in them. It is also the case that, on occasion, students wish to write projects about provision for women in Germany, and here too the *Frauenbeauftragte* will be the appropriate source for contacts.

8.2.6 *Behindertenbeauftragte(r)* (Disabled Students Officer)

Most, though not quite all, German universities have a *Behindertenbeauftragte(r)*, who is the representative for disabled students (and staff). If you are a student with a disability, then it is important for you to indicate this on your application form and to make yourself known to the *Behindertenbeauftragte(r)*, if possible by letter before you leave for Germany, or personally soon after you have arrived.

8.2.7 Computer access

If you are used to having an email address at your home institution, you will probably want to be able to maintain your links while you are in Germany, and at most institutions you will be able to obtain a local email address, once you have registered as a student, via the central computing department, which is usually called the *Rechenzentrum* (Computer Centre) or *Hochschulrechenzentrum* (University Computer Centre).

8.2.8 English and German departments

Because many students will have lectures and classes in the English and German departments of the institution they are visiting, we have given their addresses, since these are likely to be an early port of call. If you are intending to study in other departments, you need only to consult the *Vorlesungsverzeichnis* in order to discover their whereabouts (see 1.4).

8.2.9 Vacation courses

Many institutions offer summer vacation courses in German language and culture, and where these are available we have indicated them. If you can afford it or can earn enough money to finance it, taking part in such a course is an excellent introduction to life in the country, and a likewise excellent opportunity to lengthen your stay by a few weeks if you are intending to spend the winter semester in Germany.

8.3 **Universities**

Aachen

Verkehrsverein: Atrium Elisenbrunnen, Friedrich-Wilhelm-Platz, 52062
Aachen. Tel: (0241) 18 02 960
Jugendherberge: Maria-Theresia-Allee 260, 52074 Aachen. Tel: (0241) 71
101
Industrie- und Handelskammer: IHK Aachen, Theaterstr. 6–10, Postfach
650, 52007 Aachen. Tel: (0241) 44 60 0 Fax: (0241) 44 60 259 Email:
info@aachen.ihk.de
AOK: Karlshof am Markt, 52062 Aachen. Tel: (0241) 46 40 Fax: (0241)
40 36 27
Local newspapers: Aachener Nachrichten: www.an-online.de/; *Aachener
Zeitung:* www.aachener-zeitung.de/

Town, area and industry

Aachen: The name is derived from the Latin *Aquisgrani*, 'Granus's
Waters/Spa', Granus being a Celtic god. By 972 CE, the name had
been translated into a more Germanic form as *Ahha* (waters). The
town thus dates back to pre-Roman times. This was Charlemagne's
capital and the place where the Holy Roman emperors were crowned
until the Reformation. Despite much destruction in the Second
World War, much remains or was reconstructed after the war. There
is a great deal in the way of Charlemagne memorabilia. Aachen,
incidentally, has the warmest springs in Germany and is an important
Carnival centre.
Population: c. 254,000; there are *c.* 32,000 students at RWTHA, with a
further 10,200 at the FH.
Position: SE North Rhine-Westphalia. It is at the so-called *Dreiländereck*
(three country corner) – the town is on the border of both Holland
and Belgium, and it is possible to find a place just outside the town
where you can walk round in a small circle and be in three countries
in as many seconds.
Sights: Altstadt, cathedral with many treasures, many historical sites.
Culture: Museums, theatres, orchestra, galleries.
Industry: Iron, steel, machinery, foodstuffs, textiles, engineering, chemicals, glass, electronics, cosmetics, needles and pins, computers,
insurance.
Twinning: GB: Halifax; USA: Arlington

Rheinisch-Westfälische Technische Hochschule

Templergraben 55, 52056 Aachen. Tel: (0241) 801 Fax: (0241) 88 88 312
Web site: www.rwth-aachen.de

Akademisches Auslandsamt: Ahornstr. 55, 52056 Aachen. Tel: (0241) 80
41 01 Fax: (0241) 88 81 72 Email: international@aaa.rwth-aachen.de

Studentenwerk: Turmstr. 3, 52072 Aachen. Tel: (0241) 88 840 Fax: (0241)
88 84 125 Email: anja.elsen@stw.rwth-aachen.de

AStA: Turmstr. 3, 52072 Aachen. Tel: (0241) 80 37 92 Fax: (0241) 87 61 03

Frauenbeauftragte: Karmanstr. 9, Raum 314, 52062 Aachen. Tel: (0241) 80
35 76 Fax: (0241) 88 88 258 Email: frauenbeauftragte@rwth-aachen.de

Behindertenbeauftragte(r): Michael Hohenstein, Templergraben 55, 52062
Aachen. Tel: (0241) 80 40 18 Fax: (0241) 88 88 609

Computer/email access via: Rechenzentrum der RWTH, Seffenter Weg
23, 52074 Aachen. Tel: (0241) 80 49 00 Fax: (0241) 88 88 134 Email:
sekretariat@rz.rwth-aachen.de

English department: Institut für Anglistik, Karmanstr. 17/19, 52062
Aachen. Tel: (0241) 80 61 05 Fax: (0241) 88 88 350 Email: Marsden
@anglistikIII.rwth-aachen.de

German department: Germanistisches Institut der RWTH Aachen,
Templergraben 55, 52056 Aachen. Tel: (0241) 80 60 76 Fax: (0241)
88 88 269

Vacation courses: Usually in August. Emphasis on German as a foreign
language.

Augsburg

Verkehrsverein: Bahnhofstr. 7, 86150 Augsburg. Tel: (0821) 50 20 70
Fax: (0821) 50 20 745 Email: tourismus@augsburg.btl.de

Jugendherberge: Beim Pfaffenkeller 3, 886152 Augsburg. Tel: (0821) 33 909

Industrie- und Handelskammer: IHK Augsburg, Stettenstr. 1, 86150 Augsburg.
Tel: (0821) 31 620 Fax: (0821) 31 62 323 Email: info@augsburg.ihk.de

AOK: Bürgermeister-Wegele-Str. 6, 86167 Augsburg. Tel: (0821) 27 070
Fax: (0821) 27 07 200

Local newspaper: Augsburger Allgemeine: www.augsburger-allgemeine.de/

Town, area and industry

Augsburg: The town, founded by the Romans 2000 years ago and originally called *Augusta Vindelicorum*, is named after the Roman emperor
Augustus and a Celtic tribe from the area; the German word *burg* in the

sense of 'town' was added in the ninth century. By the fifteenth century Augsburg was a major banking and commercial centre, developed by the Fugger and Welser families. It was badly damaged in the Second World War; none the less many of the town's historic monuments survive.

Population: 265,000; there are *c.* 14,000 students at the university.

Position: Augsburg is the capital of Bavarian Swabia, on the River Lech, quite close to Munich.

Sights: Roman remains, medieval churches, Fuggerei (this was a socially planned living area originally financed by the Fugger banking family in the sixteenth century in order to provide former servants of the household and poor people of the town with security and decent accommodation). You will also find the house belonging to Mozart's father, which is now a Mozart museum.

Culture: Museums, theatres, galleries.

Industry: Engineering, steel, textiles, cars, aeroplane manufacture, paper, electronics, high-tech industries, chemicals, shoes.

Twinning: GB: Inverness; USA: Dayton

Universität Augsburg

Universitätsstr. 2, 86135 Augsburg. Tel: (0821) 59 80 Fax: (0821) 59 85 505. Web site: www.uni-augsburg.de

Akademisches Auslandsamt: Universitätsstr. 2, Raum 3075, 86135 Augsburg. Tel: (0821) 59 85 146

Studentenwerk: Eichleitnerstr. 30, 86135 Augsburg. Tel: (0821) 59 84 901 Fax: (0821) 59 86 250

AStA: Universitätsstr. 2, 86135 Augsburg. Tel: (0821) 59 85 169 Fax: (0821) 59 85 169 Email: asta@asta.uni-augsburg.de

Frauenbeauftragte: Marion Magg-Schwarzbäcker, Rektoratsgebäude, Zi. 3074, Universitätsstr. 2, 86135 Augsburg. Tel: (0821) 59 85 145 Fax: (0821) 59 84 20

Behindertenbeauftragte(r): Frau Agnes Hagg, Universitätsstr. 2, 86135 Augsburg. Tel: (0821) 59 85 393

Computer/email access via: Universitätsstr. 8, 86135 Augsburg. Tel: (0821) 59 82 010 Fax: (0821) 59 82 028 Web site: wwwadm@rz.uni-augsburg.de

English department: Sprachenzentrum, Universtitätsstr. 2, 86135 Augsburg. Tel: (0821) 59 85 189 Email: anthony.hornby@sz.uni-augsburg.de

German department: Sprachenzentrum, Universtitätsstr. 2, 86135 Augsburg. Tel: (0821) 59 85 227

Vacation courses: August. German as a foreign language.

Bamberg

Verkehrsverein: Geyerswörthstr. 3, 96047 Bamberg. Tel: (0951) 871161
Jugendherberge: Oberer Leinritt 70, 96049 Bamberg. Tel: (0951) 56002
 Fax: (0951) 55211
Industrie- und Handelskammer: Use: IHK Nürnberg, Hauptmarkt 25–27,
 90403 Nürnberg. Tel: (0911) 13 350 Fax: (0911) 13 35 200 Email:
 info@ihk-nuernberg.de
AOK: AOK Bayern, Pödeldorferstr. 75, 96052 Bamberg. Tel: (0951) 93
 36 0 Fax: (0951) 93 36 105 Email: info@ihk-nuernberg.de
Local newspaper: Fränkischer Tag: www.fraenkischer-tag.de/

Town, area and industry

Bamberg: The name was originally *Papinberc*, 'the castle of Papo' (or Babo,
 possibly the original name of the noble Babenberg family, whose name
 was associated with the area from 902 CE). The first book in German
 was printed in Bamberg in 1459. E. T. A. Hoffmann (as in 'Tales of ...')
 lived here for a time, and there is a museum at the house where he lived.
Population: c. 70,000; there are *c.* 8,000 students at the university.
Position: Northern Bavaria, in Upper Franconia, close to Nuremberg, the
 Steigerwald, Fränkische Schweiz.
Sights: Cathedral, *Altstadt, Neue Residenz,* churches, *Rathaus,* architec-
 ture in general.
Culture: Symphony orchestra, theatres, art collections.
Industry: Service industries, clothing, shoes, brewing, electronics, pianos,
 porcelain, market gardening.
Twinning: GB: Bedford

Otto-Friedrich-Universität

Zentrale Universitätsverwaltung, Kapuzinerstr. 16, 96045 Bamberg. Tel:
 (0951) 86 30 Fax: (0951) 86 31 005 Web site: www.uni-bamberg.de
Akademisches Auslandsamt: Markusstr. 6, 96045 Bamberg. Tel: (0951) 86
 31 049 Fax: (0951) 86 31 054 Email: auslandsamt@zuv.uni-bamberg.de
Studentenwerk: Am Studentenhaus 1, 97072 Würzburg. Tel: (0931) 80 050
 Fax: (0931) 80 05 214 Email: claudia.geyer@mail.uni-wuerzburg.de
AStA: Heumarkt 2, 96047 Bamberg. Tel: (0951) 863 1214 Fax: (0951)
 863 4214 Email: sprecherrat@sv.uni-bamberg.de
Frauenbeauftragte: Prof. Dr Ursula Hoffmann-Lange, Kapuzinerstr. 16,
 96045 Bamberg. Tel: (0951) 86 31 244 Fax: (0951) 86 31 005 Email:
 frauenbeauftragte@asv.uni-bamberg.de

Behindertenbeauftragte(r): Kapuzinerstr. 16, 96045 Bamberg. Tel: (0951) 86 31 820

Computer/email access via: Rechenzentrum, Kapuzinerstr. 16, 96045 Bamberg. Tel: (0951) 86 31 301 Fax: (0951) 86 31 302 Email: rechenzentrum@urz.uni-bamberg.de

English department: Lehrstuhl für Englische Sprachwissenschaft, Kapuzinerstr. 16, 96045 Bamberg. Tel: (0951) 86 32 166 Email: wolfgang. viereck@split.uni-bamberg.de

German department: Professur für Deutsche Sprachwissenschaft, Kapuzinerstr. 16, 96045 Bamberg. Tel: (0951) 86 32 141 Email: helmut. glueck@split.uni-bamberg.de

Vacation courses: August. Emphasis on German literature, some language and *Landeskunde.*

Bayreuth

Verkehrsverein: Tourismuszentrale, Luitpoldplatz 9, 95444 Bayreuth. Tel: (0921) 88 588 Fax: (0921) 88 555 Email: 101453,3466CompuServe

Jugendherberge und Jugendgästehaus: Universitätsstr. 28, 95447 Bayreuth. Tel: (0921) 25 12 62 Fax: (0921) 51 28 05

Industrie- und Handelskammer: IHK für Oberfranken, Bayreuth, Bahnhofstr. 25–27, Postfach 10 06 53, 95406 Bayreuth. Tel: (0921) 88 60 Fax: (0921) 12 778 Email: ihk.bt@bayreuth.ihk.de

AOK: Friedrich-Puchta-Str. 27, 95444 Bayreuth. Tel: (0921) 28 80 Fax: (0921) 28 82 11

Local newspaper: Nordbayerischer Kurier: www.bayreuth.de/deutsch/ nachrichten/navigation/bayreuth.htm You could also try *Nordbayerischer Kurier* in a search engine.

Town, area and industry

Bayreuth: The name was originally *Baierrute* 'Land cleared by Bavarians', whose name *Bayern*, incidentally, derives from that of the *Boier*, who originated in Bohemia, German *Böhmen*, 'the homeland of the *Boier*'. Names like this demonstrate how much movement of peoples there has always been and what an ethnic mix there is everywhere. This city is the capital of Upper Franconia and is especially associated with Richard Wagner and the annual opera festivals.

Population: c. 72,000; there are *c.* 8,000 students at the university.

Position: NE Bavaria, Upper Franconia (Bavaria), between the Fichtelgebirge and the Franconian Jura.
Sights: Wagner's *Festspielhaus* (festival theatre), *Park Eremitage, Altes Schloss, Neues Schloss.*
Culture: Much opera, Wagner Festival, museums.
Industry: Wagner, textiles, engineering, chemicals, pianos, porcelain, glass.
Twinning: No official links.

Universität Bayreuth

Universität Bayreuth, 95440 Bayreuth. Tel: (0921) 55–0 Fax: (0921) 55 52 90 Web site: www.uni-bayreuth.de
Akademisches Auslandsamt: Universitätsstraße 30, 95400 Bayreuth. Tel: (0921) 55 52 43/44/45 Fax: (0921) 55 52 48 Email: studienberatung @uni-bayreuth.de
Studentenwerk: Universitätsstr. 30, 95447 Bayreuth. Tel: (0921) 55 59 00 Fax: (0921) 55 59 99 Email: pressestelle@uni-bayreuth.de
AStA: Studentischer Konvent, Universitätsstraße 30, 95440 Bayreuth. Tel: (0921) 55 52 96 Fax: (0921) 55 52 97 Email: sprecherrat@uni-bayreuth.de
Frauenbeauftragte: Dr Brigitte John, Geo II, Universitätsstraße 30, 95440 Bayreuth. Tel: (0921) 55 22 84 Email: frauenbeauftragte@uni-bayreuth.de
Behindertenbeauftragte(r): Vertrauensmann für Schwerbehinderte, Richard Kastner, Universitätsstraße 30, 95440 Bayreuth. Tel: (0921) 55 52 42 Email: richard.kastner@uvw.uni-bayreuth.de
Computer/email access via: Rechenzentrum, Gebäude NWII 3.2.U1, 95440 Bayreuth. Tel: (0921) 55–0 Fax: (0921) 55 31 36 Email: www@uni-bayreuth.de
English department: Fachgruppe Anglistik, GW II Obergeschoss, Universitätstraße 30, 95447 Bayreuth. Tel: (0921) 55 35 63 Fax: (0921) 55 36 27 Email: michael.steppat@uni-bayreuth.de
German department: Deutsch als Fremdsprache, Universität Bayreuth, 95440 Bayreuth. Tel: (0921) 55 36 17 Fax: (0921) 55 36 20 Email: interkulturelle.germanistik@uni-bayreuth.de
Vacation courses: August. German language and society.

Berlin

Verkehrsverein: Europa Center, Budapesterstraße, 10787 Berlin. Tel: (030) 25 02 25

Jugendherberge: Jugendgästehaus, Kluckstraße 3, 10785 Berlin. Tel: (030) 26 11 097

Industrie- und Handelskammer: IHK zu Berlin, Hardenbergstraße 16–18, 10623 Berlin. Tel: (030) 31 51 00 Fax: (030) 31 51 02 78 Email: service @berlin.ihk.de

AOK: Rungestraße 3–6, 10179 Berlin. Tel: (030) 23 51 10 06/7/8/9 Fax: (030) 23 51 10 00

Local newspapers: Berliner Morgenpost: www.berliner-morgenpost.de/; *Berliner Zeitung*:www.berlinonline.de/aktuelles/berliner_zeitung/

Town, area and industry

Berlin: The name is probably of Slavonic origin and means 'marsh' or 'swamp'. Despite popular belief and the Berlin Bear on the city's coat of arms, the name has nothing whatsoever to do with bears (although Berlin does have a famous zoo). Berlin was a divided city from the end of the Second World War until the fall of the Wall in 1989 and has now again become the capital of a reunited Germany and the new seat of government. The Wall, which was built by the East German government in 1961 to prevent the exodus of its population, has largely disappeared, except for some sections which have been preserved as monuments. Although Berlin was largely destroyed in the Second World War, much has been reconstructed, including the *Reichstag*, which now again houses the German parliament.

Population: c. 3.5 million. Besides the *Humboldt Universität*, the *Freie Universität* and the *Technische Universität*, there are a further 12 HE institutions, with total student numbers of more than 120,000.

Position: Very much to the east of Germany, so fairly close to the Polish border.

Sights: This is a hugely historical and cultural city and a good guidebook is probably a necessity. *Kurfürstendamm* (*Ku'damm*), Wannsee, the spectacular museums.

Culture: c. 180 theatres, 17 orchestras, *c.* 150 chamber music ensembles, *c.* 80 museums, *c.* 200 galleries.

Industry: Electronics, engineering, metalwork, textiles, cigarettes, bicycles, foodstuffs, fashion, steel, chemicals, film production.

Twinning: GB: London (various districts of Berlin are linked with areas of London, e.g. Lewisham, Hammersmith, Luton, Sutton, Barnet); US: Los Angeles

Humboldt Universität zu Berlin

Unter den Linden 6, 10099 Berlin. Tel. (030) 20 930 Fax. (030) 20 93 27 70 Web site: www.hu-berlin.de/
Akademisches Auslandsamt: Unter den Linden 6, 10099 Berlin. Tel: (030) 20 93 25 65 Fax: (030) 20 93 27 80 Email: auslandsamt@uv.hu-berlin.de
Studentenwerk: Hardenbergstraße 34, 10623 Berlin. Tel: (030) 31 12–0 Fax. (030) 31 12 202 Email: studentenwerk.bln@t-online.de
AStA: Unter den Linden 6, 10099 Berlin. Tel: (030) 20 93 26 03/26 14
Frauenbeauftragte: Frau Dr Marianne Kriszio, Unter den Linden 6, 10099 Berlin. Tel: (030) 20 93 28 40 Fax: (030) 20 93 28 60 Email: marianne=kriszio@rz.hu-berlin.de
Behindertenbeauftragte(r): Dr Hans-Rüdiger Wilhelm, Dorotheenstr. 24, II. Etage, Zimmer 215, 10117 Berlin. Tel: (030) 20 93 27 28 Fax: (030) 20 93 15 64 Email: hans-ruediger.wilhelm@rz.hu-berlin.de
Computer/email access via: Rechenzentrum, Unter den Linden 6, 10099 Berlin. Tel: (030) 20 93 22 61 Fax: (030) 20 93 29 59 Email: rz-office@rz.hu-berlin.de
English department: Institut für Anglistik u. Amerikanistik, Hauptgebäude, Unter den Linden 6, 10099 Berlin. Tel. (030) 20 93 22 95/22 97 Fax: (030) 20 93 22 44 Email: peter.lucko@rz.hu-berlin.
German department: Institut für deutsche Sprache und Linguistik, Philosophische Fakultät II, Schützenstr. 21, 10117 Berlin. Tel: (030) 20 19 66 48 Fax: (030) 20 19 66 90 Email: ruediger.steinlein@rz.hu-berlin.de
Vacation courses: July/August. German language and history of Berlin.

Freie Universität Berlin

Kaiserswerther Str. 16–18, 14195 Berlin: Tel: (030) 83 81 Fax: (030) 83 87 31 07 Web site: www.fu-berlin.de
Akademisches Auslandsamt: Brümmerstr. 52, 14195 Berlin. Tel: (030) 83 87 39 00 Fax: (030) 83 87 39 01 Email: aaa@fu-berlin
Studentenwerk: Hardenbergstr. 34, 10623 Berlin. Tel: (030) 31 120 Fax: (030) 31 12 202 Email: studentenwerk.bln@t-online.de
AStA: Kiebitzweg 23, 14195 Berlin. Tel: (030) 83 90 91–0 Fax: (030) 83 14 536 Email: asta-fu@zedat.fu-berlin.de
Frauenbeauftragte: Rudeloffweg 25–27, 14195 Berlin. Tel: (030) 83 84

259 Fax: (030) 83 82 159 Email: frauenbeauftragte@fu-berlin.de
Behindertenbeauftragte(r): Raum 213, 1.OG, Thielallee 38 (Ecke Kiebitz-
weg), 14195 Berlin. Tel: (030) 83 85 292 Fax: (030) 83 84 511 Email:
gclassen@zedat.fu-berlin.de
Computer/email access via: Zentraleinrichtung für Datenverarbeitung,
Fabeckstr. 32, 14195 Berlin. Tel: (030) 83 85 42 15 Fax: (030) 83 84 511
Email: zedat@fu-berlin.de
English department: Institut für englische Philologie, Gosslerstr. 2–4,
14195 Berlin. Tel: (030) 83 87 23 21 Fax: (030) 83 87 23 23 Email:
ekuhles@zedat.fu-berlin.de
German department: Institut für Deutsche und Niederländische Philo-
logie (WE 4), Habelschwerdter Allee 45, 14195 Berlin. Tel: (030) 83
85 42 33 Email: verwaltung@germanistik.fu-berlin.de
Vacation courses: July. German language and *Landeskunde*.

Bielefeld

Verkehrsverein: Leinenmeisterhaus, Hauptbahnhof, 33602 Bielefeld. Tel:
(0521) 17 88 44
Jugendherberge: Oetzer Weg 25, 33605 Bielefeld. Tel: (0521) 22 227
Industrie- und Handelskammer: IHK Ostwestfalen zu Bielefeld, Elsa-
Brandströmstr. 1–3, Postfach 100363, 33503 Bielefeld. Tel: (0521) 55
40 Email: cbuchwald@bielefeld.ihk.de
AOK: Universitätsstr. 25, 33615 Bielefeld. Tel: (0521) 16 40 170 Fax: (0521)
16 40 172
Local newspaper: Neue Westfälische: www.nw-news.de/

Town, area and industry

Bielefeld: The name can mean either 'axe-head field', referring to the
shape of the original settlement, from Old High German *bihal*, or
'rocky field'. The town dates back to 1214. Badly damaged in the
Second World War, it has been rebuilt and remains an important
centre for the linen industry.
Population: c. 325,000; there are *c.* 19,500 students at the university, with
c. 7,300 students at other HE institutions.
Position: NE North-Rhine-Westphalia. It is at the northern edge of the
Teutoburger Wald, between Dortmund and Hanover.
Sights: Castle (Sparrenburg), churches, Gothic Crüwell House, parks.
Culture: Galleries, museums, concert hall, opera, theatres.
Industry: Textiles, clothing, sewing machines, foodstuffs, engineering,

bicycles, machine tools, pharmaceuticals, paper, electronics.
Twinning: GB: Rochdale, Enniskillen; US: Long Beach

Universität Bielefeld

Universitätsstraße 25, 33615 Bielefeld. Tel: (0521) 10 600 Fax: (0521) 10
65 844 Web site: www.uni-bielefeld.de
Akademisches Auslandsamt: Universitätsstraße 25, Bauteil A, Ebene 4,
33615 Bielefeld. Tel: (0521) 10 64 40 88 Fax: (0521) 10 64 679
Email: aaaunibi@hrz.uni-bielefeld.de
Studentenwerk: Universitätsstr. 25, Postfach 100203, 33615 Bielefeld.
Tel: (0521) 10 64 119 Fax: (0521) 10 66 446 Email: studentenwerk@uni-bielefeld.de
AStA: Universitätsstraße 25, Ebene I (C1–154), 33615 Bielefeld. Tel: (0521)
10 64 34 36 Fax: (0521) 106–3032 Email: asta@uni-bielefeld.de
Frauenbeauftragte: Universitätsstraße 25 (L3–113), 33615 Bielefeld. Tel:
(0521) 10 64 202 Fax: (0521) 10 68 066 Email: frauenbuero@uni-bielefeld.de
Behindertenbeauftragte(r): Prof. Dr Michael Brambring, Postfach 100131,
33501 Bielefeld. Tel: (0521) 10 64 345
Computer/email access via: Hochschulrechenzentrum, Universitätsstraße
25, 33615 Bielefeld. Tel: (0521) 10 64 948 Email: frank.stuckmann-@uni-bielefeld.de
English department: FB Anglistik, Universitätsstraße 25, 33615 Bielefeld.
Tel: (0521) 10 63 510 Fax: (0521) 10 66 008 Email: gibbon@spectrum.
uni-bielefeld.de
German department: Fakultät für Linguistik und Literaturwissenschaft,
Universitätsstraße 25, 33615 Bielefeld. Tel: (0521) 10 65 240 Fax: (0521)
10 62 996 Email: carla-christina.sievers@uni-bielefeld.de
Vacation courses: August, September. German language.

Bochum

Verkehrsverein: Kurt-Schumacher-Platz (am Hbf), 44728 Bochum. Tel:
(0234) 96 30 2–0 Fax: (0234) 96 30 255
Jugendherberge: JH Essen-Werden, Pastoratsberg 2, 45329 Essen. Tel:
(0201) 49 11 63
Industrie- und Handelskammer: IHK zu Bochum, Ostring 30–32, Postfach
101230, 44712 Bochum. Tel: (0234) 68 90 10 Email: kammer@bochum.
ihk.de

AOK: Universitätsstr. 150, 44801 Bochum. Tel: (0234) 95 87 477 Fax: (0234) 95 87 479
Local newspaper: Westdeutsche Allgemeine Zeitung: www.waz.de/

Town, area and industry

Bochum: The name derives from *Buockheim* – 'settlement with beech trees'. The town dates back to the eleventh century. Its historic centre was destroyed in the Second World War and was rebuilt on modern lines. Coal mining had been Bochum's major industry, but by the 1950s the industry here was in decline, and the last mine closed in 1973. The historical connection remains, and Bochum is the seat of the miners' union (*Industriegewerkschaft Bergbau und Energie*). There has been economic diversification and the town remains a thriving industrial centre.
Population: c. 400,000; there are *c.* 37,000 students at the university, and *c.* 7,600 at a further three HE institutions.
Position: North Rhine-Westphalia in the centre of the Ruhr industrial area. It is close to Essen, Hagen, and Dortmund.
Sights: Propsteikirche, underground mine open to the public, planetarium.
Culture: Museums, theatre, symphony orchestra.
Industry: Cars (Opel), metallurgy, chemicals, textiles, beer, tobacco, electronics, petroleum.
Twinning: GB: Sheffield

Ruhr-Universität

Universitätsstr. 150, 44801 Bochum. Tel: (0234) 70 0–1 Fax: (0234) 70 94 201 Web site: www.ruhr-uni-bochum.de
Akademisches Auslandsamt: Universitätsstr. 150, 44801 Bochum. Tel: (0234) 70 05 483 Fax: (0234) 70 94 684 Email: monika.sprung@uv.ruhr-uni-bochum.de
Studentenwerk: Universitätsstr. 150, Postfach 100133, 44801 Bochum. Tel: (0234) 70 04 759 Fax: (0234) 70 94 226 Email: arafoe@rz.ruhr-uni-bochum.de
AStA: Studierendenhaus, Ebene 0, Zimmer 005, Universitätsstr. 150, 44801 Bochum. Tel: (0234) 70 02 416 Fax: (0234) 70 16 23
Frauenbeauftragte: Senatsbeauftragte für Frauenfragen, Forum Nord-Ost, Zimmer 10/12, Universitätsstr. 150, 44801 Bochum. Tel: (0234) 70 07 837 Fax: (0234) 70 94 354
Behindertenbeauftragte(r): Harry Baus, Studierendenhaus, 44780 Bochum. Tel: (0234) 70 05 279

Computer/email access via: Universitätsstraße 150, 44780 Bochum. Tel: (0234) 70 04 025 Fax: (0234) 70 94 349 Email: service@ruhr-uni-bochum.de

English department: Englisches Seminar, Gebäude GB 6, Universitätsstraße 150, Postfach 102148, 44780 Bochum. Tel: (0234) 70 02 589 Fax: (0234) 70 94 26 40 Email: anglistik@rz.ruhr-unibochum.de

German department: Germanistisches Institut, Gebäude GB, Universitätsstraße 150, 44780 Bochum. Tel: (0234) 70 02 834 Fax: (0234) 70 94 254

Vacation courses: Not available.

Bonn

Verkehrsverein: Tourist-Information und Tagesvermittlung, Münsterstraße 20, 53111 Bonn. Tel: (0228) 77 34 66 Fax: (0228) 69 03 68

Jugendherberge: JH Bad Godesberg, Horionstr. 60, 53177 Bonn. Tel: (0228) 31 75 16

Industrie- und Handelskammer: IHK Bonn, Bonner Talweg 17, Postfach 1820, 53008 Bonn. Tel: (0228) 22 84–0 Fax: (0228) 22 84 170 Fax: (0228) 51 12 14 Email: email@IHKBonn/Rhein-Sieg

AOK: Heisterbacherhofstr. 4, 53111 Bonn. Tel: (0228) 51 13 61/62 Fax: (0228) 51 12 14

Local newspapers: *Bonner Rundschau*: www.rundschau-online.de/; *General-Anzeiger*: www.general-anzeiger-bonn.de/

Town, area and industry

Bonn: The name is of obscure origin; the Romans called it *Castra Bonnensia* after a Celtic word meaning, possibly, 'castle'. Bonn was the 'provisional' capital of the FRG until 1990 and the seat of government until 1999 when this status was returned to Berlin. Despite fears that the town would go into economic decline with the removal of so many of its sources of income, the transition from seat of government to provincial town seems to be proceeding successfully. Some national, international and scientific organisations will remain in Bonn, which sees itself a centre for expanding service industries. Beethoven was born here, and this in itself is an important economic factor. The town centre was badly damaged in the Second World War, but much has been restored.

Population: c. 292,000; there are c. 36,000 students at the university.

Position: On the Rhine, in the southern part of North Rhine-Westphalia, just south of Cologne, near the Eifel mountains.

Sights: Romanesque church (Münster St Martin), cathedral, Baroque architecture, *Rathaus, Residenz, Beethovenhaus.*

Culture: Excellent museums (*Museumsmeile*), especially *Haus der Geschichte der BRD* (FRG House of History), galleries, opera, orchestras, theatre, cabaret, festivals, especially *Beethovenfest.*

Industry: Service, chemicals, pharmaceuticals, printing, organs (musical), porcelain, light metal.

Twinning: GB: Oxford, Maidenhead

Rheinische-Friedrich-Wilhelms-Universität

Regina-Pacis-Weg 3, 53113 Bonn. Tel: (0228) 73–0 Fax: (0228) 73 55 79 Web site: www.uni-bonn.de

Akademisches Auslandsamt: Poppelsdorfer Allee 53, 53115 Bonn. Tel: (0228) 73 74 38/72 93 Fax: (0228) 73 77 22 Email: aaa@uni-bonn.de

Studentenwerk: Nassestraße 11, 53113 Bonn. Tel: (0228) 73 71 99 Fax: (0228) 73 71 04 Email: studentenwerk@uni-bonn.de

AStA: Mensa Nassestraße 11, 1. Stock, 53113 Bonn. Tel: (0228) 73 70 30/70 36 Fax: (0228) 26 22 10 Email: asta@uni-bonn.de

Frauenbeauftragte: Frau Dr Brigitte Mühlenbruch, Regina-Pacis-Weg 3, 53113 Bonn. Tel and Fax: (0228) 73 74 90 Email: muehfb@uni-bonn.de

Behindertenbeauftragte(r): Schwerbehindertenvertretung, Herr J Ressler, Konviktstr. 1, EG, 53113 Bonn. Tel: (0228) 73 70 30 Email: akadez1 @uni-bonn.de

Computer/email access via: Regionales Hochschulrechenzentrum, Wegelerstraße 6, 53113 Bonn. Tel: (0228) 73 34 48 Fax: (0228) 73 27 43 Email: wwwadmin@uni-bonn.de

English department: Englisches Seminar, Regina-Pacis-Weg 5, 53113 Bonn. Tel: (0228) 73 76 25 Fax: (0228) 73 95 10 Email: upp210@uni-bonn.de

German department: Deutsches Seminar, Am Hof 1/Regina-Pacis-Weg 1, 53113 Bonn. Tel: (0228) 73 75 69. Fax: (0228) 73 77 66

Vacation courses: August. German language and literature.

Braunschweig

Verkehrsverein: Langer Hof 6, 38100 Braunschweig. Tel: (0531) 27 55–0 Fax: (0521) 27 55 29

Jugendherberge: Salzdahlumer Straße 170, 38126 Braunschweig. Tel: (0531) 68 16 16 Fax: (0531) 63 654
Industrie- und Handelskammer: IHK Braunschweig, Brabandtstr. 11, 38100 Braunschweig. Tel: (0531) 47 15–0 Fax: (0531) 47 15 299 Email: postmaster@braunschweig.ihk.de
AOK: Am Fallerslebertore 3/4, 38100 Braunschweig, Tel: (0531) 12 03 361 Fax: (0531) 12 03 331
Local newspaper: Braunschweiger Zeitung: www.newsclick.de/

Town, area and industry

Braunschweig: The name in the eleventh century was *Brunesguik*, later *Bruneswich*, which looks much more like its English name, *Brunswick*: 'Bruno's village' (or 'place', or 'settlement'). This is the second largest town in Lower Saxony. It is an internationally recognised centre for scientific research, and the *Technische Hochschule* is the oldest institution of its kind in Germany. There are Federal institutes for physics and technology (*Physikalisch-Technische Bundesanstalt*), agriculture and forestry (*Bundesanstalt für Land- und Forstwirtschaft*). Braunschweig has the somewhat unfortunate distinction of being the town which gave Hitler the title of *Regierungsrat* (= senior civil servant), thereby automatically providing him with German citizenship and enabling him to run for president in 1932. 90 per cent of the town centre was destroyed in the Second World War but has been rebuilt.
Population: c. 250,000; there are *c.* 15,000 students at the technical university, with *c.* 5,500 students at a further two HE institutions.
Position: S.E. Lower Saxony, close to the Harz mountains.
Sights: Much mediaeval architecture, *Altstadt, Sankt Blasius* cathedral, oldest German railway station.
Culture: Museums, galleries, theatres, symphony orchestra.
Industry: Cars, musical instruments, publishing, electronics, office machines, sugar, gingerbread, sausages, meat and vegetable canneries.
Twinning: GB: Bath; US: Omaha

Technische Universität Braunschweig

Pockelsstr. 14, 38106 Braunschweig. Tel: (0531) 39 1–0 Fax: (0531) 39 14 577 Web site: www.tu-bs.de
Akademisches Auslandsamt: Rebenring 18, 38106 Braunschweig. Tel: (0531) 39 14 331 Fax: (0531) 39 14 273 Email: aka@tu-bs.de
Studentenwerk: Katharinenstr. 1, 38106 Braunschweig. Tel: (0531) 39 14 803 Fax: (0531) 39 14 848 Email: swbs@tu-bs.de

AStA: Katharinenstr. 1, 38106 Braunschweig. Tel: (0531) 39 14 555
Fax: (0531) 39 13 42 192 Email: asta@tu-bs.de
Frauenbeauftragte: Frau Claudia Batisweiler, Pockelsstraße 11, 38106
Braunschweig. Tel: (0531) 39 14 547/545 Fax: (0531) 39 14 81 71
Email: frauenbuero@tu-bs.de
Behindertenbeauftragte(r): Schwerbehinderten-Vertretung, Beethoven-
straße 52, 38106 Braunschweig. Tel: (0531) 39 15 427 Fax: (0531) 39
15 41 98 Email: v-a.bruns@tu-bs.de
Computer/email access via: Rechenzentrum, Pockelsstraße 14, 38106
Braunschweig. Tel: (0531) 39 14 55 10 Fax: (0531) 39 14 55 49 Email:
r.hagemeier@tu-bs.de
English department: Seminar für englische und französische Sprache,
Bültenweg 74/75, 3.OG, Zi.304, 38106 Braunschweig. Tel: (0531) 39
13 497 Fax: (0531) 39 13 59 33
German department: Sprache Seminar für deutsche Sprache u. Literatur,
Bültenweg 74/75, 3.OG, Zi.315, 38106 Braunschweig. Tel: (0531) 39
13 419 Fax: (0531) 39 13 82 31
Vacation courses: Mid-July to mid-August, mid-September to mid-October.
German language and *Landeskunde*, applied language (science and
technology).

Bremen

Verkehrsverein: Touristikzentrale, Findorffstr. 105, 28215 Bremen. Tel:
(0421) 30 800
Jugendherberge und Jugendgästehaus: Jugendgästehaus, Kalkstr. 6, 28195
Bremen. Tel: (0421) 17 13 69
Industrie- und Handelskammer: Haus Schütting, Am Markt 13, Postfach
105107, 28051 Bremen. Tel: (0421) 36 370 Fax: (0421) 36 37 299
Email: service@handelskammer-bremen.de
AOK: Bürgermeister-Smidt-Str. 95, 28195 Bremen. Tel: (0421) 17 61
447/268. Fax: (0421) 17 61 340
Local newspaper: Bremer Nachrichten: www2.nordwest.net/partner/bremer_
nachrichten_start.asp

Town, area and Industry

Bremen: The name is derived from an Old Saxon word, *bremo* ('edge')
and it refers to the location of the Carolingian cathedral at the edge
(of a sand dune). Bremen is an old Hanseatic town; hence the car

number plate is *HB* (*Hansestadt* Bremen). It became a city state in 1947 and is therefore its own Bundesland. Bremen is the second most important port in Germany (after Hamburg), even though the open sea is 113 km away. Import/export is a major economic factor. Bremen is the seat of the *Bundesamt für Auswanderung* (Federal Emigration Office). There are about thirty consulates in the town. There was much destruction in the Second World War (almost 70 per cent); much has been rebuilt.

Population: *c.* 550,000; there are *c.* 18,000 students at the university and 7,000+ students at other HE institutions.

Position: On the River Weser, close to Bremerhaven and the North Sea coast, and fairly close to Hamburg.

Sights: Cathedral, *Rathaus*, Renaissance architecture, *Böttcherstraße*, *Schnoorviertel* (reconstructed), parks.

Culture: Museums, galleries, theatres, libraries, archives.

Industry: Shipbuilding, shipping (*Norddeutscher Lloyd, Hapag*), steel, aircraft, radio and television equipment, electronics, coffee, tobacco, banking, insurance.

Twinning: Bremen has none with GB or US, but Bremerhaven, which is not too far away, has twinning arrrangements with Grimsby (GB).

Universität Bremen

Bibliothekstraße 28359 Bremen. Tel: (0421) 28–1 Fax: (0421) 21 84 283
Web site: www.uni-bremen.de

Akademisches Auslandsamt: Bibliothekstr. 1, 28359 Bremen. Tel: (0421) 21 82 732 Fax: (0421) 21 84 320 Email: hasenm@uni-bremen.de

Studentenwerk: Bibliothekstr. 3, 28359 Bremen. Tel: (0421) 22 01–0 Fax: (0421) 22 01 195

AStA: Bibliothekstr. 1, 28359 Bremen. Tel: (0421) 21 82 511 Fax: (0421) 21 82 514 Email: asta@uni-bremen.de

Frauenbeauftragte: Ulrike Rosemeier, Bibliothekstr. 1, 28359 Bremen. Tel: (0421) 21 83 064 Fax: (0421) 21 87 557 Email: ulrike.rosemeier @uni-bremen.de

Behindertenbeauftragte(r): Prof. Dr Nils Jaeger, Bibliothekstr. 1, 28359 Bremen. Tel: (0421) 21 82 500 Fax: (0421) 21 84 918 Email: jse@zfn. uni-bremen.de

Computer/email access via: Zentrum für angewandte Informationstechnologien, MZH Ebenen 1 und 4, 28334 Bremen. Tel: (0421) 21 84 978 Fax: (0421) 21 82 720 Email: uvst@zait.uni-bremen.de

English & German departments: Fachbereich 10, Sprach- und Literatur-

wissenschaften, GW2, Bibliothekstr. 1?, 28359 Bremen. Tel: (0421)
21 84 343 Fax: (0421) 21 84 283 Email: wstr@zfn.uni-bremen-de
Vacation courses: July/August/September. German applied language:
economics, law.

Darmstadt

Verkehrsverein: Neues Rathaus, Luisenplatz 5, 64283 Darmstadt. Tel:
(06151) 13 27 81
Jugendherberge: Landgraf-Georg-Str. 119, 64287 Darmstadt. Tel: (06151)
45 293
Industrie- und Handelskammer: IHK Darmstadt, Rheinstr. 89, 64295
Darmstadt. Tel: (06151) 87 1–0 Fax: (06151) 87 12 81 Email: gilke
@darmstadt.ihk.de
AOK: Neckarstr. 9, 64283 Darmstadt. Tel: (06151) 39 30 Fax: (06151)
39 33 00
Local newspaper: Darmstädter Echo: www.suedhessen-echo-online.de/

Town, area and industry

Darmstadt: The name has nothing to do with entrails, which is more or
less what *Darm* means in modern German. It is first mentioned in the
eleventh century as *Darmundestat*, the place where a man called Dar-
mund lived. Entrails might have been more interesting. Darmstadt is
a medium-sized industrial city; it was very badly damaged in the
Second World War, but much has been rebuilt. The *Zentrum für Welt-
raumforschung* (Centre for Space Research) is located here, and Darm-
stadt is also the base for the FRG's branch of the PEN (Poets,
Essayists and Novelists) association.
Population: c. 140,000; there are *c.* 16,000 students at the university, with
a further *c.* 10,000 students at two other HE institutions.
Position: Southern Hesse, convenient for and north of Mannheim and
Heidelberg and south of Frankfurt am Main.
Sights: Schloss, Rathaus, churches, *Residenzschloss,* parks.
Culture: Theatres, museums, galleries, literature and art festivals.
Industry: Chemicals, pharmaceuticals, engineering, electronics, cosmetics,
printing, publishing.
Twinning: GB: Chesterfield

Technische Hochschule Darmstadt

Karolinenplatz 5, 64289 Darmstadt. Tel: (06151) 16 22 24/16 20 21
Fax: (06151) 16 54 89 Web site: www.th-darmstadt.de
Akademisches Auslandsamt: Hochschulstr. 1, 64289 Darmstadt. Tel: (06151)
16 51 20 Fax: (06151) 16 54 74 Email: auslandsamt@pvw.tu-darmstadt.de
Studentenwerk: Alexanderstraße 4, 64283 Darmstadt. Tel: (06151) 16 3
Fax: (06151) 16 38 68 Email: studentenwerk@th-darmstadt.de
AStA: Hochschulstr. 1, 64289 Darmstadt. Tel: (06151) 16 32 17 Fax:
(06151) 16 60 26 Email: asta@asta.tu-darmstadt.de
Frauenbeauftragte: Frau von Borzyskowski, Karolinenplatz 5,2. Stock,
Raum 266, 64289 Darmstadt. Tel: (06151) 16 61 02 Fax: (06151) 16 33
28 Email: borzyskowski@pvw.th-darmstadt.de
Behindertenbeauftragte(r): Winfried Seidel, Karolinenplatz 5, 64289
Darmstadt. Tel: (06151) 16 34 24 Fax: (06151) 16 54 89 Email: seidel
@pvw.tu-darmstadt.de
Computer/email access via: Hochschulrechenzentrum, Gebäude 75 (2.
Stock), Raum 241, Karolinenplatz 5, 64289 Darmstadt. Tel: (06151)
16 20 54 Fax: (06151) 30 50 Email: webmaster@hrz.tu-darmstadt.de
English & German departments: Institut für Sprach-und Literaturwissen-
schaft, Hochschulstraße 1, 64289 Darmstadt. Tel: (06151) 16 25 97
Fax: (06151) 16 36 94 Email: sprachli@hrzl.hrz.tu-darmstadt.de
Vacation courses: No information available.

Dortmund

Verkehrsverein: Königswall 20 (am Hauptbahnhof), 44137 Dortmund.
Tel: (0231) 50 25 666
Jugendherberge und Jugendgästehaus: Bismarckallee 31, 44135 Dortmund.
Tel: (0231) 53 24 70
Industrie- und Handelskammer: IHK zu Dortmund, Märkische Str. 120,
44141 Dortmund. Tel: (0231) 54 17–0 Fax: (0231) 54 17 109 Email:
info@dortmund.ihk.de
AOK: Königswall 25–27, 44137 Dortmund. Tel. (0231) 91 580 Fax: (0231)
91 58 100
Local newspaper: Ruhr Nachrichten: www.westline.de/

Town, area and industry

Dortmund: The earliest version of the name, which dates back to the ninth
century, was *Throtmanni*; *Throt* (or *Dort*) is of obscure origin (some-

one's name?), but the *manni* or *mund* bit means 'stretch of water' or 'bog', so 'Throt's bog' perhaps. Dortmund is the second largest city in the Ruhr, a major economic, industrial and scientific research centre. It is the seat of the *Bundesanstalt für Unfallforschung und Arbeitsschutz* (Federal Institute for Research into Accidents and Industrial Health and Safety Standards). Most of Dortmund was destroyed in the Second World War; some medieval buildings have been restored, but the rest has been rebuilt as a modern city.

Population: c. 600,000; there are c. 25,000 students at the university, with a further c. 10,000 at other HE institutions.

Position: Centre of North Rhine-Westphalia, on the Dortmund-Ems Canal.

Sights: Many churches (Gothic, late Gothic, Flemish art), parks, lake, castle *Hohensyburg*, TV tower.

Culture: Museums, galleries, theatre.

Industry: Iron, steel, engineering, breweries (Dortmunder Union), bridge-building, electronics (Siemens), coal-mining, printing, service industries, banking, insurance.

Twinning: GB: Leeds; US: Buffalo, New York

Universität Dortmund

Emil-Figge-Str 50, 44221 Dortmund. Tel: (0231) 7551 Web site: www.uni-dortmund.de

Akademisches Auslandsamt: Emil-Figge-Str. 66, 44227 Dortmund (Eichling-hofen). Tel: (0231) 75 54 727/25 95/24 84 Fax: (0231) 75 55 222 Email: saemann@verwaltung.uni-dortmund.de

Studentenwerk: Vogelpothsweg 85, 44227 Dortmund. Tel: (0231) 75 53 600/01 Fax: (0231) 75 40 60

AStA: Emil-Figge-Str. 50, 44227 Dortmund. Tel: (0231) 75 52 584 Fax: (0231) 75 55 143 Email: mail@asta.uni-dortmund.de

Frauenbeauftragte: Emil-Figge-Str. 50, 44227 Dortmund. Tel: (0231) 75 52 603/10 Fax: (0231) 75 55 456 Email: frauenbt@pop.uni-dortmund.de

Behindertenbeauftragte(r): Raum 0302, Emil-Figge-Str. 50, 44221 Dortmund. Tel: (0231) 75 52 848 Fax: (0231) 75 52 848

Computer/email access via: Hochschulrechenzentrum, August Schmidt Straße 12, 44221 Dortmund. Tel: (0231) 75 52 346 Fax: (0231 75 52 371

English department: Institut für Anglistik und Amerikanistik, Emil-Figge-Straße 50, 44227 Dortmund. Tel: (0231) 7551

German department: Institut für deutsche Sprache und Literatur, Emil-Figge-Straße 50, 44227 Dortmund. Tel: (0231) 7551

Vacation courses: No information available.

Dresden

Verkehrsverein: Pragerstr. 10–11, 01069 Dresden. Tel: (0351) 49 19 20
Jugendherberge: Hübnerstr. 11, 01069 Dresden. Tel: (0351) 47 10 667
Industrie- und Handelskammer: IHK Dresden, Niedersedlitzerstr. 63, 01257
Dresden. Tel: (0351) 28 020 Fax: (0351) 28 02 280 Email: service
@dresden.ihk.de
AOK: Sternplatz 7, 01067 Dresden. Tel: (0351) 47 39 427 Fax: (0351)
47 39 470
Local Newspaper: Sächsische Zeitung: www.sz-online.de/

Town, area and industry

Dresden: The name derives from the Old Sorbian words *drezg* (wood) and
ane (settlers) and means 'settlers by the wood'. Old Sorbian was a West
Slavonic language spoken by part of the eastern German population in
the area between the upper reaches of the Elbe and Oder rivers; the
modern version of the language is still spoken, but tends to be called
Wendish. Dresden is the capital of Saxony. One of the most beautiful
cities in Germany ('the Florence on the Elbe'), it was completely
destroyed by bombing in February 1945. Many buildings have been
restored; the rest of the city has been rebuilt in modern fashion. The
Technische Universität is the seat of the *Institut für Kern- und Teilchen-
physik* (Institute for Nuclear Physics).

Population: c. 500,000; there are *c.* 22,000 students at the university, with
a further *c.* 5,800 at five other HE institutions.

Position: SE Saxony, between Meißen and Pirna and quite close to the
Czech border.

Sights: Zwinger, Residenzschloss, Semper Opera House, many churches
from various periods and styles.

Culture: 25 museums, opera, orchestras, theatres, galleries.

Industry: Chemicals, electronics, radio equipment, hydroelectrics, optics,
glass, engineering, foodstuffs including chocolate.

Twinning: GB: Coventry

Technische Universität Dresden

01062 Dresden. Tel: (0351) 46 37 044 Web site: www.tu-dresden.de
Akademisches Auslandsamt: Toeplerbau, 1. Etage, Mommsenstr. 13, 01069
Dresden. Tel: (0351) 46 34 698 Fax: (0351) 46 34 214 Email: aaa@tu-
dresden.de
Studentenwerk: 3. Geschoß, Zimmer 304, Fritz-Löffler-Str. 18, 01069

Dresden. Tel: (0351) 46 97 50 Fax: (0351) 47 18 154 Email: rpoertner.
stwdd@t-online.de
AStA: Studentenrat, TU-Kerngelände, Baracke 1, 01062 Dresden. Tel:
(0351) 46 32 042/3 Fax: (0351) 46 34 714 Email: stura@stura.tu-
dresden.de
Frauenbeauftragte: Gleichstellungsbeauftragte: Dr. Karin Reiche. Tel:
(0351) 46 36 423 Fax: (0351) 46 33 296
Behindertenbeauftragte(r): Dr Heinz Dieter Degen. Tel: (0351) 46 33
881 Fax: (0351) 46 37 171
Computer/email access via: Universitätsrechenzentrum, Willers-Bau A-
Flügel, Zellescher Weg 12–14, 01069 Dresden. Tel: (0351) 46 34 684
Fax: (0351) 46 37 116 Email: benutzer.beratung@urz.tu-dresden.de
English department: Institut für Anglistik/Amerikanistik, Zeunerstr. 1c,
1d, 01062 Dresden. Tel: (0351) 46 32 347 Fax: (0351) 46 37 166
Email: anglist@tu-tudurz.urz..tu-dresden.de
German department: Institut für Germanistik, Zeunerstr. 1e, 01062 Dresden
Tel: (0351) 46 61 75 Fax: (0351) 46 61 75 Email: germ@rcs.urz.tu-
dresden.de
Vacation courses: August, September. Applied language and *Landeskunde.*

Duisburg

Verkehrsverein: Königstr. 53, 47051 Duisburg. Tel: (0203) 28 32 189
Jugendherberge und Jugendgästehaus: Kalkweg 148, 47055 Duisburg. Tel:
(0203) 72 41 64
Industrie- und Handelskammer: Niederrheinische IHK, Duisburg–Wesel–
Kleve zu Duisburg, Mercatorstr. 22–24, 47051 Duisburg. Tel: (0203)
28 21–00 Fax: (0203) 26 533 Email: info@ihkduisburg.de
AOK: Falkstr. 35–41, 47058 Duisburg. Tel. (0203) 39 32 233 Fax: (0203)
39 32 169
Local newspaper: Rheinische Post: www.rp-online.de/news/lokales/duisburg/

Town, area and industry

Duisburg: The name is of obscure origin; in the ninth century it was
called *Diusburg.* It is thought that the name may be derived from the
Latin word *Dispargum,* the only meaning for which appears to be
Duisburg, which is not a very great help. Duisburg is a major economic centre with the biggest inland/river port in the world. The
Rhine–Herne Canal links it with the North Sea German ports. Much
of the town centre was destroyed in the Second World War. It has

been completely rebuilt, but only a few buildings have been restored. The university is named after Gerhard Mercator, a sixteenth-century cartographer, who was active in Duisburg.

Population: c. 535,000; there are *c.* 15,000 students at the university.

Position: North Rhine-Westphalia at the confluence of the Rhine and Ruhr rivers, north of Düsseldorf, close to Essen and Gelsenkirchen.

Sights: Rathaus, churches, port, zoo with biggest aquarium in Germany.

Culture: Museum, opera, theatre.

Industry: Port and transportation systems, iron, steel, heavy machinery, chemicals, textiles, oil, shipbuilding, foodstuffs.

Twinning: GB: Portsmouth, Durham/Sedgefield

Gerhard-Mercator-Universität – Gesamthochschule Duisburg

Lotharstr. 65, 47048 Duisburg. Tel: (0203) 37 90 Web site: www.uni-duisburg.de

Akademisches Auslandsamt: Gebäude LF, Raum 226/227b, Lotharstraße 65, 47048 Duisburg. Tel: (0203) 37 93 706 Fax: (0203) 37 92 470 Email: aaa@verwaltung.uni-duisburg.de

Studentenwerk: Duisburger Str. 426–428, 45478 Mülheim/Ruhr. Tel: (0208) 59 90 70 Fax: (0208) 59 90 736 Email: stw@studentenwerk-du.de

AStA: Lotharstr. 63, 47048 Duisburg. Tel: (0203) 37 00 47/35 72 74 Fax: (0203) 36 26 51 Email: asta@uni-duisburg.

Frauenbeauftragte: Ursula Ziller, Lotharstr. 65, 47048 Duisburg. Tel: (0203) 37 92 055 Fax: (0203) 37 91 875 Email: frauenbuero@uni-duisburg.de

Behindertenbeauftragte(r): Herr Gudlik, Lotharstr. 65, Gebäude LM, Raum 005b, 47048 Duisburg, Tel: (0203) 37 92 156 Email: gudlik @verwaltung.uni-duisburg.de

Computer/email access via: Hochschulrechenzentrum, Lotharstraße 65, 47048 Duisburg. Tel: (0203) 37 94 230 Fax: (0203) 37 94 366 Email: hrz@uni-duisburg.de

English department: Department of English and American Studies, Lotharstraße 65, 47048 Duisburg. Tel: (0203) 37 92 400 Fax: (0203) 37 92 399 Email: haesler@uni-duisburg.de

German department: Germanistisches Seminar, Lotharstraße 65, 47048 Duisburg. Tel: (0203) 37 92 397/490 Fax: (0203) 37 92 490 Email: amann.w@uni-duisburg.de

Vacation courses: August/September. German language and *Landeskunde.*

Düsseldorf

Verkehrsverein: Konrad-Adenauer-Platz am Bahnholf, 40210 Düsseldorf.
  Tel: (0211) 17 20 20
Jugendherberge und Jugendgästehaus: Düsseldorferstr. 1, 40545 Düsseldorf-
  Oberkassel. Tel: (0211) 57 40 41
Industrie- und Handelskammer: IHK Düsseldorf, Ernst-Schneider-Platz
  1, 40212 Düsseldorf. Tel: (0211) 35 570 Fax: (0211) 35 57 401 Email:
  ihkdus@duesseldorf.ihk.de
AOK: AOK Rheinland, Kasernenstr. 61, 40213 Düsseldorf. Tel. (0211)
  82 25 666 Fax: (0211) 82 25 600
Local newspapers: Rheinische Post: www.rp-online.de/; *Westdeutsche Zeit-
  ung* (*Düsseldorfer Nachrichten*): www.wz-ewsline.de/duesseldorf/

Town, area and industry

Düsseldorf: Originally *Dusseldorp*, the name means 'village on the River
  Düssel' (river in its smallest sense); so this town has grown somewhat.
  Düssel itself is derived from the name *Tussale*, which means 'rushing
  water', and does not appear to have anything whatsoever to do with
  the slang *Dussel* (thickie). Düsseldorf is the capital of North Rhine-
  Westphalia; it is a very wealthy, metropolitan city (*Kleinparis* – 'Little
  Paris'), a major economic and cultural centre. This was the birthplace
  of Heinrich Heine (the nineteenth-century poet who wrote *Das Lorelei-
  lied* (Song of the Lorelei, which, if you take a trip down the Rhine on
  a steamer, you will hear played as you pass the *Loreleifelsen* – Lorelei
  Rock)). There was huge destruction in the Second World War, but
  much restoration and much modernisation have taken place.
Population: c. 574,000; there are *c.* 22,000 students at the university, with
  c. 10,500 students at a further three HE institutions.
Position: On the Rhine, in SW North Rhine-Westphalia, north of Cologne.
Sights: Königsallee (*die Kö*), regarded by many as the most elegant shop-
  ping street in Germany; parks, *Schloss*, *Rathaus*, *Altstadt*, the whole city.
Culture: Vast amounts: museums, theatres, concert halls, opera, galleries.
Industry: Iron, steel, engineering (Mercedes Benz steering systems),
  motor vehicles, glass, chemicals, coal, brewing, advertising, clothing,
  electronics, publishing, trade fairs, banking.
Twinning: GB: Reading

Heinrich-Heine-Universität

Universitätsstr. 1, 40225 Düsseldorf. Tel: (0211) 81 00 Fax: (0211) 34 22 29 Web site: www.uni-duesseldorf.de

Akademisches Auslandsamt: Gebäude 16.11, Universitätsstr. 1, 40225 Düsseldorf. Tel: (0211) 81 12 238

Studentenwerk: Gebäude 21.12, Universitätsstr. 1, 40225 Düsseldorf. Tel: (0211) 81 13 298 Fax: (0211) 81 15 299 Email: studentenwerk @uni-duesseldorf.de

AStA: Studierendenschaft, Gebäude 21.12, Universitätsstr. 1, 40225 Düsseldorf. Tel: (0211) 81 13 172 Fax: (0211) 81 13 290

Frauenbeauftragte: Heike Thulmann, Gebäude 16.11, Ebene 03, Raum 24–28, Universitätsstr. 1, 40225 Düsseldorf. Tel: (0211) 81 11 526 Fax: (0211) 81 15 239

Behindertenbeauftragte(r): Professor Dr Matthias Franz, Institut für Psychosomatische Medizin und Psychotherapie, Moorenstr. 5, 41225 Düsseldorf. Tel: (0211) 81 18 338 Fax: (0211) 81 16 250 Email: matthias.franz@uni-duesseldorf.de

Computer/email access via: Universitätsrechenzentrum, Gebäude 25.41, Universitätsstr. 1, 40225 Düsseldorf. Tel: (0211) 81 13 926

English department: Anglistisches Institut, Universitätsstr. 1, 40225 Düsseldorf. Tel: (0211) 81 12 963 Fax: (0211) 81 15 292 Email: Anglistik @phil-fak.uni-duesseldorf.de

German department: Germanistisches Seminar, Universitätsstr. 1, 40225 Düsseldorf. Tel: (0211) 81 12 944

Vacation courses: July/August. German language, economics.

Erfurt

Verkehrsverein: Schlösserstr. 44, 99084 Erfurt. Tel: (0361) 56 26 267

Jugendherberge: Hochheimerstr. 12, 99094 Erfurt. Tel: (0361) 56 26 705

Industrie- und Handelskammer: IHK Erfurt, Friedrich-List-Str. 36, 99096 Erfurt. Tel: (0361) 34 56/58 Fax: (0361) 34 81 299 Email: krepuska @erfurt.ihk.de

AOK: Augustinerstr. 38, 99084 Erfurt. Tel: (0361) 65 740 Fax: (0361) 65 74 10 000

Local newspaper: Thüringer Allgemeine: www.thueringer-allgemeine.de/

Town, area and industry

Erfurt: Earlier forms of the name were: *Erphort, Erphesfurt, Erpesfurt,* which looks as though it might have been the name of a nasty disease, but which is likely to mean 'ford across the river Erphesa', a section of the River Gera. The *Erf/Erph* bit appears to be derived from an Old High German word meaning 'dark' or 'brownish'. Erfurt is the capital of Thuringia. Historically important, Erfurt was the site of the famous Congress of Erfurt attended by Napoleon and Alexander I of Russia. There was war damage, but the *Altstadt* was largely spared.

Population: c. 210,000; there are *c.* 2,500 students at the university, with a further *c.* 3,500 at the FH.

Position: Central Thuringia, in the *Thüringer Becken* (Thuringian Basin) on the River Gera, north of Bavaria.

Sights: Cathedral, Luther monument, medieval churches and architecture.

Culture: Amploniana collection of medieval manuscripts, museums, theatres.

Industry: Metalwork, electricals, shoes, clothing, agriculture.

Twinning: GB: Bradford; US: Shawnee

Universität Erfurt*

Nordhäuser Straße 63, 99089 Erfurt. Tel: (0361) 73 70 Fax: (0361) 73 71 999 Web site: www.uni-erfurt.de

* NB: From January 2001 the old Pädagogische Hochschule Erfurt will be integrated into the university. The letters *ph* in E-mail addresses will probably change to *uni.*

Akademisches Auslandsamt: Internationales Büro, Nordhäuser Straße 63, 99089 Erfurt. Tel: (0361) 73 71 008 Fax: (0361) 73 71 902 Email: manuela.linde@uni-erfurt.de

Studentenwerk: Studentenwerk Erfurt-Ilmenau, AöR, Postfach 307, 99006 Erfurt. Tel: (0361) 73 71 800 Fax: (0361) 73 71 990 Email: swe-I@swe.ph-erfurt.de

AStA: Studentenrat, Nordhäuser Straße 63, 99089 Erfurt. Email: studentenrat@uni-erfurt.de

Frauenbeauftragte: Gleichstellungsbeauftragte: Heidi Richter, Nordhäuser Straße 63, 99089 Erfurt. Tel: (0361) 73 71 160 Fax: (0361) 73 71 924 Email: heidi.richter@uni-erfurt.de

Behindertenbeauftragte(r): Dr Frank Peukert, Nordhäuser Strasse 63, 99089 Erfurt. Tel: (0361) 73 71 042 Fax: (0361) 73 71 028

Computer/email access via: Hochschul-Rechenzentrum, Nordhäuser Strasse 63, 99089 Erfurt. Tel: (0361) 67 00 123 Fax: (0361) 67 00 133 Email: schmidt@hrz.fh-erfurt.de

English department: Institut für Anglistik/Amerikanistik, Nordhäuser Straße 63, 99089 Erfurt. Tel: (0361) 73 71 099 Fax: (0361) 73 71 914 Email: anglistik@ifangl.ph-erfurt.de

German department: Institut für Germanistik, Nordhäuser Straße 63, 99089 Erfurt. Tel: (0361) 73 71 086 Fax: (0361) 73 71 910 Email: dumont@igerm.ph-erfurt.de

Vacation courses: July. Language, literature and *Landeskunde.*

Erlangen

Verkehrsverein: Rathausplatz 1, 91054 Erlangen. Tel: (09131) 89 510 Fax: (09131) 89 51 51

Jugendherberge: Südliche Stadtmauerstr. 35, 91054 Erlangen. Tel: (09131) 86 25 55

Industrie- und Handelskammer: Geschäftsstelle Erlangen, Äußere Brucker Str. 51, 91052 Erlangen. Tel: (09131) 260–96 Fax: (09131) 260–95 Email: *ihgerlg@aol.com*

AOK: Schuhstr. 36, 91054 Erlangen. Tel: (09131) 81 020 Fax: (09131) 81 02 88

Local newspaper: Fränkischer Tag: www.fraenkischer-tag.de/

Town, area and industry

Erlangen: The name is derived from two Old High German words, *erila* (alder) and *ang* (field/meadow) so: 'field of alders'. Erlangen dates back to the eighth century. This is a remarkable example of Baroque town planning, with the original layout remaining more or less as it was in the seventeenth century, when a 'new town' was built there as a haven for Huguenot refugees. The town has been a centre for bee-keeping since the eleventh century.

Population: c. 100,000; there are 19,000 students on the Erlangen campus with a further 6,000 in Nuremberg (*Nürnberg*).

Position: Southern Germany in Bavaria (Central Franconia), on the river Regnitz.

Sights: Baroque town centre, churches; Schloss, Schlossgarten, Orangery.

Culture: Theatre, music, museum, various international festivals.

Industry: Micro-electronics, medical technology, leather, textiles, gloves, hats, paper.

Twinning: GB: Stoke-on-Trent

Friedrich-Alexander-Universität – Erlangen-Nürnberg

Schlossplatz 4, 91054 Erlangen. Tel: (09131) 85–0 Fax: (09131) 85 21 31
Web site www.uni-erlangen.de

Akademisches Auslandsamt: Schlossplatz 3, I. Stock, Raum 1.026, 1.025,
Postfach 3520, 91023 Erlangen. Tel: (0931) 85 24 810 Fax: (0931) 85
26 335 Email: gerhard.mischel@zuv.uni-erlangen.de

Studentenwerk: Studentenwerk Erlangen-Nürnberg, Langemarckplatz 4,
91054 Erlangen. Tel: (09131) 80 020 Fax: (09131) 80 02 18 Email:
stw.orb@rzmail.uni-erlangen.de

AStA: Büro der Studentenvertretung, Turnstr. 7, 91054 Erlangen. Tel:
(09131) 85 26 695 Fax: (09131) 85–6760 Email: sprecherrat@rzmail.
uni-erlangen.de

*Frauenbeauftragte:*Büro der Frauenbeauftragten, Bismarckstr. 6, 91054
Erlangen. Tel: (09131) 85 22 951 Fax: (09131) 85 22 951 Email:
frauenbuero@phil.uni-erlangen.de

Behindertenbeauftragte(r): Frau von Künsberg, Halbmondstr. 6, 91023
Erlangen. Tel: (09131) 85 24 130 Email: msvkuensberg@groopwese.
uni-erlangen.de

Computer/email access via: Regionales Rechenzentrum Erlangen,
Martinsstraße 1, 91058 Erlangen. Tel: (09131) 85 27 031 Fax: (09131)
30 29 41 Email: beratung@rrze.uni-erlangen.de

English department: Institut für Anglistik und Amerikanistik, Universität
Erlangen-Nürnberg, Bismarckstraße 1, 91054 Erlangen. Tel: (09131)
85 22 436 Fax: (09131) 85 29 362

German department: Institut für Germanistik, Universität Erlangen-
Nürnberg, Bismarckstraße 1B, 91054 Erlangen. Tel: (09131) 85 22
423 Fax: (09131) 85 69 97

Vacation courses: August. Language and society.

Essen

Verkehrsverein: Am Hauptbahnhof 2, 45127 Essen. Tel: (0201) 23 54 27
Fax: (0201) 81 06 081

Jugendherberge: Pastoratsberg 2, 45329 Essen-Werden, Tel: (0201) 49 11
63 Fax: (0201) 49 25 05

Industrie- und Handelskammer: IHK zu Essen, Am Waldthausenpark 2,
45127 Essen. Tel: (0201) 18 92–0 Fax: (0201) 20 78 66 Email: ihkessen
@essen.ihk.de

AOK: AOK-Rheinland, Jägerstr. 25, 45127 Essen. Tel: (0201) 20 110
Fax: (0201) 20 11 650

Local newspapers: Neue Ruhr Zeitung: www.nrz.de/free/nrz.lokales.set–000.html; *Westdeutsche Allgemeine Zeitung*: www.waz.de/free/waz.staedte.set–000.html

Town, area and industry

Essen: The name has nothing to do with food, so don't go there expecting it to be a gourmet's paradise. It may well be, but 'Essen' is first mentioned in 874 as *Astnide*, meaning 'the place where the smelting furnaces are', which shows how the area has been an industrial base from time immemorial. Essen is the largest city in the Ruhr area and the sixth largest in Germany. It is no longer a great producer of coal and iron, but is a major centre for heavy industrial processing and is a service and business management base. It suffered much destruction in the Second World War and was rebuilt as a modern town.

Population: c. 617,400; there are *c.* 24,000 students at the university, and a further 1000+ at two other small HE institutions.

Position: North Rhine-Westphalia, in the industrial Ruhr area, close to Duisburg and Bochum and north of Düsseldorf.

Sights: Münster (minster) with museum containing important ecclesiastical treasures, *Gruga Park*, *Margarethenhöhe* garden city, *Villa Hügel*, the former home of the Krupp family, now a museum.

Culture: Wide variety of museums, galleries, concerts, theatre, opera.

Industry: Technology, engines, lorries, locomotives, steel, glass, textiles, brewing, chemicals, service; headquarters for many major concerns, e.g. Krupp, Karstadt, Ruhrkohle, Ruhrgas, ALDI, Thyssen.

Twinning: GB: Sunderland

Universität-Gesamthochschule Essen

Universitätsstr. 2, 45141 Essen. Tel: (0201) 18 31 Fax: (0201) 18 32 151
  Web site: www.uni-essen.de
Akademisches Auslandsamt: Raum T03 R00 C24, Universitätsstraße 2, 45141 Essen. Tel: (0201) 18 34 128 Fax: (0201) 18 32 257 Email: aaa@uni-essen.de
Studentenwerk: Westendhof 5, 45143 Essen. Tel: (0201) 82 01 00 Fax: (0201) 82 01 066 Email: swe@uni-essen.de
AStA: Universitätsstr. 2, 45141 Essen. Tel: (0201) 18 3–1 Fax: (0201) 18 32 151 Email: universitaet@uni-essen.de
Frauenbeauftragte: R09 R00 H35, Universitätsstr. 2, 45141 Essen. Tel: (0201) 18 34 014 Fax: (0201) 18 34 013 Email: m.werner-schaub @uni-essen.de

Behindertenbeauftragte(r): Herr Hiedl, Universitätsstr. 12, 45141 Essen.
Tel: (0201) 18 32 004
Computer/email access via: Hochschulrechenzentrum der Uni-GH
Essen, Schützenbahn 70, 45117 Essen. Tel: (0201) 18 32 890 Email:
webmaster@hrz.uni-essen.de
English department: Institut für Anglistik, Fachbereich 3, Universitäts-
straße 12, 45117 Essen. Tel: (0201) 18 33 580 Fax: (0201) 18 33 959
German department: Institut für Germanistik, Fachbereich 3, Universitäts-
straße 12, 45117 Essen. Email: daz@uni-essen.de
Vacation courses: July, August, September. Intensive German language
course and *Landeskunde.*

Flensburg

Verkehrsverein: Norderstr. 6, 24939 Flensburg. Tel: (0461) 23 090
Jugendherberge: Fichtestr. 16, 24943 Flensburg. Tel. (0461) 37 742
Industrie- und Handelskammer: IHK zu Flensburg, Heinrichstr. 28–34.
Postfach 1942, 24909 Flensburg. Tel. (0461) 80 60 Fax: (0461) 80 61
71 Email: ihk@flensburg.ihk.de
AOK: Helenenallee 4, 24937 Flensburg. Tel: (0461) 86 70 Fax: (0461)
86 73 82
Local newspaper: Flensburger Tagblatt: www.shz.de/

Town, area and industry

Flensburg: The name is first mentioned in 1196 as *Flensborgh.* The first
part of the name will be derived from an Old Danish word *flen*, the
apex of a gable, and *aa* from Old High German *aha*, water, so that
Flensburg means 'castle on the stretch of water with a pointy bit',
which probably refers to a local coastal inlet of that shape. Flensburg
is Germany's most northern port and an important naval base. The
capital of Danish-occupied Schleswig from 1848, it became Prussian
from 1864, and the citizens voted to remain part of Germany in 1920.
The town, which for the last days of the Third Reich harboured the
government of Hitler's successor Doenitz, sustained little damage in
the Second World War.
Population: c. 90,000; there are *c.* 1,700 students at the university, and a
further 2,500 at the FH.
Position: Northern Schleswig-Holstein, close to the Danish border, by
the Flensburger Förde, a sort of fjord.

Sights: Gabled houses, *Nikolai-Kirche* with huge Renaissance organ, *Südermarkt, Nordermarkt* (South Market, North Market).
Culture: Galleries, museums.
Industry: Shipbuilding, metalworking, paper, rum production, smoked eels, services.
Twinning: GB: Carlisle

Universität Flensburg

Mürwiker Straße 77, 24943 Flensburg. Tel: (0461) 31 30 0 Fax: (0461) 38 543
Akademisches Auslandsamt: Ulrike Bischoff-Parker, Zi.H54, Mürwiker Straße 77, 24943 Flensburg. Tel: (0461) 31 30 226
Studentenwerk: Studentenwerk Schleswig-Holstein, Westring 385, 24118 Kiel. Tel. (0431) 80 54 16 Fax: (0431) 40 00 81 09 Email: studentenwerk. s-h@t-online.de
AStA: Mürwiker Str. 77, 24943 Flensburg. Tel: (0461) 31 30 149 Fax: (0461) 31 30 170 Email: asta@uni-flensburg.de
Frauenbeauftragte: Dr Ursula Kneer, Mürwiker Str. 77, 24943 Flensburg. Tel: (0461) 31 30 182 Email: ukneer@uni-flensburg.de
Behindertenbeauftragte(r): Vertrauensfrau der Schwerbehinderten, Viola Miehe-Werk, Mürwiker Straße 77, 24943 Flensburg. Tel: (04631) 6 21 19 Fax: (04631) 6 21 17
Computer/email access via: Zentrum für Informations- und Medientechnologie, Mürwiker Straße 77, 24943 Flensburg
English department: Englisches Seminar, Mürwiker Straße 77, 24943 Flensburg
German department: Institut für Germanistik, Mürwiker Straße 77, 24943 Flensburg. Tel: (0461) 57 01 311 Fax: (0461) 57 01 312
Vacation courses: Not available.

Frankfurt am Main

Verkehrsverein: im Hauptbahnhof. Tel: (069) 21 23 88 49
Jugendherberge: Haus der Jugend, Deutschherrnufer 12, 60594 Frankfurt am Main. Tel: (069) 61 90 58
Industrie- und Handelskammer: Börsenplatz 4, 60313 Frankfurt am Main. Tel: (069) 21 97–0 Fax: (069) 21 97 14 24 Email: info@frankfurt-main.ihk.de

AOK: Battonnstr. 40–42, 60311 Frankfurt am Main. Tel: (069) 13 630
Fax: (069) 13 63 31 99

Local newspapers: Frankfurter Neue Presse: www.rhein-main.net/; *Frankfurter
Rundschau*: www.fr-aktuell.de/; *Frankfurter Allgemeine Zeitung* is not
listed because, at the time of writing, this newspaper still does not
publish on its website.

Town, area and industry

Frankfurt am Main: The name is first mentioned in 794 CE (although it
probably had been in existence since the sixth century) as
Franconofurd, 'the ford (i.e. crossing place) of the Franks (on the
River Main)'. The name of the river, the *Main* is derived from an old,
general European term for 'water'. There are similar river names in
Ireland, the Maín, and in Poland, the Mien. Frankfurt is the major
European banking city and the seat of the European Central Bank. All
the main German banks have their head offices here, and many
foreign banks their German headquarters. The main German stock
exchange is also based here. It is the centre of economic activity in the
Rhine–Main area and is the seat of a number of Federal authorities:
Bundesamt für Ernährung und Wirtschaft (Federal Food and Economics
Department), *Deutsche Bundesbank* (German Federal Bank), *Bundes-
rechnungshof* (Federal Audit Office), *Zentralstelle für Arbeitsvermittlung
der Bundesanstalt für Arbeit* (Federal Institute of Employment Central
Job Agency) and *Hauptverwaltung der Deutschen Bundesbahn* (Administrative Headquarters of the Federal German Railways). Frankfurt is
also an extremely important trade fair centre. Much of the old part of
the town was razed to the ground in the Second World War; it has
been partly restored.

Population: c. 660,000; there are *c.* 36,000 students at the university, and
c. 11,500 students at a further five HE institutions.

Position: Southern Hesse, on the River Main, at the foot of the Taunus
mountains.

Sights: The house where Goethe was born, cathedral, *Römer*, *Eschen-
heimer Turm*.

Culture: Theatres, many museums and galleries, opera, book fairs.

Industry: Engineering, chemicals, pharmaceuticals, printing, leather, foodstuffs, electronics; banking, insurance; trade fairs; huge airport.

Twinning: GB: Birmingham

Johann Wolfgang Goethe Universität

Senckenberganlage 31, 60054 Frankfurt am Main. Tel: (069) 79 81 Web site: www.uni-frankfurt.de
Akademisches Auslandsamt: Sencckenberganlage 31, 0325 Frankfurt am Main. Tel: (069) 79 82 84 01 Fax: (069) 79 82 39 83 Email: international@em.uni-frankfurt.de
Studentenwerk: Vorzimmer 317, Bockenheimer Landstr. 133, 60325 Frankfurt am Main. Tel: (069) 79 82 30 51
AStA: Senckenberganlage 31, 60054 Frankfurt am Main. Tel: (069) 79 8–1 Email: asta@stud.uni-frankfurt.de
Frauenbeauftragte: Senckenberganlage 31, 60054 Frankfurt am Main. Tel: (069) 79 8–1
Behindertenbeauftragte(r): Dr Michael Dietrich, Zimmer 138, Senckenberganlage 15, 60054 Frankfurt am Main. Tel: (069) 79 82 21 92 Fax: (069) 79 82 38 05
Computer/email access via: Hochschulrechenzentrum, Gräfstr. 38, 60054 Frankfurt am Main. Tel: (069) 79 82 35 90 Fax: (069) 79 82 83 13 Email: hrz@rz.uni-frankfurt.de
English department: Institut für England- und Amerikastudien, Kettenhofweg 130, 60325 Frankfurt am Main. Tel: (069) 79 82 22 66
German department: Institut für Deutsche Sprache und Literatur, Georg-Voigt-Straße 12, 60325 Frankfurt am Main. Tel: (069) 79 82 25 98 Fax: (069) 79 82 25 97
Vacation courses: August. Intermediate and advanced language: history and literature.

Freiburg

Verkehrsverein: Rotteckring 14, 79098 Freiburg i/B. Tel: (0761) 38 81 880
Jugendherberge: Karthäuserstraße 151, 79104 Freiburg i/B. Tel: (0761) 67 656
Industrie- und Handelskammer: IHK Freiburg, Schnewlinstr. 11–13, Postfach 86079008, 79098 Freiburg im Breisgau. Tel: (0761) 38 580 Fax: (0761) 38 58 222 Email: ihk@freiburg.ihk.de
AOK: Fahnenbergplatz 6, 79089 Freiburg im Breisgau. Tel: (0761) 21 03 207 Fax: (0761) 23 281
Local newspaper: Badische Zeitung: www.badische-zeitung.de/

Town, area and industry

Freiburg im Breisgau: The name is formed from Middle High German _vri_, 'free', and _burg_, 'fortified place'. Freiburg's inhabitants were granted unusual freedoms, being allowed to elect their own vicars and sheriffs. The words _Burg_ (castle) and _Berg_ (hill/mountain) are related to each other, and will originally have meant 'high place' (since a high place would give a castle a commanding position). The people of Freiburg live in the _Gau_ (a medieval word for 'region', a name which, incidentally, the Nazis resuscitated to indicate an administrative district in the Third Reich) where the Brisgavi (Roman auxiliary troops) had been stationed. Freiburg is a traditional old university town, founded in 1120. The medieval town centre was destroyed in the Second World War, but the cathedral was spared and there has been much reconstruction.

Population: c. 200,000; there are 23,000 students at the university, with a further 5,000+ students at other HE institutions in the city.

Position: Southern Baden-Württemberg, in the western part of the Black Forest, close to France and Switzerland.

Sights: Altstadt, Gothic Freiburger Münster, many medieval churches, towers, gateways.

Culture: Theatres, museums, art galleries.

Industry: Wine growing, timber, tourism, publishing, electronics, pharmaceuticals, banking, insurance.

Twinning: GB: Guildford; US: Madison

Albert-Ludwigs-Universität

Fahnenbergplaz, 79085 Freiburg im Breisgau. Tel: (0761) 20 30 Web site: www.uni-freiburg.de

Akademisches Auslandsamt: Fahnenbergplatz, 79098 Freiburg im Breisgau. Tel: (0761) 20 34 375 Email: scheidler@verwaltung.uni-freiburg.de

Studentenwerk: Schreiberstr. 12–16, 79085 Freiburg im Breisgau. Tel: (0761) 21 01 200 Fax: (0761) 38 30 30 Email: swfr@studentenwerk. uni-freiburg.de

AStA: Bertoldstr. 26, 79085 Freiburg im Breisgau. Tel: (0761) 20 32 032 Fax: (0761) 20 32 034 Email: asta@sun2.ruf.uni-freiburg.de

Frauenbeauftragte: Frau Prof. Dr Elisabeth Cheauré, Werderring 8, 79098 Freiburg im Breisgau. Tel: (0761) 20 34 222 Fax: (0761) 20 34 256 Email: cheaure@ubi-freiburg.de

Behindertenbeauftragte(r): Bruno Zimmermann, Zentrale Studienberatung Raum 02.024, Sedanstraße 6, 79085 Freiburg im Breisgau. Tel: (0761) 20 34 244 Fax: (0761) 20 34 409 Email: zsw@uni-freiburg.de

Computer/ email access via: Rechenzentrum der Universität Freiburg, Hermann-Herder-Str. 10, 79104 Freiburg. Tel: (0761) 20 34 626 Fax: (0761) 20 34 643 Email: sek@uni-freiburg.de

English department: Englisches Seminar der Universität Freiburg, 79085 Freiburg. Tel: (0761) 20 33 350 Fax: (0761) 20 33 40

German department: Deutsches Seminar der Universität Freiburg, 79085 Freiburg. Tel: (0761) 20 33 241 Fax: (0761) 20 33 55

Vacation courses: August, September. Literature, language, economics.

Germersheim

Verkehrsverein: Verkehrsverein der Stadt Germersheim, Ritter von Schmauß 18, 76726 Germersheim. Tel: (07274) 13 575 Fax: (07274) 13 575 Email: tourist@germersheim.de

Jugendherberge: Jugendgästehaus, Geibstraße 5, 76726 Germersheim.

Industrie- und Handelskammer: IHK für Rheinhessen, Schillerplatz 7, Postfach 2509, 55015 Mainz. Tel: (06131) 26 20 Fax: (06131) 26 21 69 Email: ihkmainz@mainz.ihk.de

AOK: Josef-Probst-Str. 1, 76726 Germersheim. Tel: (07274) 95 50 Fax: (07274) 95 51 00/95 54 00

Local newspaper: Germersheimer Stadtanzeiger: www.germersheim.de/aktuell/

Town, area and industry

Germersheim: The name contains the old German proper name *Germar* (possibly 'spear famous') and *heim* (home), so: 'the home of the man who was famous for his spear(manship)'. Incidentally: it was thought until recently that the original meaning of 'German' was 'man with spear', but the *Ger* syllable is now thought to be of Celtic origin and to mean 'shouting', so 'German' probably means 'noisy man' instead. The town was originally a Roman settlement called *Iulius vicus*, which has absolutely nothing to do with its new eleventh-century name. A small town, it does have some local industry, but is probably best known for its interpreting institute, the FASK, which is a branch of the University of Mainz.

Population: c. 20,000; there are *c.* 2,500 students at the FASK.

Position: In the Rhineland-Palatinate, where the River Queich flows into the Upper Rhine.

Sights: Parts of the medieval fortress, Weißenburger Tor, arsenal.

Culture: Museums, theatre, chamber music, ballet.
Industry: Furniture, glass, textiles, Rhine port.
Twinning: No formal twinning arrangements with GB or US.

Fachbereich Angewandte Sprach- und Kulturwissenschaft (FASK) in Germersheim

An der Hochschule 2, 76711 Germersheim. Tel: (07274) 50 80 Fax: (07274)
50 83 54 29 Web site: www.fask.uni-mainz.de
Akademisches Auslandsamt: Zimmer 118, An der Hochschule 2, 76726
Germersheim. Tel: (07274) 50 83 51 18 Fax: (07274) 50 83 54 28
Email: voelkel@mail.fask.uni-mainz.de
Studentenwerk: Staudingerweg 21, 55128 Mainz. Tel: (06131) 39 0 Fax:
(06131) 39 49 07 Email: stwmzwv@mail.uni-mainz.de
AStA: Zimmer 140, An der Hochschule 2, 76726 Germersheim. Tel:
(07274) 50 83 51 40 Fax: (07274) 88 82 Email: asta@mail. fask.uni-
mainz.de
Frauenbeauftragte: Angelika Hüttenberger, Zimmer 101, An der Hoch-
schule 2, 76726 Germersheim. Tel: (07274) 50 83 51 01 Fax: (07274)
50 83 54 03 Email: huettena@mail.fask.uni-mainz.de
Behindertenbeauftragte(r): Giulio Gilmozzi, Zimmer 343, An der Hochschule 2, 76726 Germersheim. Tel: (07274) 50 83 51 47 Fax: (07274)
50 83 54 29
Computer/email access via: Computeranlagen für Forschung und Lehre,
An der Hochschule 2, 76726 Germersheim. Tel: (07274) 50 83 51 50
Fax: (07274) 50 83 54 38 Email: kurowska@nfask2.fask.uni-mainz.de
English department: Institut für Anglistik u. Amerikanistik, An der Hochschule 2, 76711 Germersheim. Tel: (07274) 50 83 52 47 Fax: (07274)
50 83 54 47
German department: Germanistisches Institut, An der Hochschule 2,
76711 Germersheim. Tel: (07274) 50 83 53 22 Fax: (07274) 50 83 54
29 Email: info@nfask2.fask.uni-mainz.de
Vacation courses: July: *Deutsch für Konferenzdolmetscher*; August: language,
literature, culture.

Gießen

Verkehrsverein: Berlinerplatz 2, 35390 Gießen. Tel: (0641) 30 62 489
Jugendherberge: Gießen an der Lahn JH, Richard-Schirrmann-Weg 53,
35398 Gießen/Lahn. Tel: (0641) 65 879 Fax: (0641) 65 879
Industrie- und Handelskammer: IHK Gießen, Lonystr. 7, 35390 Gießen
Tel: (0641) 79 540 Fax: (0641) 75 914 Email: zentrale@giessen-
friedberg.ihk.de
AOK: Gartenstr. 10, 35390 Gießen. Tel: (0641) 70 090 Fax: (0641) 70
09 199
Local newspaper: Gießener Anzeiger: www.anzeiger.net/start.html

Town, area and industry

Gießen: The name means just what it looks like (*gießen* = to pour). In
1196 it is mentioned as *burc ze din Giezzen* (castle by the streams), so
if you're doing your residence there, don't worry: the reference is to
flowing water rather than to rain. Gießen, a garden city, dates back to
the twelfth century. Its centre suffered large-scale destruction (70 per
cent) in the Second World War, but much has been rebuilt and
restored. The university is named after its most famous professor, the
chemist, Justus Liebig.

Population: c. 74,000; there are *c.* 21,500 students at the university, and
c. 7,000 at the FH.

Position: On the River Lahn, in central Hesse between Marburg and
Frankfurt am Main.

Sights: Altes and *Neues Schloss*, botanical gardens.

Culture: Theatre, opera, ballet, museums.

Industry: Machinery, tool-making, textiles, pharmaceuticals, foodstuffs,
pottery, rubber, tobacco.

Twinning: GB: Winchester; US: Waterloo.

Justus Liebig Universität

Ludwigstraße 23, 35390 Gießen. Tel: (0641) 99–0 Fax: (0641) 99 12 289
Web site: www.uni-giessen.de
Akademisches Auslandsamt: Gutenbergstr. 6, 35390 Gießen. Tel: (0641)
99 12 140 Fax: (0641) 99 12 149 Email: akademisches.auslandsamt
@admin.uni-giessen.de
Studentenwerk: Otto-Behaghel-Str. 23–27, 35394 Gießen. Tel: (0641) 40
00 80 Fax: (0641) 40 00 821

AStA: Haus D, Otto-Behaghel-Str. 25, 35394 Gießen. Tel: (0641) 99 14 800 Fax: (0641) 47 113 Email: asta@uni-giessen.de

Frauenbeauftragte: Gerda Weigel-Greilich, Ludwigstraße 28a, 35390 Gießen. Tel: (0641) 99 12 050 Fax: (0641) 99 12 059 Email: gerda. weigelgreilich@admin.uni-giessen.de

Behindertenbeauftragte(r): Frau Ulrike Wittmann, Ludwigstraße 28a, 35390 Gießen. Tel: (0641) 99 16 223 Email: ulrike.wittmann@zil.uni-giessen.de

Computer/email access via: Hochschulrechenzentrum, Heinrich-Buff-Ring 44, 35392 Gießen. Tel: (0641) 99 13 001 Fax: (0641) 99 13 009 Email: frage@hrz.uni-giessen.de

English department: FB 10 Anglistik, Otto-Behaghel-Straße 10g, 35394 Gießen. Tel: (0641) 99 30 000 Fax: (0641) 99 30 000 Email: charlotte.e.beck@anglistik.uni-giessen.de

German department: Institut für deutsche Sprache, Otto-Behaghel-Straße 10b, 35394 Gießen. Tel: (0641) 99 29 031 Fax: (0641) 99 29 049 Email: otfried.ehrismann@germanistik.uni-giessen.de

Vacation courses: September. Language and *Landeskunde*.

Göttingen

Verkehrsverein: Fremdenverkehrsverein Göttingen e.V., Altes Rathaus, Markt 9, 37073 Göttingen. Tel: (0551) 54 000

Jugendherberge: Habichtsweg 2, 37073 Göttingen. Tel: (0551) 57 622 Fax: (0551) 43 887

Industrie- und Handelskammer: IHK Hannover-Hildesheim, Schiffgraben 49, Postfach 3029, 30030 Hannover. Tel: (0511) 31 070 Fax: (0511) 31 07 333 Email: bebek@hannover.ihk.de

AOK: Godehardstr. 24, 37081 Göttingen. Tel: (0551) 50 61 600 Fax: (0551) 50 61 690

Local newspaper: Göttinger Tageblatt: www.gtonline.de/

Town, area and industry

Göttingen: The name, first mentioned as *Gutingi* in 953, is derived from the Old Saxon words *gota* (water channel) and *-ingi-* (people), so it means 'people by the channel of water'. Göttingen is a prestigious university town. The Brothers Grimm, Bismarck, Max Planck, Heisenberg, et al. (more than thirty Nobel Prize winners among them), studied here. The university is named after Georg August,

Elector of Hanover, who was also George II of England. The town survived the Second World War more or less unscathed.

Population: c. 133,000; there are *c.* 30,000 students at the university.

Position: S.E Lower Saxony on the River Leine.

Sights: Many buildings from the fourteenth, fifteenth and sixteenth centuries, churches, *Altes Rathaus, Gänseliesel* (Lizzie the Goose Girl) statue, allegedly the most kissed girl in Germany, as all newly qualified PhDs of the university have to give her a kiss.

Culture: Theatres, symphony orchestra, galleries, museums, university library, literature, jazz, film festivals.

Industry: Printing, publishing, optical and precision instruments, film production, musical instruments, ceramics.

Twinning: GB: Cheltenham

Georg-August Universität

Wilhelmsplatz 1, 37073 Göttingen. Tel: (0551) 39 0 Web site: www.uni-goettingen.de

Akademisches Auslandsamt: Wilhelmsplatz 4, 37073 Göttingen. Tel: (0551) 39 0 Fax: (0551) 39 25 91 Email: aaa@zvw.uni-goettingen.de

Studentenwerk: Platz der Göttinger Sieben 4, 37073 Göttingen. Tel: (0551) 39 0 Fax: (0551) 39 51 86 Email: info@studentenwerk.stud. uni-goettingen.de

AStA: Goßlerstraße 16a, 37073 Göttingen. Tel: (0551) 39 45 64 Fax: (0551) 39 45 64 Email: info@asta.stud.uni-goettingen.de

Frauenbeauftragte: Dr Dorothea Mey, Humboldtallee 3, 37073 Göttingen. Tel: (0551) 39 39 50 Fax: (0551) 39 25 57

Behindertenbeauftragte(r): Dr Jochen Krohn, Humboldtalle 15, 37073 Göttingen. Tel: (0551) 39 27 25 Fax: (0551) 39 21 85 Email: vertrauensmann.schwerbehinderte@zvw.uni-goettingen.de

Computer/email access via: Rechenzentrum, Platz der Göttinger Sieben 5, 37073 Göttingen. Tel: (0551) 39 73 47 Fax: (0551) 39 73 46 Email: mpforr@uni-goettingen.de

English department: Seminar für englische Philologie, Humboldtallee 13, 37073 Göttingen. Tel: (0551) 39 75 57

German department: Seminar für deutsche Philologie, Jacob-Grimm-Haus, Käte-Hamburger-Weg 3, 37073 Göttingen. Tel: (0551) 39 75 10 Fax: (0551) 39 75 11 Email: uhdp@uni-goettingen.de

Vacation courses: August. Language and *Landeskunde.*

Greifswald

Verkehrsverein: Schuhhagen 22, 17493 Greifswald. Tel: (03834) 34 60
Jugendherberge: No YH, but this is inexpensive: Schipp in, Am Hafen 3,
   17493 Greifswald. Tel: (03834) 84 00 26
Industrie- und Handelskammer: IHK Rostock, Ernst-Barlach-Straße 1–3,
   18055 Rostock. Tel: (0381) 33 80 Fax: (0381) 45 91 156 Email: info
   @rostock.ihk.de
AOK: Vulkanstr. 16, 17489 Greifswald. Tel: (03834) 57 71 43 34 Fax:
   (03834) 57 71 43 12
Local newspaper: Ostsee-Zeitung: www.ostsee-zeitung.de Click on *Aus der
   Region,* then *Greifswald.*

Town, area and industry

Greifswald: The name is first mentioned in the thirteenth century as
   Gripheswald 'Griffin wood' after the mythical bird on the coat of arms
   of the dukes of Pomerania. *Wald,* incidentally, is directly related to
   the English *wold,* as in Cotswolds. The town grew up as a settlement
   around a Cistercian abbey around the year 1200. It was a member of
   the Hanseatic League. The university is named after Ernst Moritz
   Arndt, who was a professor of history and philology at Greifswald.
Population: c. 60,000; there are *c.* 5,000 students at the university.
Position: In eastern Mecklenburg-West Pomerania, on the Baltic, so
   good for water sports.
Sights: Cathedral, thirteenth- and fourteenth-century churches including
   Gothic *Marienkirche,* Renaissance architecture.
Culture: Music festivals, jazz, theatre, orchestras, cinemas.
Industry: Machinery, textiles, foodstuffs.
Twinning: US: Bryan

Ernst-Moritz-Arndt-Universität

Domstr. 11, 17487 Greifswald. Tel: (03834) 86 0 Web site: www.uni-
greifswald.de
Akademisches Auslandsamt: Domstr. 11, 17487 Greifswald. Tel: (03834)
   86 11 16 Fax: (03834) 86 11 20 Email: aaa@mail.uni-greifswald.de
Studentenwerk: Am Schießwall 1–4, 17489 Greifswald. Tel: (03834) 86
   17 00 Fax: (03834) 86 17 02 Email: studwerk@mail.uni-greifswald.de
AStA: Rubenowstr. 1, 17489 Greifswald. Tel: (03834) 86 17 50 Fax: (03834)
   86 17 52 Email: asta@mail.uni-greifswald.de
Frauenbeauftragte: Gleichstellungsbeauftragte: Heike Völcker, Löfflerstr.

23, 17487 Greifswald. Tel: (03834) 86 69 42

Behindertenbeauftragte(r): Dr Martin Domm, Institut für Mathematik/ Informatik, Jahnstr. 15a 17489 Greifswald. Tel: (03834) 86 46 19

Computer/email access via: Universitätsrechenzentrum, Friedrich-Ludwig-Jahn-Str. 14d, 17487 Greifswald. Tel: (03834) 86 14 00 Fax: (03834) 86 14 01 Email: callcent@rz.uni-greifswald.de

English department: Institut für Anglistik u. Amerikanistik, Steinbecker Str. 15, 17489 Greifswald. Tel: (03834) 86 33 54 Fax: (03834) 86 33 65 Email: ifaa@rz.uni-greifswald.de

German department: Institut für Deutsche Philologie, Bahnhofstr. 46–47, 17487 Greifswald. Tel: (03834) 86 34 04 Fax: (03834) 86 34 23 Email: philosek@mail.uni-greifswald.de

Vacation courses: July. Language and literature.

Halle

Verkehrsverein: Roter Turm, Am Marktplatz, 06108 Halle. Tel: (0345) 2023340

Jugendherberge: August-Bebel-Str. 48a, 06108 Halle. Tel: (0345) 124716

Industrie- und Handelskammer: IHK Halle-Dessau, Georg-Schumann-Platz, 06110 Halle. Tel: (0345) 2126–0 Fax: (0345) 2029649 Email: info@halle.ihk.de

AOK: AOK, Robert-Franz-Ring 16, 06108 Halle. Tel: (0345) 2143 Fax: (0345) 2145999

Local newspaper: Mitteldeutsche Zeitung: At the time of writing, this newspaper does not have an online news site.

Town, area and industry

Halle: The name can mean 'salt', although another theory is that it just means 'hall'. However, given that there is evidence of there having been a settlement here since pre-historic times (Iron and Bronze Ages) because of the presence of salt, the first meaning seems more likely. Halle is a major industrial city and a scientific and cultural centre. The university, which was amalgamated with its Wittenberg counterpart in 1817, is thus named after Martin Luther (you will remember that he nailed his 95 theses to the door of the Wittenberg *Schlosskirche*). Händel (the composer) was born here. There was some damage in the Second World War, but reconstruction was successful, and much was preserved.

Population: c. 290,000; there are c. 12,000 students at the university, with a further c. 750 at two other HE institutions.

Position: Southern Saxony-Anhalt, south of Magdeburg, northwest of Leipzig, close to the Harz mountains, and, of course, Wittenberg.

Sights: Castles, *Altstadt*, *Rathaus*, churches, cathedral.

Culture: Gallery, museums (including museum devoted to salt), theatres, music, opera house.

Industry: Engineering, coachbuilding, chemicals, pharmaceuticals, food-stuffs, rock salt, sugar refining, brewing, cement, brown coal, potash.

Twinning: No formal links.

Martin-Luther-Universität Halle-Wittenberg

06099 Halle (Saale). Tel: (0345) 55 20 Fax: (0345) 55 27 077 Web site: www.uni-halle.de

Akademisches Auslandsamt: Universitätsring 3, 06108 Halle. Tel: (0345) 55 21 313 Fax: (0345) 55 27 052 Email: m.pichier@verwaltung.uni-halle.de

Studentenwerk: Selkestraße 9, 06122 Halle. Tel: (0345) 21 80 91 02 Fax: (0345) 21 80 91 48 Email: swhalle@t-online.de

AStA: StudentInnenrat, Universitätsplatz 7, 06108 Halle. Tel: (0345) 55 21 411 Fax: (0345) 55 27 086 Email: stura@uni-halle.de

Frauenbeauftragte: Gleichstellungsbeauftragte, Moritzburgring 10, 06108 Halle. Tel: (0345) 55 21 359 Fax: (0345) 55 27 099 Email: gleichstellungsbuero@uni-halle.de

Behindertenbeauftragte(r): Dr Detlev Rieder, Ernst-Gruber-Straße 40, 06099 Halle. Tel: (0345) 55 72 396 Email: behindertenbeauftragter @uni-halle.de

Computer/email access via: Universitätsrechenzentrum, Kurt-Mothes-Straße 1, 06120 Halle. Tel: (0345) 55 21 801 Fax: (0345) 55 27 008 Email: hotline@urz.uni-halle.de

English department: Institut für Anglistik und Amerikanistik. Gimritzer Damm 2, 06099 Halle. Tel: (0345) 55 23 511 Fax: (0345) 55 27 044 Email: dziubiel@amerikanistik.uni-halle.de

German department: Germanistisches Institut, Herweghstraße 96, 06099 Halle. Tel: (0345) 55 23 601 Fax: (0345) 55 21 707 Email: drosdziok @germanistik.uni-halle.de

Vacation courses: Not available.

Hamburg

Verkehrsverein: Hauptbahnhof–Kirchenallee, 20099 Hamburg. Tel: (040) 30 05 12 01
Jugendherberge: Jugendgästehaus 'Horner Rennbahn', Rennbahnstr. 100, 22111 Hamburg. Tel: (040) 65 11 671
Industrie- und Handelskammer: Handelskammer Hamburg, Adolphsplatz 1, 20457 Hamburg. Tel: (040) 36 13 80 Fax: (040) 36 13 84 01 Email: service@hamburg.handelskammer.de
AOK: Grindelallee 100, 20146 Hamburg. Tel: (040) 20 23 22 12 Fax: (040) 20 23 22 13
Local newspapers: Hamburger Morgenpost: www.mopo.de/; *Hamburger Abendblatt*: www.abendblatt.de/

Town, area and industry

Hamburg: The name, originally *Hammaburg* (836 CE), comes from Old High German *hamma* (hollow of the knee, i.e. when your leg is bent) and is used metaphorically to indicate a bend in a river, and *burg* (castle). So Hamburg is the 'castle over a bend in the river'. Hamburg is a city state, so it is its own *Bundesland*. It is a vast cosmopolitan city and Germany's main port. It is the seat of various Federal agencies, including the *Bundesforschungsanstalt für Fischerei* (Federal Fishery Research Institute), the *Bundesamt für Seeschifffahrt und Hydrologie* (Federal Department for Maritime Fishing), and the *Deutscher Wetterdienst* (German Meteorological Office). It is one of the most important industrial locations in Germany, and there are more than 3000 import and export firms based there. Hamburg is a Hanseatic town, and this is reflected in its HH car number plates (*HH = Hansestadt Hamburg*). It took twenty years to rebuild Hamburg after the Second World War destruction.

Population: c. 1.7 million; there are *c.* 43,000 students at the university, and a further 24,000+ students at seven other HE institutions.

Position: On the River Elbe, *c.* 100 km from the North Sea. Fairly close to Bremen and Lübeck.

Sights: Large amounts, e.g. many churches, *Rathaus*, markets, *Hanseviertel* (Hansa Quarter), *St. Pauli* (this is probably like recommending Soho in the 1960s); see the guidebooks.

Culture: Theatres, museums, galleries, opera (the oldest German opera house is here, founded in 1678), nightlife.

Industry: Shipping (HAPAG), foodstuffs, tobacco, chemicals, petroleum products (Deutsche BP, Deutsche Shell), engineering, furniture, coffee (Tchibo), publishing, tourism.

Twinning: US: Chicago

Universität Hamburg

Edmund-Siemers-Allee 1, 20146 Hamburg. Tel: (040) 42 83 80 Fax: (040) 42 83 82 449 Web site: www.uni-hamburg.de

Akademisches Auslandsamt: Edmund-Siemers Allee 1, 20146 Hamburg. Tel: (040) 42 83 83 305 Fax: (040) 42 83 82 142 Email: akahh@ni-hamburg.de

Studentenwerk: Von-Melle-Park 2, 20146 Hamburg. Tel: (040) 41 90 20 Fax: (040) 41 90 21 00 Email: stw@mail.whm.hamburg.de

AStA: Von-Melle-Park 5, 20146 Hamburg. Tel: (040) 45 02 040 Fax: (040) 41 07 224 Email: oeff@asta.uni-hamburg.de

Frauenbeauftragte: Prof. Dr Ursula Platzer, Martinistr. 52, 20146 Hamburg. Tel: (040) 42 80 32 282 Email: platzer@uke.uni-hamburg.de

Behindertenbeauftragte(r): Frau Prof. Dr. Rath, Institut für Behindertenpädagogik, Sedanstr. 19, 20146 Hamburg. Tel: (040) 41 23 37 64 Fax: (040) 42 83 83 392 Email: Behinderte.Studierende @erzwiss.uni-hamburg.de

Computer/email access via: Regionales Rechenzentrum, Schlüterstraße 70, 20146 Hamburg. Tel: (040) 42 83 84 132 Fax: (040) 42 83 86 270 Email: beratung@rrz.uni-hamburg.de

English department: Institut für Anglistik und Amerikanistik, Von-Melle-Park 6, 20146 Hamburg. Tel: (040) 42 83 84 858 Fax: (040)42 83 84 856 Email: fs0a002@uni-hamburg.de

German department: Germanistisches Seminar, Von-Melle-Park 6, 20146 Hamburg. Tel: (040) 42 83 84 779 Fax: (040) 42 83 84 785 Email: fs6a085@uni-hamburg.de

Vacation courses: August, September. Language and *Landeskunde.*

Hannover

Verkehrsverein: Ernst-August-Platz, 30159 Hannover. Tel: (0511) 30 140

Jugendherberge: Ferdinand-Wilhelm-Fricke-Weg 1, 30169 Hannover. Tel: (0511) 32 29 41

Industrie- und Handelskammer: IHK Hannover-Hildesheim, Postfach 3029, Schiffgraben 49, 30030 Hannover. Tel: (0511) 31 070 Fax: (0511) 31 07 333 Email: rathert@hannover.ihk.de

AOK: Hans-Böckler-Allee 30, 30173 Hannover. Tel: (0511) 13 819 Fax: (0511) 28 52 980

Local newspaper: Hannoversche Allgemeine Zeitung: www.haz.de/

Town, area and industry

Hannover (Hanover): The derivation of this name is not easy to guess unless you happen to know some Low German, and even then you might have some trouble. Hanover was founded in the eleventh century as a market settlement at a crossing point on the River Leine. The name appears for the first time around 1150 CE as *vicus* (Latin for a place or settlement) *Honovere* (Middle Low German *hohen over* = *am hohen Ufer:* 'on the high river bank'). Note that the English version is closer to the early spelling, while modern German has added an 'n'. This town is the capital of Lower Saxony, seat of the *Bundesanstalt für Geo-Wissenschaften* (Federal Geo-Science Institute). Much of the city was destroyed in the Second World War. Having been rebuilt, it is now a modern garden city and trade fair centre.

Population: c. 500,000; there are *c.* 32,000 students at the university, with *c.* 13,300 at a further six HE institutions.

Position: On the River Leine, more or less in the centre of Lower Saxony, close to Hildesheim and Hamlyn (*Hameln*).

Sights: Altes and *Neues Rathaus, Schloss,* churches.

Culture: Many museums, theatre, opera.

Industry: Engineering, textiles, leather, paper, chemicals, motor vehicles, rubber, foodstuffs, printing; site of trade fairs, and EXPO 2000. Firms such as AEG, Continental, Sennheiser, Varta have bases here.

Twinning: GB: Bristol

Universität Hannover

Welfengarten 1, 30167 Hannover Tel: (0511) 76 20 Fax: (0511) 76 23 456 Web site: www.uni-hannover.de

Akademisches Auslandsamt: Welfengarten 1a, 30167 Hannover. Tel: (0511) 76 20 Fax: (0511) 76 24 090 Email: auslandsamt@uni-hannover.de

Studentenwerk: Jägerstr. 3–5, 30167 Hannover. Tel: (0511) 76 88 022 Fax: (0511) 76 88 949 Email: sinfo@studentenwerk.hannover.de

AStA: Welfengarten 2c, 30167 Hannover. Tel: (0511) 76 25 061 Fax: (0511) 71 74 41 Email: asta@stud.uni-hannover.de

Frauenbeauftragte: Helga Gotzmann, Wilhelm-Busch-Straße 4, 30167 Hannover. Tel: (0511) 76 24 058 Fax: (0511) 76 23 564 Email: frauenbuero@uni-hannover.de

Behindertenbeauftragte(r): Schwerstbehindertenvertretung, Barbara Zadow, Am Puttenserfelde 2, 30167 Hannover. Tel: (0511) 76 23 074 Fax: (0511) 76 23 075

Computer/email access via: Regionales Rechenzentrum für Niedersachsen, Universität Hannover, Schlosswenderstraße 5, 30159 Hannover. Tel: (0511) 76 22 883 Fax: (0511) 76 23 003 Email: hotline@rrzn.uni-hannover.de

English department: Englisches Seminar, Königsworther Platz 1, 30167 Hannover. Tel: (0511) 76 22 209 Fax: (0511) 76 23 229 Email: nhtnanne@mbox.anglistik.uni-hannover.de

German department: Seminar für Deutsche Literatur und Sprache, Königsworther Platz 1, 30167 Hannover. Tel: (0511) 76 25 464 Fax: (0511) 76 28 243

Vacation courses: Not available.

Heidelberg

Verkehrsverein: Bahnhofsplatz, 69115 Heidelberg. Tel: (06221) 21 341

Jugendherberge: Tiergartenstr. 5, 69120 Heidelberg, Tel: (06221) 41 20 66

Industrie- und Handelskammer: IHK Hauptgeschäftsstelle Heidelberg, Hans-Böckler-Str. 4, 69115 Heidelberg. Tel: (06221) 90 17 0 Fax: (06221) 90 17

AOK: Friedrich-Ebert-Platz 3, 69117 Heidelberg. Tel: (06221) 52 96 00 Fax: (06221) 52 96 99

Local newspaper: Rhein Neckar Zeitung: www.rnz.de/

Town, area and industry

Heidelberg: The name, first mentioned as *Heidelberch* in 1196, probably refers to the bilberries (*Heidelbeeren*) growing on the hills surrounding the town. This is the oldest university town in Germany, with many renowned scientific institutes. The university was founded in 1386 at the instigation of a Palatinate count, Ruprecht I; owing to various religious–political problems, it kept being closed down and then reopened. In 1803 it was reopened (presumably permanently now) under Grand Duke Karl-Friedrich of Baden, hence the hybrid name *Ruprecht-Karl Universität*. Heidelberg is as picturesque as its reputation suggests, thus attracting (literally) millions of tourists every year.

Population: c. 140,000; there are *c.* 28,000 students at the university, with a further 5,000+ students at other HE institutions in the city.

Position: In Baden-Württemberg, SW Germany, in the Neckar valley close to Mannheim and the Odenwald.

Sights: Altstadt, Schloss, in which there is a huge wine cask with a capacity of 185,000 litres, *Alte Brücke* (Old Bridge), *Heiliggeistkirche* (Church of the Holy Ghost), Baroque *Rathaus,* above the town the *Thingstätte,* an eerie amphitheatre built by the Nazis to hold mystical gatherings.

Culture: Theatres, museums, including the house where Ebert was born, much music.

Industry: Tourism, electronics, steel, machinery, surgical instruments, leather, tobacco, wood, building materials (*Heidelberger Zement*), pens (*Lamy*), publishing (*Springer Verlag*).

Twinning: GB: Cambridge

Ruprecht-Karls-Universität

Rektorat, Grabengasse 1, 69117 Heidelberg. Tel: (06221) 54 21 47 Fax: (06221) 54 23 15 Web site: www.uni-heidelberg.de

Akademisches Auslandsamt: Seminarstr. 2, 69117 Heidelberg. Tel: (06221) 54 23 35 Fax: (06221) 54 23 32 Email: aaa@zuv.uni-heidelberg.de

Studentenwerk: Marstallhof 1–5, 69117 Heidelberg. Tel: (06221) 54 26 40 Fax: (06221) 54 27 41 Email: gf.stw@urz.uni-heidelberg.de

AStA: Lauerstr. 1, 69117 Heidelberg. Tel: (06221) 54 24 56 Fax: (06221) 54 24 57 Email: fsk@urz.uni-heidelberg.de

Frauenbeauftragte: Hauptstr. 126, 69117 Heidelberg. Tel: (06221) 54 76 97 Fax: (06221) 54 72 71 Email: a65@uni-heidelberg.de

Behindertenbeauftragte(r): Eckhard Behrens, Seminarstr. 2, 69117 Heidelberg. Tel: (06221) 54 23 13 Fax: (06221) 54 35 76 Email: behrens @zuv.uni-heidelberg.de

Computer/email access via: Universitätsrechenzentrum, Im Neuenheimer Feld 293, 69120 Heidelberg. Tel: (06221) 54 45 09 Fax: (06221) 54 55 81 Email: beratung@urz.uni-heidelberg.de

English department: Anglistisches Seminar, Kettengasse 12, 69117 Heidelberg. Tel: (06221) 54 28 10 Fax: (06221) 54 28 77 Email: andreas. hoefele@urz.uni-heidelberg.de

German department: Germanistisches Seminar, Hauptstr. 207–209, 69117 Heidelberg. Tel: (06221) 54 32 01 Fax: (06221) 54 32 55 Email: sekretariat@novell1.gs.uni-heidelberg.de

Vacation courses: July, August. Language and *Landeskunde.*

Jena

Verkehrsverein: Jena-information, Holzmarkt 8, Postfach 10 03 38, 07703 Jena. Tel: (03641) 58 630 Fax: (03641) 58 63 22
Jugendherberge: Internationales Jugendgästehaus, Am Herrenberge 3, 07745 Jena. Tel: (03641) 68 70
Industrie- und Handelskammer: IHK Erfurt, Friedrich-List-Str. 36, 99096 Erfurt. Tel: (0361) 34 840 Fax: (0361) 34 81 299 Email: krepuska @erfurt.ihk.de
AOK: August-Bebel-Str. 27a–b, 07743 Jena. Tel: (03641) 58 50 Fax: (03641) 58 51 03
Local newspaper: Thüringische Landeszeitung: www.thueringische-landeszeitung.de/ Click on *Lokales,* then *Jena.*

Town, area and industry

Jena: The name comes from the Old High German word *jani,* meaning 'strip of mowed grassland'. Jena is a medieval town, the site of the battle in 1806, when Napoleon defeated the Prussian army. The university, which at one time had Fichte, Hegel, Schlegel, and Schiller on its teaching staff, is named after Friedrich Schiller. The town centre was destroyed in the Second World War, but there has been much restoration.
Population: c. 100,000; there are *c.* 12,000 students at the university, and a further *c.* 2,500 at the FH.
Position: Eastern Thuringia, on the River Saale, between Erfurt and Gera.
Sights: Churches, *Rathaus, Schillerhaus,* mediaeval towers, university.
Culture: Theatres, museums, philharmonic orchestra.
Industry: Optics (Zeiss), glassware (Jenaer Glas, Schott), pharmaceuticals, electronics, precision instruments.
Twinning: US: Berkeley

Friedrich-Schiller-Universität

Fürstengraben 1, 07743 Jena. Tel: (03641) 90 Fax: (03641) 93 11 02 Web site: www.uni-jena.de
Akademisches Auslandsamt: Dr Jürgen Hendrich, Fürstengraben 1, 07743 Jena. Tel: (03641) 93 11 60 Fax: (03641) 93 11 62 Email: hhj@sokrates. verwaltung.uni-jena.de
Studentenwerk: Studentenwerk Jena/Weimar, Philosophenweg 22, 07743 Jena. Tel: (03641) 93 05 00 Fax: (03641) 93 05 202 Email: studentenwerk @stw.uni-jena.de

AStA: Büro des Studentenrates, Fürstengraben 1, 07743 Jena. Tel: (03641) 93 09 90/91 Fax: (03641) 93 09 92

Frauenbeauftragte: Dr Gisela Horn, Gleichstellungsstelle, Fürstengraben 1, 07743 Jena. Tel: (03641) 30 980 Fax: (03641) 93 09 82 Email: hhg@sokrates.verwaltung.uni-jena.de

Behindertenbeauftragte(r): Veronika Schmidt, Stoystraße 3, 07743 Jena. Tel: (03641) 93 09 70 Fax: (03641) 93 09 72 Email: sbvmail@rz.uni-jena.de

Computer/email access via: Universitätsrechenzentrum, Am Johannis-friedhof 2, 07743 Jena. Tel: (03641) 93 09 70 Fax: (03641) 94 05 02 Email: lhs@rz.uni-jena.de

English department: Institut für Anglistik/Amerikanistik. Tel: (03641) 94 45 00 Fax: (03641) 94 45 02 Email: x6huax@rz.uni-jena.de

German department: Institut für Germanistische Sprachwissenschaft. Tel: (03641) 94 43 00 Fax: (03641) 94 43 02 Email: x6gohe@rz.uni-jena.de

Vacation courses: July, August. Language, culture and *Landeskunde*.

Karlsruhe

Verkehrsverein: Verkehrsverein Karlsruhe e.V., Bahnhofplatz 6, 76137 Karlsruhe. Tel: (0721) 35 530 Fax: (0721) 35 5343

Jugendherberge: Moltkestr. 24, 76133 Karlsruhe. Tel: (0721) 28 248 Fax: (0721) 27 647

Industrie- und Handelskammer: IHK Karlsruhe, Lammstr. 13–17, 76133 Karlsruhe. Tel: (0721) 17 40 Fax: (0721) 17 42 90 Email: info@karlsruhe. ihk.de

AOK: Kriegsstr. 41, 76133 Karlsruhe. Tel: (0721) 37 11 255 Fax: (0721) 37 11 550

Local newspaper: Badische Neueste Nachrichten: At the time of writing, this newspaper does not have an online news site.

Town, area and industry

Karlsruhe: The name means exactly what it looks like: Karl-Wilhelm, Margrave of Baden-Durlach, made his royal residence here, so they called it *Carols-Ruhe* (1715), then *Carlsruhe*, finally replacing the 'C' with a 'K': 'Karl's Repose'. Karlsruhe is the seat of the *Bundes-verfassungsgericht* (Federal Constitutional Court), of the *Bundesgerichtshof* (Federal Supreme Court), the *Bundesanwaltschaft* (Federal Supreme

Court Prosecutors) and the *Bundesanstalt für Wasserbau* (Federal
Institute of Hydraulic Engineering). There was much destruction in
the Second World War, but many buildings have been restored.

Population: c. 270,000; there are 18,000 students at the university, with a
further 7,000+ at other HE institutions.

Position: Baden-Württemberg, on the Rhine, situated between the
Vosges Mountains (*Vogesen*) and the Black Forest (*Schwarzwald*).
Close to Alsace and the Palatinate.

Sights: Baroque *Schloss* with street layout fanning out from it, churches,
orangery, architecture in general.

Culture: Many museums, galleries, theatres, music.

Industry: High-tech (Siemens), electrical products, oil refineries,
machinery, bicycles, perfumes, pharmaceuticals, foodstuffs, clothing,
local nuclear reactor, paper (Holtzmann), steel.

Twinning: GB: Nottingham

Universität Karlsruhe (Technische Hochschule)

Postfach 6980, 76128 Karlsruhe. Tel: (0721) 60 80 Fax: (0721) 60 84 290
Web site: www.uni-karlsruhe.de

Akademisches Auslandsamt: Karlstr. 42/44, 76133 Karlsruhe. Tel: (0721)
60 84 911 Fax: (0721) 60 84 918 Email: pc04@rz.uni-karlsruhe.de

Studentenwerk: Adenauerring 7, 76131 Karlsruhe. Tel: (0721) 69 090
Fax: (0721) 69 09 292 Email: studentenwerk@stud.uni-karlsruhe.de

AStA: UstA der Uni Karlsruhe, Adenauerring 7, 76131 Karlsruhe. Tel:
(0721) 96 40 30 Fax: (0721) 69 21 56 Email: info@usta.de

Frauenbeauftragte: Kaiserstr. 12, 76128 Karlsruhe. Tel: (0721) 60 84 700
Fax: (0721) 60 84 701 Email: Frauenbeauftragte@verwaltung.uni-
karlsruhe.de

Behindertenbeauftragte(r): Joachim Klaus, Kaiserstr. 12, 76128 Karlsruhe.
Tel: (0721) 93 20 70 Fax: (0721) 93 20 711 Email: joachim.klaus
@fsz.uni-karlsruhe.de

Computer/email access via: Rechenzentrum, Kaiserstr. 12, 76128 Karlsruhe. Tel: (0721) 60 83 754 Fax: (0721) 32 550 Email: leitung
@rz.uni-karlsruhe.de

English department: Via: Sprachenzentrum beim Studienkolleg, Karlstr.
42/44, 76133 Karlsruhe. Tel: (0721) 60 84 922 Fax: (0721) 60 84 938

German department: Institut für Literaturwissenschaft. Tel: (0721) 60 82
150 Fax: (0721) 60 84 778 Email: ea14@rz.uni-karlsruhe.de

Vacation courses: Not available.

Kassel

Verkehrsverein: Kassel Service Gesellschaft für Tourismus und Marketing mbH, Königsplatz 53, 34117 Kassel. Tel: (0561) 70 77 07 Fax: (0561) 70 77 200

Jugendherberge: Jugendherberge Kassel, Schenkendorfstr. 18, 34119 Kassel. Tel: (0561) 77 64 55/77 69 33

Industrie- und Handelskammer: IHK Kassel, Kurfürstenstr. 9, 34117 Kassel. Tel: (0561) 78 910 Fax: (0561) 78 91 290 Email: moeller@kassel.ihk.de

AOK: Holländische Str. 17, 34127 Kassel. Tel: (0561) 89 00 409 Fax: (0561) 83 901

Local newspaper: Hessische Niedersächsische Allgemeine: www.hna.de/

Town, area and industry

Kassel: The name means just what it sounds like: 'castle', 'fortress'. First mentioned as *Chassalla* in 913 CE, the word goes back ultimately to Latin *castellum*. However, Kassel appears to have absolutely no connection with the Romans and was founded by the Franks. This is an industrial town, the old centre of which was destroyed in the Second World War; while there has been much reconstruction, little remains of the medieval parts. Kassel is the seat of the *Bundessozialgericht* (Federal Social Welfare Court).

Population: c. 200,000; there are *c.* 18,000 students at the university.

Position: Northern Hesse on the River Fulda to the northeast of Frankfurt am Main, but a good 150 km away.

Sights: Wilhelmshöhe Schloss and parks, *Ottoneum*, reputed to be the oldest building to have housed a theatre in Germany (1607).

Culture: Many museums, including *Brüder-Grimm-Museum*, theatres, *documenta* art exhibitions, galleries.

Industry: Public transport vehicle production, optical and precision instruments, textiles, oil refining, gas.

Twinning: No formal links.

Universität-Gesamthochschule Kassel

Mönchebergstr. 19, 34109 Kassel. Tel: (0561) 80 40 Fax: (0561) 80 42 330 Web site: www.uni-kassel.de

Akademisches Auslandsamt: Mönchebergstr. 19, 34125 Kassel. Tel: (0561) 80 42 103 Fax: (0561) 80 43 513 Email: aaa@hrz.uni-kassel.de

Studentenwerk: Wolfhagerstr. 10, 34117 Kassel. Tel: (0561) 80 42 550 Fax: (0561) 80 43 520 Email: verwaltg@studentenwerk.uni-kassel.de

AStA: Nora-Platiel-Straße 2, 34109 Kassel. Tel: (0561) 80 42 886 Fax: (0561) 85 660

Frauenbeauftragte: Gisela Noll, Möncheberstr. 11, 34109 Kassel. Tel: (0561) 80 42 268 Fax: (0561) 80 43 814 Email: frauenbe@hrz.uni-kassel.de

Behindertenbeauftragte(r): Klaus Raabe, Möncheberstr. 19, 34109 Kassel. Tel: (0561) 80 42 201 Fax: (0561) 80 47 202 Email: kraabe@hrz.uni-kassel.de

Computer/email access via: Hochschulrechenzentrum, Möncheberstraße 1, 34109 Kassel. Tel: (0561) 80 42 287 Fax: (0561) 80 42 297 Email: sekretariat@hrz.uni-kassel.de

English department: Fachbereich Anglistik, Georg-Forster-Straße 3, 34109 Kassel. Tel: (0561) 80 43 340 Fax: (0561) 80 43 341 Email: dekanat8 @uni-kassel.de

German department: Fachbereich 9 Germanistik, Georg-Forster-Straße 3, 34109 Kassel. Tel: (0561) 80 43 322 Fax: (0561) 80 42 812 Email: dekan-09@hrz.uni-kassel.de

Vacation courses: September. Language, literature, *Landeskunde.*

Kiel

Verkehrsverein: Sophienblatt 30, 24103 Kiel. Tel: (0431) 67 91 00

Jugendherberge: Johannesstr. 1, 24143 Kiel. Tel: (0431) 73 14 88

Industrie- und Handelskammer: IHK zu Kiel, Lorentzendamm 24, Postfach 2640, 24025 Kiel. Tel: (0431) 51 940 Fax: (0431) 51 94 234 Email: ihk@kiel.ihk.de

AOK: Gartenstr. 9, 24103 Kiel. Tel: (0431) 59 030 Fax: (0431) 59 03 505

Local newspaper: Kieler Nachrichten: www.kn-online.de/

Town, area and industry

Kiel: Originally *to dem Kyle,* the name is Low German, meaning 'at the narrow bay'. The town is the capital and administrative centre of Schleswig-Holstein and a Baltic port. There is much sailing activity owing to its geographical position. It is the seat of the *Bundesanstalt für Milchforschung* (Federal Milk Research Institute). The university is named after its founder, Duke Christian-Albrecht of Schleswig-Holstein-Gottdorf. It is said by some that the enormous destruction which Kiel suffered during the Second World War had the unusually positive effect of giving the town a chance to de-uglify itself.

Population: c. 246,000; there are *c.* 23,000 students at the university, with a further *c.* 5,600 at other HE institutions.

Position: NE Schleswig-Holstein, on the Baltic at the southern end of the 17 km long *Förde* (coastal inlet or firth), close to Scandinavia.

Sights: The *Förde*, churches, *Rathaus* tower, *Schloss*, *Kieler Woche* (sailing festival and competition).

Culture: Museums, galleries, opera, theatre.

Industry: Shipping, engineering, textiles, optics, fisheries, printing, brewing, textiles.

Twinning: GB: Coventry

Christian-Albrechts-Universität zu Kiel

Olshausenstr. 40, 24118 Kiel. Tel: (0431) 88 000 Web site: www.uni-kiel.de

Akademisches Auslandsamt: Olshausenstr. 40, 24118 Kiel. Tel: (0431) 88 03 715 Fax: (0431) 88 01 666 Email: aaa@zentr-verw.uni-kiel.de

Studentenwerk: Studentenwerk Schleswig-Holstein, Westring 385, 24118 Kiel. Tel: (0431) 88 160 Fax: (0431) 80 54 16 Email: studentenwerk.s-h@t-online.de

AStA: Innenhof Mensa I, 24098 Kiel. Tel: (0431) 88 02 647 Fax: (0431) 88 01 721 Email: thj@asta.uni-kiel.de

Frauenbeauftragte: Verwaltungshochhaus der CAU, Raum 1001, Olsenhausenstr. 40, 24098 Kiel. Tel: (0431) 88 02 651 Fax: (0431) 88 01 661 Email: ldrewing@frauenbeauftragte.uni-kiel

Behindertenbeauftragte(r): Reinhard Eckstein, Olshausenstr. 40, 24098 Kiel. Tel: (0431) 88 03 012 Fax: (0431) 88 07 326 Email: re@zentr-verw.uni-kiel.de

Computer/email access via: Rechenzentrum, Ludewig-Meyn-Str. 4, 24118 Kiel. Tel: (0431) 88 02 765 Email: beratung@rz.uni-kiel.de

English department: Englisches Seminar, Leibnitzstr. 10, 24098 Kiel. Tel: (0431) 88 02 244 Fax: (0431) 88 01 512 Email: anglistik@mail.uni-kiel.de

German department: Germanistisches Seminar, Olshausenstr. 40, 24098 Kiel. Tel: (0431) 88 02 313 Fax: (0431) 88 07 302 Email: puetz @germsem.uni-kiel.de

Vacation courses: July. Language and communication.

Köln

Verkehrsverein: Unter Fettenhennen 19 (am Dom). Tel: (0221) 33 45
Jugendherberge: Jugendherberge Köln-Deutz, Siegesstr. 5A, 50679 Köln
Tel: (0221) 81 47 11
Industrie- und Handelskammer: IHK zu Köln, Unter Sachsenhausen 10–
26, 50448 Köln. Tel: (0221) 16 400 Fax: (0221) 16 40 123 Email:
webmaster@ihk-koeln.de
AOK: Machabäerstr. 19–27, 50668 Köln. Tel: (0221) 94 15 760 Fax: (0221)
16 18 580
Local newspaper: Kölner Stadt-Anzeiger: www.ksta.de/; *Kölnische Rund-
schau:* www.rundschau-online.de/

Town, area and industry

Köln (Cologne): The name was originally *Colonia Claudia Ara Agrippinensium* (Settlement of Claudius Altar of Agrippa). Agrippa was the
wife of Claudius and she was born here. The name was clearly felt to
be a bit of a mouthful by the fourth century and was reduced to
Colonia Agrippina and in the fifth century to *Colonia*, whence eventually *Köln*. Cologne is a major economic centre, filled with monuments
to the city's Roman history. Despite the horrific devastation in the
Second World War, much of the town has been restored, the bomb
damage and consequent excavations revealing more and more of its
Roman origins. The town is the seat of the *Bundesverfassungsschutz*
(Federal Office for the Protection of the Constitution).
Population: c. one million; there are *c.* 63,000 students at the university,
17,000 at the FH, with a further 12,300 at five other HE institutions.
Position: On the Rhine, south of Düsseldorf, north of and very close to
Bonn.
Sights: Cathedral, *Praetorium* (preserved underneath the *Rathaus*), all the
museums, medieval *mikvah* (Jewish ritual bath), *Altstadt*, *Gestapo* cells
with preserved graffiti drawn by victims.
Culture: All the museums and galleries, philharmonic orchestra, opera,
theatres. Although it is unfair to pick anything out, it has to be said
that the *Römisch-Germanisches Museum* is an astonishing experience.
Industry: Banking, insurance, engineering, motor vehicles (Ford),
technology, textiles, foodstuffs, brewing, printing, publishing, trade
fairs, inland port, television and radio stations (*Westdeutscher Rundfunk*,
Deutschlandfunk, Deutsche Welle).
Twinning: GB: Liverpool, London, Portsmouth; US: Indianopolis

Universität zu Köln

Albertus-Magnus-Platz, 50923 Köln. Tel: (0221) 47 00 Fax: (0221) 47 05
153 Web site: www.uni-koeln.de

Akademisches Auslandsamt: Kerpener Straße 4, 50937 Köln. Tel: (0221)
47 02 332 Fax: (0221) 47 05 016 Email: aaa@verw.uni-koeln.de

Studentenwerk: Universitätsstr. 16, 50937 Köln. Tel: (0221) 94 26 50
Fax: (0221) 94 26 51 15 Email: arst1@uni-koeln.de

AStA: Universitätsstr. 16, 50937 Köln. Tel: (0221) 47 02 993 Fax: (0221)
47 05 071 Email: asta@uni-koeln.de

Frauenbeauftragte: Eckertstr. 4, 50931 Köln. Tel: (0221) 47 04 830 Fax:
(0221) 47 05 138 Email: frauenbeauftragte@uni-koeln.de

Behindertenbeauftragte(r): Herr Faßbender, Kosterstraße 79b, 50937
Köln Tel: (0221) 51 06 908

Computer/email access via: Regionales Rechenzentrum, Berrenrather
Straße 136, 50937 Köln. Tel: (0221) 47 04 563 Fax: (0221) 47 05 881

English department: Englisches Seminar, Albertus-Magnus-Platz, 50923
Köln. Tel: (0221) 47 02 793 Fax: (0221) 47 05 109

German department: Institut für Deutsche Sprache und Literatur,
Albertus-Magnus-Platz, 509234 Köln. Tel: (0221) 47 02 460 Fax: (0221)
47 05 107

Vacation courses: August. *Landeskunde*, economics, law.

Konstanz

Verkehrsverein: Bahnhofplatz 13, 78462 Konstanz. Tel: (07531) 13 30
30/28 43 76

Jugendherberge: Zur Allmannshöhe 18, 78464 Konstanz. Tel: (07531) 32
260

Industrie- und Handelskammer: IHK Hochrhein-Bodensee, Schützenstr.
8, Postfach 100943, 78409 Konstanz. Tel: (07531) 28 600 Email: info
@konstanz.ihk.de

AOK: Inselgasse 30, 8462 Konstanz. Tel: (07531) 28 30 Fax: (07531) 28
32 89

Local newspaper: Südkurier: www.skol.de/lokales/konstanz/

Town, area and industry

Konstanz: The name is derived from the Latin *civitas Constantia* (citizens
of Constantine). In 1251 the name had been shortened to *Costinze*,
and in modern times the missing 'n' has returned. This is a very old

town, founded by the Romans in 260 CE, but there had been a Celtic settlement here previously. Zeppelin, the airship designer, was born here. The location makes it a place for water sports activities, and the proximity to Austria and Switzerland means that there is the opportunity to ski.

Population: c. 78,000; there are *c.* 8,500 students at the university, with a further 2,700+ students at the FH.

Position: S. Baden-Württemberg, on the Rhine and Lake Constance (*Bodensee*), very close to both Austria and Switzerland.

Sights: Altstadt, Münster (minster) with tenth century crypt, *Rathaus*, Lake Constance.

Culture: Museums, theatre.

Industry: Pharmaceuticals, engineering, printing, publishing, information technology (Siemens), tourism.

Twinning: GB: Richmond

Universität Konstanz

Rektorat, 78457 Konstanz. Tel: (07531) 88 0 Fax: (07531) 88 36 88 Web site: www.uni-konstanz.de

Akademisches Auslandsamt: Auslandsreferat, Universität Konstanz, 78457 Konstanz. Tel: (07531) 88 30 89 Fax: (07531) 88 30 37 Email: ausref @uni-konstanz.de

Studentenwerk: Universitätsstraße 10, 78464 Konstanz. Tel: (07531) 88 1 Fax: (07531) 88 39 99

AStA: Raum D410, Universitätsstraße, 78464 Konstanz. Tel: (07531) 88 25 17 Fax: (07531) 88 31 Email: asta@uni-konstanz.de

Frauenbeauftragte: Frauenrat, Fach D94, 78457 Konstanz. Tel: (07531) 88 20 32 Fax: (07531) 88 36 88 Email: frauenrat@uni-konstanz.de

Behindertenbeauftragte(r): Ursula Lindel, Raum V405, Universitätsstraße, 78464 Konstanz. Tel: (07531) 88 307 Email: ursula.lindel@uni-konstanz.de

Computer/email access via: Rechenzentrum, Universitätsstraße, 78464 Konstanz. Email: support@uni-konstanz.de

English department: Fachgruppe Sprachwissenschaft Anglistik, 78457 Konstanz. Tel: (07531) 88 25 52 Fax: (07531) 88 27 41 Email: ines.eckerle@uni-konstanz.de

German department: Fachbereich Sprachwissenschaft, Fach D185, 78457 Konstanz. Fax: (07531) 88 27 41

Vacation courses: Not available.

Leipzig

Verkehrsverein: Leipzig Tourist Service e.V., Richard-Wagner-Str. 1, 04109 Leipzig. Tel: (0341) 71 04 260/265 Fax: (0341) 71 04 271/276 Email: lipsia@aol.com

Jugendherberge: Jugendherberge Leipzig-Centrum, Käthe-Kollwitz-Str. 64, 04109 Leipzig. Tel: (0341) 47 05 30 Fax: (0341) 47 58 88

Industrie- und Handelskammer: IHK zu Leipzig, Goerdelerring 5, 04109 Leipzig. Tel: (0341) 12 670 Fax: (0341) 12 67 421 Email: schultz @leipzig.ihk.de

AOK: Willmar-Schwabe-Str. 2, 04109 Leipzig. Tel: (0341) 12 11 100 Fax: (0341) 12 11 137

Local newspaper: Leipziger Volkszeitung: www.lvz-online.de/

Town, area and industry

Leipzig: In the early eleventh century the name was *in urbe Libzi vocata* (in the town called Libzi), which was derived from an Old Sorbian word *lipa* (limetree), via Slavic Lipc. It thus means 'the place where lime trees grow'. Leipzig is an important city well known for its trade fairs. It is also a major cultural centre. Much of the city centre was destroyed in the Second World War, but there are still many monuments to the city's past. The demonstrations (*Montagsdemonstrationen*) against the government of the former German Democratic Republic that took place in Leipzig in 1989 played a large part in bringing about the fall of the Wall and of the East German regime.

Population: c. 470,000; there are *c.* 21,000 students at the university, and a further *c.* 6,200 at six other HE institutions.

Position: NW Saxony, SE of Halle.

Sights: Rathaus, churches, *Auerbachs Keller* (as in *Faust*).

Culture: Museums, galleries, theatres, opera, orchestra, important libraries.

Industry: Trade fairs, technology, engineering, textiles, chemicals, printing, publishing.

Twinning: GB: Birmingham; US: Houston, Texas

Universität Leipzig

Ritterstr. 26, 04109 Leipzig. Tel: (0341) 97 108/109 Fax: (0341) 97 30 099 Web site: www.uni-leipzig.de

Akademisches Auslandsamt: Goethestr. 6, 04109 Leipzig. Tel: (0341) 97 32 020 Fax: (0341) 97 32 049 Email: aaa@rz.uni-leipzig.de

Studentenwerk: Goethestr. 6, 04109 Leipzig. Tel: (0341) 96 595 Fax: (0341) 96 59 684 Email: swl@rz.uni-leipzig.de

AStA: StudentInnenRat (StuRa), Augustusplatz 10/11, 04109 Leipzig. Tel: (0341) 9737 850 Fax: (0341) 97 37 859 Email: stura@uni-leipzig.de

Frauenbeauftragte: Prof. Dr Ilse Nagelschmidt, Augustusplatz 10/11, 04109 Leipzig. Tel: (0341) 97 30 090/091/092

Behindertenbeauftragte(r): Eberhard Fischer, Theologische Fakultät, Emil-Fuchs-Str. 1, 04105 Leipzig. Tel: (0341) 97 35 400

Computer/email access via: Universitätsrechenzentrum, Augustusplatz 10/11, 04109 Leipzig. Tel: (0341) 97 33 300 Fax: (0341) 97 33 399 Email: wwwserv@wwwrz.uni-leipzig.de

English department: Institut für Anglistik, Brühl 34–50, 04109 Leipzig. Tel: (0341) 97 37 310 Fax: (0341) 97 37 347 Email: anglistik@rz.uni-leipzig.de

German department: Institut für Germanistik, Brühl 34–50, 04109 Leipzig. Tel: (0341) 97 37 351 Fax: (0341) 97 37 398 Email: hbrandt @rz.uni-leipzig.de

Vacation courses: July. Language.

Magdeburg

Verkehrsverein: Alter Markt 12, 39104 Magdeburg. Tel: (0391) 54 04 903

Jugendherberge: Apparently no YH but, if stuck: Tagungs- und Bildungshotel, Lorenzweg 57, 39124 Magdeburg. Tel: (0391) 25 15 065 Fax: (0391) 22 34 30

Industrie- und Handelskammer: Industrie- und Handelskammer Magdeburg, Alter Markt 8, 39104 Magdeburg. Tel: (0391) 56 93 0 Fax: (0391) 56 93 105 Email: internet@magdeburg.ihk.de

AOK: Lüneburger Str. 4, 39106 Magdeburg. Tel: (0391) 54 15 206 Fax: (0391) 54 15 207

Local newspaper: Volksstimme: At the time of writing, this newspaper does not have an online news site.

Town, area and industry

Magdeburg: The name is derived from Old High German *magad* (maiden, virgin) and *burg*: 'castle/fortress of the virgin'; it will have been associated with either a Christian or pre-Christian cult or ritual. This town is the capital of Saxony-Anhalt. A major industrial city, much of it was destroyed in the Second World War, but much has been restored. Otto von Guericke, the physicist after whom the university is named, was born here, as was the composer Telemann.

Population: c. 250,000; there are c. 5,500 students at the university, with a further c. 2,600 at the FH.

Position: Central Saxony-Anhalt, on the River Elbe.

Sights: Cathedral, Baroque *Rathaus, Alter Markt, Magdeburger Reiter* (thirteenth-century statue), zoological gardens.

Culture: Theatres, music, museum.

Industry: Agricultural products, engineering, sugar refining, chocolate, engineering, chemicals, textiles, diesel engines, inland port.

Twinning: No formal links.

Otto-von-Guericke-Universität

Universitätsplatz 2, 39106 Magdeburg. Tel: (0391) 67 01 Fax: (0391) 67 11 156 Web site: www.uni-magdeburg.de

Akademisches Auslandsamt: Frau Eva Böhning, Universitätsplatz 2, 39106 Magdeburg. Tel: (0391) 67 12 580 Fax: (0391) 67 11 132 Email: eva.boehning@verwaltung.uni-magdeburg.de

Studentenwerk: Studentenwerk Magdeburg, Universitätsplatz 1, 39106 Magdeburg. Tel: (0391) 67 03 Fax: (0391) 67 11 555 Email: studentenwerk-magdeburg@swmd.uni-magdeburg.de

AStA: Studentenrat der Uni-Magdeburg, Postfach 4120, 39016 Magdeburg. Tel: (0391) 67 12 630 Fax: (0391) 67 11 421 Email: stura@uni-magdeburg.de

Frauenbeauftragte: Gleichstellungsbeauftragte der Uni-Magdeburg, Dr Gudrun Goes. Tel: (0391) 67 16 690 Email: gudrun.goes@gse-w.uni-magdeburg.de

Behindertenbeauftragte(r): Gert Dehne. Tel: (0391) 67 14 564 Email: gert.dehne@mb.uni-magdeburg.de

Computer/email access via: Universitätsrechenzentrum, Universitätsplatz 2, 39016 Magdeburg. Tel: (0391) 67 18 553 Fax: (0391) 67 11 134 Email: iris.schneider@urz.uni-magdeburg.de

English department: Institut für Anglistik, Universitätsplatz 2, 39106 Magdeburg. Tel: (0391) 67 16 669 Fax: (0391) 67 16 668

German department: Institut für Germanistik, Virchowstr. 24, 39104 Magdeburg. Tel: (0391) 67 16 616 Fax: (0391) 67 16 559 Email: iger@uni-magdeburg.de

Vacation courses: July. Language, linguistics, literature, *Landeskunde.*

Mainz

Verkehrsverein: Brückenturm am Rathaus, Rheinstraße, 55116 Mainz.
  Tel: (06131) 28 62 10
Jugendherberge: Otto-Brunfels-Schneise 4, 55130 Mainz. Tel: (06131) 85
  332
Industrie- und Handelskammer: IHK für Rheinhessen, Schillerplatz 7,
  55015 Mainz. Tel: (06131) 26 20 Fax: (06131) 26 21 69 Email:
  ihkmainz@mainz.ihk.de
AOK: Hintere Bleiche 59, 55116 Mainz. Tel: (06131) 38 79 41 Fax:
  (06131) 25 61 60
Local newspaper: Mainzer Rhein-Zeitung: www.mainz-online.de/

Town, area and industry

Mainz: The name has been written like this since about 1550. In the
  thirteenth century it was *Megenze*, in the seventh century *Magáncia*,
  in the sixth century *Mogontiacum*, and in the first century it is
  mentioned by Tacitus as *Moguntiacum*: 'estate belonging to Moguntios',
  or possibly not that at all, but instead a place dedicated to a goddess
  called Mogontia, which would be slightly more fun. Mainz is the
  capital of Rhineland-Palatinate. As you can see from the derivation of
  its name, it is a Roman town, founded in 38 BCE. It was the home of
  Johannes Gutenberg, inventor of the first printing press, hence the
  university's name. 80 per cent of town was destroyed in the Second
  World War. There has been much restoration.
Population: c. 187,000; there are *c.* 29,000 students at the university, with
  c. 4,500 at a further two HE institutions.
Position: Eastern Rhineland-Palatinate, on the Rhine, close to Wiesbaden
  and Frankfurt am Main, on the border with Hesse.
Sights: Altstadt, cathedral (with styles of architecture from various
  periods), *Rathaus*, Gutenberg memorabilia, Roman remains.
Culture: Museums, libraries, theatre.
Industry: Chemicals, pharmaceuticals (Novo Nordisk), engineering, glass
  (Schott), musical instruments, technology (IBM), cement, printing,
  publishing, media (ZDF), wine.
Twinning: GB: Watford; US: Louisville, Kentucky

Johannes-Gutenberg-Universität

Saarstraße 21, 55099 Mainz. Tel: (06131) 39 0 Web site: www.uni-mainz.de

Akademisches Auslandsamt: Forum universitatis, Becherweg 2, 55128 Mainz. Tel: (06131) 39 22 81/39 25 25 Fax: (06131) 39 55 48 Email: aaa@verwaltung.uni-mainz.de

Studentenwerk: Staudingerweg 21, 55128 Mainz. Tel: (06131) 39 0 Fax: (06131) 39 49 07 Email: stwmzwv@mail.uni-mainz.de

AStA: Staudingerweg 21, 55128 Mainz. Tel: (06131) 39 48 01 Fax: (06131) 37 18 57 Email: asta@uni-mainz.de

Frauenbeauftragte: Frauenbüro, Saarstraße 21, 55099 Mainz. Tel: (06131) 39 22 988 Fax: (06131) 39 35 747 Email: frauenbuero@verwaltung.uni-mainz.de

Behindertenbeauftragte(r): Johanna Ehlers, Forum 1, 55099 Mainz. Tel: (06131) 39 23 085

Computer/email access via: Zentrum für Datenverarbeitung, Postfach 3980, 55099 Mainz. Tel: (06131) 39 63 00 Fax: (06131) 39 64 07 Email: btisch@mail.uni-mainz.de

English department: Seminar für Englische Philologie, Jakob-Welder-Weg 18, 55099 Mainz. Tel: (06131) 39 27 63 Fax: (06131) 39 38 08

German department: Deutsches Institut, Jakob-Welder-Weg 18, 55099 Mainz. Tel: (06131) 39 22 60 Fax: (06131) 39 33 66 Email: illy@mail.uni-mainz.de

Vacation courses: August. Language and *Landeskunde.*

Mannheim

Verkehrsverein: Willy-Brandt-Platz 4, 68161 Mannheim. Tel: (0621) 10 10 11

Jugendherberge: Rheinpromenade 21, 68163 Mannheim. Tel: (0621) 82 27 18

Industrie- und Handelskammer: IHK Rhein-Neckar, L1,2, Postfach 10 16 61, 68016 Mannheim. Tel: (0621) 17 090 Fax: (0621) 17 09 100 Email: quiddeg@mannheim.ihk.de

AOK: Renzstr. 11–13, 68161 Mannheim. Tel: (0621) 17 66 65 Fax: (0621) 17 64 40

Local newspaper: Mannheimer Morgen: www.mamo.de/ When you reach the site, click on the *Mannheimer Morgen* logo.

Town, area and industry

Mannheim: The name in the eighth century was *Manninheim*, and means the 'Residence of Manno' (*Manno* being a very old Germanic man's name meaning 'man' and demonstrating a certain lack of imagination amongst early Germanic parents). Mannheim is an old Kurpfalz (Electoral Palatinate) residence town. It suffered more than 50 per cent destruction in the Second World War, a fate which had befallen the town twice before in seventeenth century wars. The most recent rebuilding has preserved the alphabetical and numerical grid of the street layout, which was designed in 1606. Mannheim has a very large inland port. This is also the seat of the *Institut für Deutsche Sprache* (German Language Institute) and of various publishers of dictionaries and encyclopaedias.

Population: c. 300,000; there are 12,000+ students at the university, with a further 3,500+ at other HE institutions.

Position: Baden-Württemberg, at the point where the Neckar flows into the Rhine; it is opposite the highly industrialised Ludwigshafen (BASF) and close to Heidelberg and the Odenwald.

Sights: Baroque castle (seat of the university) and buildings, parks, *Wasserturm* (water tower).

Culture: Museums, art galleries, theatres.

Industry: Industrial river port, heavy industries, brewing, chemicals (Rhein Chemie-Bayer), foodstuffs, textiles, publishing (Duden, Brockhaus, Meyer), printing.

Twinning: GB: Swansea; US: Wichita

Universität Mannheim

Schloss Ostflügel, 68131 Mannheim. Tel: (0621) 18 11 006 Fax: (0621) 18 11 010 Web site: www.uni-mannheim.de

Akademisches Auslandsamt: L9, 6, 68161 Mannheim. Tel: (0621) 29 25 507 Fax: (0621) 29 23 174 Email: berg@verwaltung.uni-mannheim.de

Studentenwerk: Parkring 39, 68159 Mannheim. Tel: (0621) 29 20 Fax: (0621) 29 22 940 Email: swma@rumms.uni-mannheim.de

AStA: L4, 12, 68131 Mannheim. Tel: (0621) 18 13 372 Fax: (0621) 18 13 371 Email: asta@rumms.uni-mannheim.de

Frauenbeauftragte: Dr Dorothee Dickenberger, Lehrstuhl für Sozialpsychologie, 68131 Mannheim. Tel: (0621) 18 12 037 Fax: (0621) 18 12 038 Email: ddickenberger@sowi.uni-mannheim.de

Behindertenbeauftragte(r): Wolfgang Hauss, Tattersallstr. 2, 68131 Mannheim. Tel: (0621) 18 13 314 Fax: (0621) 18 13 313 Email: persrat @rumms. uni-mannheim.de

Computer/email access via: Rechenzentrum der Universität Mannheim, 68131 Mannheim. Tel: (0621) 18 13 170 Fax: (0621) 18 13 170 Email: hans-guenther.kruse@rz.uni-mannheim.de

English department: Lehrstuhl Anglistik II, Schloss Ehrenhof West, 68131 Mannheim. Tel: (0621) 29 25 657 Fax: (0621) 29 25 658 Email: kopke@rummelplatz.uni-mannheim.de

German department: Lehrstuhl Neuere Germanistik II, Schloss Ehrenhof West (Zimmer 247), 68131 Mannheim. Tel: (0621) 18 12 320

Vacation courses: September. Language, literature, *Landeskunde.*

Marburg

Verkehrsverein: Neue Kasselerstr. 1, 35039 Marburg. Tel: (06421) 20 12 62

Jugendherberge: Jahnstr. 1, 35037 Marburg. Tel: (06421) 23 461

Industrie- und Handelskammer: IHK Gießen, Lonystraße 7, 35357 Gießen. Tel: (0641) 79 540 Fax: (0641) 75 914 Email: zentrale@giessen-friedberg.ihk.de

AOK: Universitätsstr. 13, 35037 Marburg. Tel: (06421) 17 490 Fax: (06421) 17 49 19

Local newspaper: Marburger Neue Zeitung: www.lahn-dill.de/2000/mar/index.html Or more simply: www.lahn-dill.de/. Then click on *Marburger Neue Zeitung* in the lower part of the left-hand margin.

Town, area and industry

Marburg: The name was originally something like *Marbachburg*, the Marbach being the name of a local river, and was shortened to Marburg. The first part of the name is derived from the Old High German word *marca* (boundary) so Marburg is the 'castle on the boundary formed by the river'. Marburg is the home of the oldest Protestant university, which is named after the Landgrave (*Landgraf)* Philipp (called *der Großmütige*, the Magnanimous) and which is the focal point of the town.

Population: c. 78,000; there are *c.* 17,500 students at the university.

Position: On the River Lahn in western Hesse, in the Lahn valley, close to the Westerwald.

Sights: Important Gothic church (*Elisabethkirche*), *Altstadt*, half-timbered houses, *Schloss.*

Culture: Museums, galleries, open-air theatre.
Industry: Tourism, pottery, chemicals, precision instruments, clothing
Twinning: GB: Northampton

Philipps-Universität

Biegenstr. 10, 35032 Marburg. Tel: (06421) 28 0 Fax: (06421) 28 25 00
Web site: www.uni-marburg.de
Akademisches Auslandsamt: Biegenstr. 12, 35032 Marburg. Tel: (06421)
28 26 129 Fax: (06421) 28 28 998 Email: auslbera@verwaltung.uni-marburg.de
Studentenwerk: Erlenring 5, 35037 Marburg. Tel: (06421) 29 60 Fax: (06421)
15 761 Email: emmeric2@mailer.uni-marburg.de
AStA: Erlenring 5, 35037 Marburg. Tel: (06421) 17 030 Fax: (06421) 17
03 33 Email: asta@stud-mailer.uni-marburg.de
Frauenbeauftragte: Biegenstr. 10, 35032 Marburg. Tel: (06421) 28 61 16
Fax: (06421) 28 22 500 Email: frauenb@verwaltung.uni-marburg.de
Behindertenbeauftragte(r): Clemens Schwan, Biegenstr. 10, 35032 Marburg.
Tel: (06421) 28 61 86
Computer/email access via: Hochschulrechenzentrum, Hans-Meerwein-Straße, 35032 Marburg. Tel: (06421) 28 21 551 Fax: (06421) 28 26
994 Email: sekretariat@hrz.uni-marburg.de
English department: Institut für Anglistik und Amerikanistik, Wilhelm-Röpke-Straße 6D, 35032 Marburg. Tel: (06421) 28 24 761 Fax: (06421)
28 27 020 Email: voemel@mailer.uni-marburg.de
German department: Germanistik und Kunstwissenschaften, Wilhelm-Röpke-Straße 6A, 35032 Marburg. Tel: (06421) 28–0
Vacation courses: July, August. Language (including for beginners),
Landeskunde.

München

Verkehrsverein: Bahnhofsplatz 2, 80335 München. Tel: (089) 23 33 02 56
Jugendherberge: Jugendherberge München, Wendl-Dietrich-Str. 20, 80335
München. Tel: (089) 23 33 02 56
Industrie- und Handelskammer: IHK für München und Oberbayern,
Max-Joseph PH Str. 2, 80333 München. Tel: (089) 51 160 Fax: (089)
51 16 306 Email: ihkmail@muenchen.ihk.de
AOK: Maistr. 43–47, 80337 München. Tel: (089) 54 440 Fax: (089) 53
28 222

Local newspaper: Münchner Merkur: www.merkur-online.de/; *Süddeutsche Zeitung:* www.sueddeutsche.de/

Town, area and industry

München (Munich): The name has not changed much since the twelfth century *apud Munichen* (at the monks), so 'the place where the monks live'. Munich is the capital of Bavaria and is like a national rather than a regional capital – but then, this is Bavaria, which tends to think of itself as its own country. Munich is the place where Hitler's *Bierhaus-Putsch* (coup and attempt to overthrow the Bavarian government) failed in 1923, and the site of major destruction in the Second World War. Rebuilding has been very successful and has preserved the town's character. There is much to attract students to this city, but it is very expensive and accommodation is difficult to obtain. The university is named after two nineteenth-century kings of Bavaria.

Population: c. 1.3 million; there are *c.* 60,000 students at the university, which is the biggest in Germany; there are eight more HE institutions in Munich with a further *c.* 50,000 students.

Position: On the River Isar, close to the Allgäu, the Bavarian Alps, Austria, and Switzerland.

Sights: Vast amounts – churches, e.g. *Frauenkirche*, many historical buildings, e.g. the *Feldherrnhalle* (which Hitler marched on and which was the scene of a small massacre of his henchmen, who became the Nazis' martyrs), *Neue* and *Alte Pinakothek* (art galleries), *Glyptothek* (sculpture gallery), *Hofbräuhaus, Englischer Garten.*

Culture: Theatre, music, art galleries, museums, libraries; everything that such a cosmopolitan city can offer; the famous/notorious *Oktoberfest* (beer festival).

Industry: Brewing, foodstuffs, engineering (Bosch-Siemens), tourism, optics (Rodenstock), textiles, cars (BMW), tobacco, fashion, cosmetics, publishing (dtv), printing, television production, banking, finance.

Twinning: GB: Edinburgh; US: Cincinatti, Ohio

Ludwig-Maximilians-Universität

Geschwister-Scholl-Platz 1, 80539 München. Tel: (089) 21 80 0 Fax: (089) 21 80 23 22 Web site: www.uni-muenchen.de

Akademisches Auslandsamt: Ludwigstr. 27, 80539 München. Tel: (089) 21 80 28 23 Fax: (089) 21 80 31 36 Email: auslandsamt@lrz.uni-muenchen.de

Studentenwerk: Leopoldstr. 15, 80802 München. Tel: (089) 38 19 61
   Fax: (089) 38 19 61 33 Email: stuwerk@studentenwerk.mhn.de
AStA: Studentischer Sprecherrat, Leopoldstraße 15, EG, 80802 München.
   Tel: (089) 21 80 20 72
Frauenbeauftragte: Schellingstraße 10/II, 80799 München. Tel: (089) 21
   80 36 44 Fax: (089) 21 80 37 66 Email: Frauenbeauftragte@lrz.uni-
   muenchen.de
Behindertenbeauftragte(r): Professor Dr Willi H. Butollo, Leopoldstraße
   13, 80802 München. Tel: (089) 21 80 51 73
Computer/email access via: Leibnitz-Rechenzentrum, Barerstraße 21,
   80333 München. Tel: (089) 28 92 88 00 Email: lrzpost@lrz.de
English department: Institut für Englische Philologie, Schellingstr. 3,
   80799 München Tel: (089) 21 80 21 99
German department: Institut für Deutsche Philologie, Schellingstr. 3,
   80799 München. Tel: (089) 21 80 33 76
Vacation courses: August. Life and society.

Münster

Verkehrsverein: Klemensstr. 9, 48143 Münster. Tel: (0251) 49 22 710
Jugendherberge: Bismarckallee 31, 48151 Münster. Tel: (0251) 53 24 70
Industrie- und Handelskammer: IHK zu Münster, Sentmaringer Weg 61,
   Postfach 40 24, 48022 Münster. Tel: (0251) 70 70 Fax: (0251) 70 73
   25 Email: muenster@muenster.ihk.de
AOK: Königsstr. 18/20, 48143 Münster. Tel: (0251) 59 50 Fax: (0251)
   59 51 11
Local newspapers: Westfälische Nachrichten: www.wnonline.de/l/ms/
   Münstersche Zeitung: At the time of writing, this newspaper is prepar-
   ing an online website at www.westline.de/

Town, area and industry

Münster: The settlement here was originally called after a Germanic
   water spirit and the ford it guarded: *Mimigernaford* (820 CE) and later
   the somewhat long-drawn-out *Mimmigardevurdensis* (1017 CE), which
   probably explains why it was renamed *Monasterium* (1068 CE) after
   the monastery around which the town grew, whence *Münster.* Münster
   is the fourth biggest university town in Germany. It is a historical city
   – the Treaty of Westphalia was signed here to end the Thirty Years
   War. 90 per cent of the *Altstadt* was destroyed in the Second World

War, but many buildings have been restored or reconstructed. The university is named after Franz Wilhelm Freiherr von Fürstenberg, its founder.

Population: c. 280,000; there are c. 45,000 students at the university, with a further c. 9,500 students at three other HE institutions.

Position: Northern North Rhine-Westphalia, centre of the Münsterland, close to the Dutch border and Enschede.

Sights: Cathedral, many churches, especially the *Lambertikirche* (which has cages hanging from its tower in which the hanged bodies of executed Anabaptists were exhibited in the sixteenth century), *Schloss*, parks.

Culture: Many museums, theatres, opera, festivals.

Industry: Brewing, agricultural machinery, engineering, chemicals, pharmaceuticals, furniture, printing, publishing, textiles.

Twinning: GB: York; US: Fresno

Westfälische Wilhelms-Universität

Schloßplatz 2, 48149 Münster. Tel: (0251) 83–0 Fax: (0251) 83 32 090 Web site: www.uni-muenster.de

Akademisches Auslandsamt: Schloßplatz 2, 48149 Münster. Tel: (0251) 83 21 520 Fax: (0251) 83 22 226 Email: auslandsamt@uni-muenster.de

Studentenwerk: Hauptverwaltung, Am Stadtgraben 48, 48143 Münster. Tel: (0251) 83 1 Fax: (0251) 83 79 207 Email: stwsekr@uni-muenster.de

AStA: Schloßplatz 1, 48149 Münster. Tel: (0251) 83 22 280 Fax: (0251) 51 92 89 Email: asta.vorsitz@uni-muenster.de

Frauenbeauftragte: Georgskommende 26, 48143 Münster. Tel: (0251) 83–29701 Fax: (0251) 83–29700 Email: Frauenbuero@uni-muenster.de

Behindertenbeauftragte(r): Prof Dr Friedrich Udo Schmälzler, Huefferstr. 27, 48149 Münster. Tel: (0251) 22 635 Fax: (0251) 83 30 037

Computer/email access via: Zentrum für Informationsverarbeitung, Röntgenstr. 9–13, 48149 Münster. Tel: (0251) 83 31 551 Fax: (0251) 83 31 555 Email: giermann@uni-muenster.de

English department: Englisches Seminar, Johannisstraße 12–20, 48143 Münster. Tel: (0251) 83 24 500 Fax: (0251) 83 24 827 Email: englsem @uni-muenster.de

German department: Institut für Deutsche Sprache und Literatur, Philippistr. 17, 48149 Münster. Tel: (0251) 83 39 142 Fax: (0251) 83 31 755 Email: hamachc@uni-muenster.de

Vacation courses: July, August. Language, *Landeskunde.*

Oldenburg

Verkehrsverein: Wallstr. 14, 26122 Oldenburg. Tel: (0441) 15 744
Jugendherberge: Alexanderstr. 65, 26121 Oldenburg. Tel: (0441) 87 135
Industrie- und Handelskammer: Oldenburgische IHK, Moslestr. 6,
Postfach 2545, 26105 Oldenburg. Tel: (0441) 22 200 Fax: (0441) 22
20 111 Email: info@oldenburg.ihk.de
AOK: Gartenstr. 10, 26122 Oldenburg. Tel: (0441) 77 020 Fax: (0441)
77 02 300
Local newspaper: Oldenburger Nachrichten/ Nordwest-Zeitung: www2.
nordwest.net/

Town, area and industry

Oldenburg: The name, originally *Aldenburg* means just what it looks like:
'old castle'. Oldenburg is the capital of the Weser-Ems district. The
Carl von Ossietzky-University is named after the Nobel Peace Prize
winner, who was murdered by the Nazis in the local concentration camp.
Population: c. 155,000; there are *c.* 13,000 students at the university, and
a further *c.* 1,650 at the FH.
Position: Northern Lower Saxony, on the River Hunte and the Weser-
Ems canal.
Sights: Altstadt, Schloss, Fachwerkhäuser (half-timbered houses), churches.
Culture: Theatres, symphony orchestra, museums, galleries, festivals.
Industry: Glass, engineering, foodstuffs, textiles, energy supply, meat
processing, shipbuilding, glass.
Twinning: No formal links.

Carl von Ossietzky-Universität

Ammerländer Heerstr. 114–118, 26111 Oldenburg. Tel: (0441) 79 8–0
Fax: (0441) 79 83 000 Web site: www.uni-oldenburg.de
Akademisches Auslandsamt: Ammerländer Heerstr. 121, 26129 Oldenburg.
Tel: (0441) 79 82 478 Fax: (0441) 79 82 461 Email: info.aaa.@uni-
oldenburg.de
Studentenwerk: Uhlhornsweg 49–55, 26129 Oldenburg. Tel: (0441) 79 82
709 Fax: (0441) 79 82 615 Email: swo@uni-oldenburg.de
AStA: Astra-Trakt, M1–154. Tel: (0441) 79 82 573 Fax: (0441) 79 83
164 Email: asta@uni-oldenburg.de
Frauenbeauftragte: Büro der Gleichstellungsstelle, A10 Raum 0–018.
Tel: (0441) 79 82 632 Fax: (0441) 79 82 249 Email: frauenbuero@uni-
oldenburg.de

Behindertenbeauftragte(r): Astra-Trakt, M1–154. Tel: (0441) 79 83 100
Fax: (0441) 79 82 615 Email: bref@uniken.hrz.uni-oldenburg.de
Computer/email access via: Hochschulrechenzentrum. Tel: (0441) 79 80
Fax: (0441) 79 84 012 Email: beratung@uni-oldenburg.de
English department: Fachsekretariat Anglistik, A10, Ammerländer Heer-
straße 114, 26111 Oldenburg. Tel: (0441) 79 82 301 Fax: (0441) 79 83
771 Email: anglist@anglistik.uni-oldenburg.de
German department: Fachsekretariat Germanistik, A10, Ammerländer Heer-
straße 114, 26111 Oldenburg. Tel: (0441) 79 82 903 Fax: (0441) 79 82 953
Vacation courses: July, August. Language, *Landeskunde.*

Osnabrück

Verkehrsverein: Krahnstr. 54, 49074 Osnabrück. Tel: (0541) 32 32 202
Jugendherberge und Jugendgästehaus: Iburgerstr. 183a, 49082 Osnabrück.
Tel: (0541) 54 284
Industrie- und Handelskammer: IHK Osnabrück-Emsland, Postfach 3080,
Neuer Graben 38, 49074 Osnabrück. Tel: (0541) 35 30 Fax: (0541) 35
31 71 Email: ihk@osnabrueck.ihk.de
AOK: Neuer Graben 27, 49074 Osnabrück. Tel: (0541) 34 80 Fax: (0541)
34 83 90
Local newspaper: Neue Osnabrücker Zeitung: www.neue-oz.de/information/
noz_print/stadt_osnabrueck/ Writing *Neue Osnabrücker Zeitung* inside
inverted commas into your search engine should give you a direct 'hit'.

Town, area and industry

Osnabrück: The name is of obscure origin. In the eighth century it was
called *Osnabruggi. Osna* may simply be an earlier name for the local
River Hase, so that this was a 'bridge over the River Hase'. This river
looks as though it has something to do with hares, but its name is in
fact derived from an Old High German word *hasan,* meaning 'shiny
and grey', which is a bit disappointing if you were thinking this might
have been a bridge used by hares of unusual intelligence. Osnabrück
is a town famous (like Münster) for the signing of the Treaty of
Westphalia, which ended the Thirty Years War in 1648. Much of the
town was destroyed in the Second World War, but much has been
restored. The town has its own port on the *Mittellandkanal.*
Population: c. 162,000; there are *c.* 12,000 students at the university, with
c. 6,000 students at a further two HE institutions.

Position: Western Lower Saxony, close to the *Teutoburger Wald* (Teutoburger Forest).

Sights: Medieval churches, cathedral, *Friedenssaal* (Peace Hall) in the
Rathaus, where the Treaty of Westphalia was signed, churches, *Schloss.*

Culture: Museums, theatre, music.

Industry: Steel, car accessories, tools, chemicals, textiles, paper, service
industries.

Twinning: GB: Derby; US: Evansville

Universität Osnabrück

Neuer Graben/Schloß, 49069 Osnabrück. Tel: (0541) 96 90 Fax: (0541)
96 94 888 Web site: www.uni-osnabrueck.de

Akademisches Auslandsamt: Neuer Graben 19/21, 49074 Osnabrück. Tel:
(0541) 96 94 655 Fax: (0541) 96 94 495 Email: aaa@uni-osnabrueck.de

Studentenwerk: Ritterstraße 10, 49074 Osnabrück. Tel: (0541) 33 10 70
Fax: (0541) 33 10 731 Email: studentenwerk@uni-osnabrueck.de

AStA: Alte Münze 12, 49074 Osnabrück. Tel: (0541) 96 94 193 Fax: (0541)
96 94 808 Email: asta@rz.uni-osnabrueck.de

Frauenbeauftragte: Frauenbüro, Neuer Graben/Schloss, 49074 Osnabrück.
Tel: (0541) 96 94 686 Fax: (0541) 96 94 852 Email: frauenbuero@uni-
osnabrueck.de

Behindertenbeauftragte(r): Herr F. Schütz, Neuer Graben/Schloss, 49074
Osnabrück. Tel: (0541) 96 94 102 Fax: (0541) 96 94 666

Computer/email access via: Rechenzentrum, Albrechtstr. 28, 49076 Osnabrück. Tel: (0541) 96 92 341 Fax: (0541) 96 92 470 Email: office
@rz.uni-osnabrueck.de

English & German department: Fachbereich Sprach- und Literaturwissenschaft für Deutsch und Englisch, Neuer Graben 40, 49074 Osnabrück.
Tel: (0541) 96 94 194 Fax: (0541) 96 94 256 Email: aterborg@uni-
osnabrueck.de

Vacation courses: August. Language, *Landeskunde.*

Paderborn

Verkehrsverein: Marienplatz 2a, 33098 Paderborn. Tel: (05251) 26 461

Jugendherberge: Meinwerkstr. 16, 33098 Paderborn. Tel: (05251) 22 055

Industrie- und Handelskammer: IHK zu Münster, Sentmaringer Weg 61,
Postfach 40 24, 48022. Tel: (0251) 70 70 Fax: (0251) 70 73 25
Email: muenster@muenster.ihk.de

AOK: Friedrichstr. 17–19, 33102 Paderborn. Tel: (05251) 12 40 Fax: (05251) 12 44 99

Local newspaper: Neue Westfälische: www.nw-news.de/news/lokal/pb/

Town, area and industry

Paderborn: The name refers to the 200 or so springs which are the source of the River Pader. The second part of the name goes back to an Old High German word *brunno* (source). As a matter of interest, the linguistic name for the transposition of a letter (like the 'r' here) is metathesis. The river name *Pader* is of obscure origin. Paderborn is a historical town, which has come down in the world somewhat; the Holy Roman Empire was born here and it is the site of one of Charlemagne's palaces, which was excavated in the 1960s and 1970s. Often badly damaged in its history, 85 per cent of Paderborn was destroyed in the Second World War. There has been much restoration.

Population: c. 140,000; there are *c.* 16,500 students at the university, and a further *c.* 700 students at two other HE institutions.

Position: NE North-Rhine-Westphalia, close to the Egge mountains and the *Teutoburger Wald* (Teutoburger Forest).

Sights: Cathedral, *Schloss, Rathaus, Altstadt*, medieval excavations.

Culture: Museums, theatres.

Industry: Computers (Nixdorf), electronics, engineering, steel, chemicals, furniture, printing, paper, foodstuffs.

Twinning: GB: Bolton; US: Belleville, Illinois

Universität-Gesamthochschule

Warburger Str. 100, 33098 Paderborn. Tel: (05251) 60 0 Web site: www. uni-paderborn.de

Akademisches Auslandsamt: Warburgerstr. 100, 33098 Paderborn. Tel: (05251) 60 24 55 Fax: (05251) 60 35 37 Email: brebeck@zv.uni-paderborn.de

Studentenwerk: Warburgerstr. 100, 33098 Paderborn. Tel: (05251) 60 24 55 Fax: (05251) 60 35 37 Email: info@studentenwerk-pb.de

AStA: Warburger Str. 100, 33098 Paderborn. Tel: (05251) 60 31 74 Fax: (05251) 60 31 75 Email: asta@uni-paderborn.de

Frauenbeauftragte: Frauenbeauftragte des Senats, Warburger Str. 100, 33098 Paderborn. Tel: (05251) 60 20 78 Fax: (05251) 60 42 11 Email: pilgrim@hrz.uni-paderborn.de

Behindertenbeauftragte(r): Elmar Jonk, Warburgerstr. 100, 33098 Paderborn. Tel: (05251) 60 21 50 Email: ej@chemie.uni-paderborn.de

Computer/email access via: Hochschulrechenzentrum, Warburger Str.

100, 33098 Paderborn. Tel: (05251) 60 24 02 Fax: (05251) 60 42 06
Email: benutzerberatung@hrz.upb.de

English department: Anglistisches Seminar, Warburgerstr. 100, 33098 Paderborn 33098. Tel: (05251) 60 28 61 Fax: (05251) 60 35 41 Email: chuba2
@hrz.uni-paderborn.de

German department: Germanistisches Seminar, Warburgerstr. 100, 33098
Paderborn. Tel: (05251) 60 28 77 Fax: (05251) 60 42 02 Email: cried1
@hrz.uni-paderborn.de

Vacation courses: Not available.

Passau

Verkehrsverein: Bahnhofstr. 36, 94032 Passau. Tel: (0851) 95 59 80

Jugendherberge: Oberhaus 125, 94034 Passau. Tel: (0851) 41 351 Fax: (0851)
43 709

Industrie- und Handelskammer: IHK für Niederbayern in Passau, Niebel-
ungenstr. 15, Postfach 1727, 94007 Passau. Tel: (0851) 50 70 Fax: (0851)
50 72 80 Email: ihk@passau.ihk.de

AOK: Neuburgerstr. 92, 94032 Passau. Tel: (0851) 53 020 Fax: (0851)
53 02 100

Local newspaper: Passauer Neue Presse: www.pnp.de/

Town, area and industry

Passau: This town was the site of a Roman garrison called *Castra Batava*,
whose members, *Cohors IX. Batavorum* (Ninth Batavian Cohort)
belonged to a Germanic tribe called the Batavians, who lived in this
area. The name has changed a great deal since Roman times: *Batauis
> Patavium > Pazzau >* Passau, with quite a number of intermediate
stages. The name *Batauis* means 'at the Batavians' (place)'. Passau is
one of the most southerly towns in Germany. It is the economic
centre for SE Bavaria and has a steamship link to Vienna.

Population: c. 52,000; there are *c.* 8,000 students at the university.

Position: Bavaria, on the rivers Danube (*Donau*), Inn, and Ilz, very close
to the Czech Republic and Austria.

Sights: Cathedral, churches, Baroque town centre, Oberhaus fortress.

Culture: Museums, art, music.

Industry: Brewing, tobacco, leather, optical instruments, textiles, tourism.

Twinning: GB: Dumfries; US: Hackensack

Universität Passau

94030 Passau. Tel: (0851) 50 90 Fax: (0851) 50 91 005 Web site: www. uni-passau.de

Akademisches Auslandsamt: Heuwieserstr. 1, 94032 Passau. Tel: (0851) 50 91 160 Fax: (0851) 50 91 102 Email: auslandamt@uni-passau.de

Studentenwerk: Innstr. 40, 94032 Passau. Tel: (0851) 50 91 902 Fax: (0851) 55 020

AStA: SprecherInnenrat, Innstraße 40, Nikolakloster 227/228, 94032 Passau. Tel: (0851) 50 91 970 Fax: (0851) 50 91 971 Email: sprecher innenrat@uni-passau.de

Frauenbeauftragte: Frauenbüro, Innstraße 40, Zimmer 555, Nikolakloster, 94032 Passau. Tel: (0851) 50 91 965 Fax: (0851) 50 91 966 Email: frauen01@fsuni.rz.uni-passau.de

Behindertenbeauftragte(r): Detlev Houben, Heuwieserstr. 1, 94032 Passau. Tel: (0851) 50 91 120

Computer/email access via: Rechenzentrum Universität Passau, 94030 Passau. Tel: (0851) 50 91 801 Fax: (0851) 50 91 802 Email: rz@rz. uni-passau.de

English department: Fachbereich Anglistik & Amerikanistik, Innstraße 25, 94032 Passau. Tel: (0851) 50 92 607 Fax: (0851) 50 92 857 Email: jutta.pfoerdtner@uni-passau.de

German department: Fachbereich Germanistik, Innstraße 25, 94032 Passau. Tel: (0851) 50 92 781 Fax: (0851) 50 92 203 Email: eroms@uni-passau.de

Vacation courses: Not available.

Potsdam

Verkehrsverein: Friedrich-Ebert-Str. 5, 14467 Potsdam. Tel: (0331) 29 11 00

Jugendherberge und Jugendgästehaus: Jugendgästehaus, Kluckstraße 3, 10785 Berlin Tel: (030) 26 11 097

Industrie- und Handelskammer: IHK Potsdam, Große Weinmeisterstr. 59, 14469 Potsdam. Tel: (0331) 21 591/592 Fax: (0331) 27 86 111 Email: online@potsdam.ihk.de

AOK: Friedrich-Ebert-Str. 113, Postfach 600163, 14467 Potsdam. Tel: (0331) 27 720 Fax: (0331) 27 72 229

Local newspaper: Potsdamer Neueste Nachrichten: pnn.potsdam.de/

Town, area and industry

Potsdam: The name is first mentioned in 993 CE as *Poztupimi.* It is of Slavic origin and may mean 'at the press' (as in a machine used to press things flat). Potsdam is the capital of Brandenburg. It is well known as the place where the Potsdam Agreement was signed in 1945. Despite much destruction in the Second World War, many buildings were preserved and many have been restored. The Babelsberg film studios are here, as are many scientific institutes.

Population: c. 140,000; there are *c.* 10,000 students at the university, and a further 2,000 students at other HE institutions.

Position: Very close to and closely linked with Berlin, so very much to the east of Germany and close to Poland.

Sights: Schloss Sanssouci, Schloss Charlottenhof, Dutch quarter, Baroque architecture, observatory.

Culture: Museums (including museum of film), galleries, theatre.

Industry: Locomotive building, boat-building, engineering, electronics, textiles, food processing.

Twinning: US: Sioux Falls

Universität Potsdam

Am Neuen Palais 10, 14469 Potsdam. Tel: (0331) 97 70 Fax: (0331) 97 21 63 Web site: www.uni-potsdam.de

Akademisches Auslandsamt: Komplex 1 am Neuen Palais, Am Neuen Palais 10, 14469 Potsdam. Tel: (0331) 97 71 533 Fax: (0331) 97 71 798 Email: neum@rz.uni-potsdam.de

Studentenwerk: Breite Straße 9–11, 14467 Potsdam. Tel: (0331) 37 060 Fax: (0331) 37 06 36 Email: studentenwerk@potsdam.de

AStA: Büro Neues Palais, Haus 06, 14469 Potsdam. Tel: (0331) 97 71 225 Fax: (0331) 97 71 795 Email: asta@rz.uni-potsdam.de

Frauenbeauftragte: Monika Stein, Büro der Gleichstellungsbeauftragten, 14469 Potsdam. Tel: (0331) 12 11 Fax: (0331) 97 71 338 Email: mostein @rz.uni-potsdam.de

Behindertenbeauftragte(r): Dr Katrin Becher, Am Neuen Palais 10, 14469 Potsdam. Tel: (0331) 97 72 443 Fax: (0331) 97 72 199 Email: becher @rz.uni-potsdam.de

Computer/email access via: Zentrale Einrichtung für Informationsverarbeitung und Kommunikation, Am Neuen Palais 10, 14469 Potsdam Tel: (0331) 97 71 216 Fax: (0331) 97 71 750 Email: beutke@rz.uni-potsdam.de

English department: Institut für Anglistik und Amerikanistik, Karl-

Liebknecht-Straße 24–25, 14476 Potsdam. Tel: (0331) 97 72 525
Fax: (0331) 97 72 088 Email: caroll@rz.uni-potsdam.de
German department: Institut für Germanistik, Karl-Liebknecht-Straße
24–25, 14476 Potsdam. Tel: (0331) 97 72 468 Fax: (0331) 97 72 370
Email: kiesant@rz.uni-potsdam.de
Vacation courses: August. Language, literature, *Landeskunde.*

Regensburg

Verkehrsverein: Altes Rathaus, 93047 Regensburg. Tel: (0941) 50 74 410
Jugendherberge: Wöhrdstr. 60, 93059 Regensburg. Tel: (0941) 57 402
Fax: (0941) 52 411
Industrie- und Handelskammer: IHK Regensburg, Martin-Luther-Str. 12,
Postfach 110355, 93016 Regensburg. Tel: (0941) 56 940 Email: info
@regensburg.ihk.de
AOK: Bruderwöhrdstr. 9, 93055 Regensburg. Tel: (0941) 79 60 60 Fax:
(0941) 79 60 62 12
Local newspaper: Mittelbayrische Zeituing: www.donau.zet.net/ The online
version of the newspaper calls itself *Donau-Zet-Net.*

Town, area and industry

Regensburg: The name makes it sound as though it is a town whose
weather you might want to avoid, but there is only a tenuous connection with rain, since Regensburg is at the confluence of the River
Regen with the Danube. The town was a Roman settlement called
Castra Regina, and the German name is a direct translation from it:
'the castle by the (river) Regen', the latter word coming from a word
meaning 'damp'. The town is on an ancient Celtic site which was
called something like *Radasbona*. A Roman cohort was based there
from about 80 CE. Although the town was bombed in the Second
World War, most of the medieval buildings survived more or less
unscathed.

Population: c. 141,000; there are *c.* 17,000 students at the university, with
a further 5,000 at the FH.

Position: On the Danube (*Donau*) in eastern Bavaria. Fairly close to Hof,
Ingolstadt, Munich, Nuremberg.

Sights: Cathedral, *Altstadt* (regarded as one of the most beautiful in Germany), *Patrizierhäuser* (patricians' houses), twelfth-century *Steinerne
Brücke* (Stone Bridge), architecture in general.

Culture: Many museums, theatres, art galleries.

Industry: Breweries, sugar, wood, chemicals, engineering, vehicles (BMW), electronics (Toshiba), tourism.
Twinning: GB: Aberdeen; US: Tempe

Universität Regensburg

Universitätsstr. 31, 93053 Regensburg. Tel: (0941) 94 301 Fax: (0941) 94 32 305 Web site: www.uni-regensburg.de

Akademisches Auslandsamt: Universtitätsstr. 31, 93053 Regensburg. Tel: (0941) 94 32 373 Fax: (0941) 94 33 882 Email: marianne.sedlmeier @verwaltung.uni-regensburg.de

Studentenwerk: Wohnheimverwaltung des Studentenwerks, Niederbayern-Oberpfalz, Albertus-Magnus-Str. 4, 93053 Regensburg. Tel: (0941) 94 32 201 Fax: (0941) 94 31 937

AStA: Studentischer SprecherInnenrat, Universitätsstr. 31, 93053 Regensburg. Tel: (0941) 94 32 243 Fax: (0941) 94 32 242

Frauenbeauftragte: Büro der Frauenbeauftragten, Universitätsstr. 31, 93053 Regensburg. Tel: (0941) 94 33 581 Fax: (0941) 94 32 451 Email: frauen. beauftragte@tz.uni-regensburg.de

Behindertenbeauftragte(r): Dr Tilmann Pfeiffer, Universitätsstr. 31, 93053 Regensburg. Tel: (0941) 94 33 772

Computer/email access via: Rechenzentrum am Campus, Universitätsstr. 31, 93053 Regensburg. Tel: (0941) 94 34 898 Fax: (0941) 94 34 857 Email: karl.wuerfl@rz.uni-regensburg.de

English department: Institut für Amerikanistik und Anglistik, Universitätsstr. 31, 93053 Regensburg. Tel: (0941) 94 33 477 Fax: (0941) 94 33 590 Email: udo.hebel@sprachlit.uni-regensburg.de

German department: Institut für Germanistik, Universitätsstr. 31, 93053 Regensburg. Tel: (0941) 94 33 673 Fax: (0941) 94 31 733 Email: maria. thurmair@sprachlit.uni-regensburg.de

Vacation courses: July. *Landeskunde.*

Saarbrücken

Verkehrsverein: Großherzog-Friedrich-Str. 1, 66111 Saarbrücken. Tel: (0681) 36 515

Jugendherberge: Meerwiesertalweg 31, 66123 Saarbrücken. Tel: (0681) 33 040 Fax: (0681) 37 49 11

Industrie- und Handelskammer: IHK des Saarlandes, Franz-Josef-Röder-Str. 9, Postfach 136/137, 66001 Saarbrücken. Tel: (0681) 95 200

Fax: (0681) 95 20 888 Email: info@saarland.ihk.de
AOK: Halbergstr. 1, 66121 Saarbrücken. Tel: (0681) 60 010 Fax: (0681)
60 01550/360
Local newspaper: Saarbrücker Zeitung: www.sz-newsline.de/aktion/hot.htm

Town, area and industry

Saarbrücken: The name, first mentioned in 999 CE as *Sarabruca,* derives
from the Latin for the River Saar, *Saravus,* 'something that flows' and
the bridge which spanned it at Saarbrücken. Just as a matter of interest:
Saar and *Sara* are related to the word *serum,* which is actually the
Latin for 'whey'. Saarbrücken is the capital of the Saarland and a major
industrial location, the centre of the Saar coal-mining area. Much of
the town was destroyed in the Second World War, but much has been
rebuilt or restored.

Population: c. 200,000; there are *c.* 20,000 students at the university, and
a further 3,600 at four other HE institutions.

Position: Southern Saarland, very close to the French border.

Sights: Alte Brücke, Rathaus, Schloss, churches, zoo.

Culture: Museums, galleries, theatre.

Industry: Iron, steel, engineering, vehicles, brewing, foodstuffs, printing,
optics, paper, soap, lime, cement, coal-mining.

Twinning: No formal links.

Universität des Saarlandes

Im Stadtwald, 66123 Saarbrücken. Tel: (0681) 30 20 Fax: (0681) 17 16
81 753 Web site: www.uni-saarland.de

Akademisches Auslandsamt: Gebäude 4, Postfach 151150, 66041 Saarbrücken. Tel: (0681) 30 24 487 Fax: (0681) 30 24 489 Email: aaa@univw.
uni-saarland.de

Studentenwerk: Gebäude 28, 66123 Saarbrücken. Tel: (0681) 30 22 801
Fax: (0681) 30 22 890 Email: a.oswald@stw.uni-sb.de

AStA: Postfach 151131, 66041 Saarbrücken. Tel: (0681) 30 22 900   Fax:
(0681) 30 24 324 Email: sekretariat@asta.uni-sb.de

Frauenbeauftragte: Dr Phil Bärbel Miemietz, Gebäude 31, 66123 Saarbrücken. Tel: (0681) 30 24 795 Fax: (0681) 30 24 794 Email: frauenbuero
@rz.uni-saarland.de

Behindertenbeauftragte(r): Klaus Hirschberg, Gebäude 14, 66123 Saarbrücken 66123. Tel: (0681) 30 23 022 Fax: (0681) 30 24 527 Email:
k.hirschberg@univw.uni-saarland.de

Computer/email access via: Rechenzentrum, Gebäude 36.2, 66123 Saar-

brücken. Tel: (0681) 30 22 586 Fax: (0681) 30 24 462 Email: d.neisius
@rz.uni-saarland.de

English & German departments: Angewandte Sprachwissenschaft, Postfach 151150, 66041 Saarbrücken. Tel: (0681) 30 22 501 Fax: (0681) 30
24 440 Email: aswued@rz.uni-sb.de

Vacation courses: July. Language.

Stuttgart

Verkehrsverein: i-Punkt, Königstr. 1a, 70173 Stuttgart. Tel: (0711) 22 28
240/241

Jugendherberge: Haussmannstr. 27, 70188 Stuttgart. Tel: (0711) 24 15 83

Industrie- und Handelskammer: IHK Region Stuttgart, Jägerstr. 30, 70020
Stuttgart. Tel: (0711) 20 050 Fax: (0711) 20 05 354 Email. info
@stuttgart.ihk.de

AOK: Breitscheidstr. 20, 70176 Stuttgart. Tel: (0711) 20 690 Fax: (0711)
20 69 445

Local newspapers: Stuttgarter Nachrichten: www.stuttgarter-nachrichten.de/
Stuttgarter Zeitung: www.stuttgarter-zeitung.de/ These two newspapers seem to share a site.

Town, area and industry

Stuttgart: The name is derived from the Middle High German *stuotgarte*
(stud farm), around which the city grew. Stuttgart is the capital of
Baden-Württemberg. Founded in the Middle Ages, it was the residence of the Württemberg kings. It was so badly damaged in the
Second World War that only some parts around the *Schlossplatz* have
been restored. None the less, Stuttgart has been rebuilt as a fine
modern city, metropolitan and cosmopolitan. It is situated in a valley,
so that green slopes and vineyards are visible from the town centre. It
is a highly important industrial location.

Population: c. 560,000; there are *c.* 18,000 students at the university, with
a further 11,000+ students at seven other HE institutions.

Position: Stuttgart is in the centre of Baden-Württemberg, close to the
Schwäbische Alb (Swabian Mountains) and the *Schwarzwald* (Black Forest),
also to Tübingen, Schwäbisch Hall, and various other Swabian towns.

Sights: Stiftskirche, Schloss, palaces, railway station, botanical gardens,
TV tower, mineral springs in the Bad Cannstatt suburb.

Culture: Many museums, galleries, theatres, ballet, concert hall.

Industry: Cars (Daimler-Benz, Mercedes, Porsche), engineering (Bosch), banking, publishing houses (more than 130), printing, computers (IBM Deutschland, Siemens Nixdorf, Hewlett-Packard), textiles, technology (Sony), musical instruments, furniture, optics (Kodak), foodstuffs, beer, chemicals, wine production.

Twinning: GB: Cardiff, St Helens; US: St Louis

Universität Stuttgart

Universitätsbereich, Keplerstr. 7, 70173 Stuttgart. Tel: (0711) 12 10 Fax: (0711) 12 13 500 Web site: www.uni-stuttgart.de

Akademisches Auslandsamt: Geschwister-Scholl-Str. 24, 70174 Stuttgart. Email: burger.gertrud@po.uni-stuttgart.de

Studentenwerk: Höhenstr. 10, 70736 Fellbach. Tel: (0711) 95 74 410 Fax: (0711) 95 74 400 Email: studentenwerk.sws@t-online.de

AStA: Universitätsbereich Stadtmitte, Keplerstr. 17, K11, Stock 2a, Zi. 234, 70173 Stuttgart.

Frauenbeauftragte: Prof. Dr Anna-Margarete Sändig, Mathematisches Institut A, Pfaffenwaldring 57, 70569 Stuttgart. Tel: (0711) 68 55 536 Fax: (0711) 68 55 597 Email: saendig@mathematik.uni-stuttgart.de

Behindertenbeauftragte(r): Thomas Adamek, Institut für Bioverfahrenstechnik. Tel: (0711) 68 56 475 Fax: (0711) 68 56 957 Fax: (0711) 67 87 626 Email: thomas.adamek@po.uni-stuttgart.de

Computer/email access via: Rechenzentrum Uni Stuttgart, Allmandring 30, 70550 Stuttgart. Tel: (0711) 68 55 391 Fax: (0711) 67 87 626 Email: helpdesk@rus.uni-stuttgart.de

English department: Institut für Linguistik: Anglistik, Keplerstr. 17/4b (K11), 70174 Stuttgart. Tel: (0711) 12 13 120 Fax: (0711) 12 13 122 Email: elsa.salter@po.uni-stuttgart.de

German department: Institut für Linguistik: Germanistik, Postfach 10 60 37, 70049 Stuttgart. Tel: (0711) 12 13 139 Fax: (0711) 12 13 141 Email: vikner@rus.uni-stuttgart.de

Vacation courses: August. Language and *Landeskunde.*

Trier

Verkehrsverein: An der Porta Nigra, 54292 Trier. Tel: (0651) 97 80 80
Jugendherberge: Jugendgästehaus, An der Jugendherberge 4, 54292 Trier
Tel: (0651) 14 66 20
Industrie- und Handelskammer: IHK Trier, Kornmarkt 6, Postfach 2240, 54212
Trier. Tel: (0651) 71 030 Fax: (0651) 97 77 153 Email: info @trier.ihk.de
AOK: Paulinstr. 21, 54292 Trier. Tel: (0651) 20 950 Fax: (0651) 20 95 302
Local newspaper: Trierischer Volksfreund: www.intrinet.de/

Town, area and industry

Trier: The name, first mentioned in a similar form in the tenth century
as _Triera_, is derived from the Latin word for the town's inhabitants,
the Treveri. Around the year 300 CE, it was in fact called _ad Treveros_
(with the Treveri). This version is preserved in the French name for
the town, _Trèves._ Trier is said to be the oldest town in Germany. It
was founded by the Roman emperor Augustus in 16 BCE as _Colonia
Augusta in Treveris._ There are many surviving monuments to the
Roman period, which remained more or less unscathed despite the
fact that 40 per cent of the town centre was destroyed in the Second
World War. Much has been restored, and there has also been some
modernisation.

Population: c. 100,000; there are _c._ 11,000 students at the university, with
_c._ 4,800 at other HE institutions.

Position: SW Rhineland-Palatinate, very close to the border with
Luxemburg and France, and not far from Belgium, on the Moselle.

Sights: Porta Nigra (preserved Roman gateway), amphitheatre, Roman
baths, basilica, cathedral.

Culture: Museums, galleries, opera, ballet, theatre.

Industry: Tourism, wine, tobacco, leather, foodstuffs, brewing, textiles,
tyres.

Twinning: GB: Gloucester; US: Fort Worth

Universität Trier

Universitätsring 15, 54286 Trier. Tel: (0651) 20 10 Fax: (0651) 20 14
299 Web site: www.uni-trier.de
Akademisches Auslandsamt: Universitätsring 15, 54286 Trier. Tel: (0651)
20 12 807 Fax: (0651) 20 13 914 Email: haungs@uni-trier.de
Studentenwerk: Universitätsring 12a, 54296 Trier. Tel: (0651) 20 13 560
Fax: (0651) 20 13 918 Email: studwerk@uni-trier.de

AStA: Universitätsring 12b, 54296 Trier. Tel: (0651) 20 12 116/117
Fax: (0651) 20 13 902 Email: asta@uni-trier.de

Frauenbeauftragte: Frauenbüro der Uni Trier, Universitätsring, 54286
Trier. Tel: (0651) 20 13 196 Fax: (0651) 20 13 197 Email: frauenbuero
@uni-trier.de

Behindertenbeauftragte(r): Schwerbehindertenbeauftragter Walter Ziefer,
Universitätsring 15, 54286 Trier. Tel: (0651) 20 12 259 Fax: (0651)
20 13 940 Fax: (0651) 20 13 921 Email: ziefer@uni-trier.de

Computer/email access via: Rechenzentrum, Universitätsring 15, 54286
Trier. Tel: (0651) 20 13 417 Fax: (0651) 20 13 921 Email: urt@uni-
trier.de

English department: FB 2 Anglistik, Universität Trier, Universitätsring.
54286 Trier. Tel: (0651) 20 12 277 Fax: (0651) 20 13 928 Email: strietho
@uni-trier.de

German department: FB II Germanistik, Universität Trier, Universitätsring,
54286 Trier. Tel: (0651) 20 12 324 Fax: (0651) 20 13 909 Email: gelhaus
@uni-trier.de

Vacation courses: August. Language and *Landeskunde*.

Tübingen

Verkehrsverein: Karlstr./Eberhardsbrücke, 72072 Tübingen. Tel: (07071)
91 360

Jugendherberge und Jugendgästehaus: Gartenstr. 22, 72074 Tübingen.
Tel: (07071) 23 002

Industrie- und Handelskammer: IHK Reutlingen, Hindenburgstraße 54,
Postfach 1944, 72709 Reutlingen. Tel: (07121) 20 10 Fax: (07121) 20
11 81 Email: ihk@reutlingen.ihk.de

AOK: Europastr. 4, 72072 Tübingen. Tel: (07071) 91 40 Fax: (07071) 32
643

Local newspaper: Schwäbisches Tagblatt: www.cityinfonetz.de/tagblatt/

Town, area and industry

Tübingen: In medieval times the name was *Tuingia* (1078 CE), then
Twingen, then *Tuwingen*, meaning 'people belonging to the settlement
of (someone with a name looking like) Tuwo'. The Eberhard-Karls-
Universität is one of the oldest German universities (1477), named
after the Württemberg duke, Eberhard, who founded it, and Duke
Karl-Eugen, who added his name in 1769. Tübingen is an archetypal

university town with hordes of famous alumni (e.g. Kepler the astronomer, the poets Hölderlin and Mörike, Hegel the philosopher). The town's primary industry is probably the university and its students.

Population: c. 85,000; there are c. 23,000 students at the university.

Position: Baden-Württemberg, on the River Neckar, close to Stuttgart.

Sights: Stiftskirche, university buildings, *Schloss, Altstadt.*

Culture: Theatres, music, museums.

Industry: Publishing, engineering, textiles, woodworking, paper, surgical instruments. Much trade is based on the student population.

Twinning: GB: County Durham; US: Ann Arbor

Eberhard-Karls-Universität

Wilhelmstr. 5, 72074 Tübingen. Tel: (07071) 29 0 Web site: www.uni-tuebingen.de

Akademisches Auslandsamt: Amt für Internationale Beziehungen, Wilhelmstr. 9, 72074 Tübingen. Tel: (07071) 29 72 938 Fax: (07071) 29 54 04 Email: axel.markert@uni-tuebingen.de

Studentenwerk: Wilhelmstr. 15, 72074 Tübingen. Tel: (07071) 29 73 830 Fax: (07071) 29 38 36 Email: studentenwerk@studentenwerk.uni-tuebingen.de

AStA: Wilhelmstr. 30, 72074 Tübingen. Tel: (07071) 29 72 636 Fax: (07071) 29 57 61

Frauenbeauftragte: Dr Maja Heiner, Wilhelmstr. 26, 72074 Tübingen. Tel: (07071) 29 74 958 Fax: (07071) 29 52 02 Email: frauenbuero @uni-tuebingen.de

Behindertenbeauftragte(r): Klaus Heinrich, Wilhelmstr. 30, 72074 Tübingen. Tel: (07071) 29 74 209 Fax: (07071) 29 42 09 Email: klaus. heinrich@abz.uni-tuebingen.de

Computer/email access via: Zentrum für Datenverarbeitung der Universität, Wächterstraße 76, 72074 Tübingen. Tel: (07071) 29 70 201 Fax: (07071) 29 59 12 Email: sekretariat@zdv.uni-tuebingen.de

English department: Englisches Seminar, Wilhelmstr. 50, 72074 Tübingen. Tel: (07071) 29 72 959 Fax: (07071) 29 57 60 Email: christopher. harvie@uni-tuebingen.de

German department: Deutsches Seminar, Wilhelmstr. 50, 72074 Tübingen. Tel: (07071) 29 72 372 Fax: (07071) 29 53 21 Email: juergen.hauff @uni-tuebingen.de

Vacation courses: August. Language and *Landeskunde.*

Wuppertal

Verkehrsverein: Am Döppersberg, 42103 Wuppertal. Tel: (0202) 19 433
Jugendherberge: Obere Lichtenplotzerstr. 70, 42287 Wuppertal. Tel: (0202)
  55 23 72
Industrie- und Handelskammer: IHK Wuppertal–Solingen–Remscheid, HG
  Wuppertal, Heinrich-Kamp-Platz 2, Postfach 13 01 52, 42028
  Wuppertal. Tel: (0202) 24 900 Fax: (0202) 24 90 999 Email: ihk
  @wuppertal.ihk.de
AOK: Bundesallee 265, 42103 Wuppertal. Tel: (0202) 48 20 Fax: (0202)
  48 21 00
Local newspaper: Westdeutsche Zeitung: www.wz-newsline.de/wuppertal/
  Click on *Lokales* to get to Wuppertal.

Town, area and industry

Wuppertal: Since this is a twentieth-century new town, there is no
  problem with its etymology: the name means 'valley of the Wupper
  (river)'. The *Wupper* is, however, an old name. It is mentioned in the
  eighth century as *Wippera* and is connected with a group of Germanic
  words meaning 'skip', 'swing' or 'hop', so *Wupper* is 'skipping/leaping
  water'. Wuppertal is a major industrial conurbation, which was
  created from six small towns in 1929. 50 per cent of it was destroyed
  in the Second World War; some buildings have been preserved and it
  has been rebuilt with parks and gardens.
Population: c. 385,000; there are *c.* 16,000 students at the university.
Position: North Rhine-Westphalia, south of Bochum and north of
  Solingen and Remscheid.
Sights: Famous *Schwebebahn* (monorail), zoo, much parkland despite
  industry, *Rathaus*, churches.
Culture: Museums, opera, theatre, concerts.
Industry: Chemicals, engineering, electronics, textiles, rubber, printing,
  publishing, brewing.
Twinning: GB: South Tyneside

Bergische Universität-Gesamthochschule Wuppertal

Gaußstr. 20, 42119 Wuppertal. Tel: (0202) 43 91 Fax: (0202) 43 92 901
  Web site: www.uni-wuppertal.de
Akademisches Auslandsamt: Gebäude O, Ebene 6, Raum 12, 13, Gaußstr.
  20, 42119 Wuppertal. Tel: (0202) 43 92 406
Studentenwerk: Hochschul-Sozialwerk, Max-Horkheimer-Str. 15, 42119

Wuppertal. Tel: (0202) 43 92 561 Fax: (0202) 43 92 568 Email: hsw @uni-wuppertal.de

AStA: Gebäude ME (Mensa), Ebene 4, Max-Horkheimer-Str. 15, 42119 Wuppertal. Tel: (0202) 43 49 30 Fax: (0202) 87 42 Email: asta@asta. uni-wuppertal.de

Frauenbeauftragte: Gebäude O, Ebene 11, Gaußstr. 20, 42119 Wuppertal. Tel: (0202) 43 92 308

Behindertenbeauftragte(r): Prof. Dr Ing. Jürgen Schlingensiepen, Gebäude K, Ebene 01, Gaußstr. 20, 42119 Wuppertal. Tel: (0202) 43 93 003 Fax: (0202) 43 92 039 Email: schlinge@uni-wuppertal.de

Computer/email access via: Hochschulrechenzentrum, Raum Gebäude P, Ebene 09, Gaußstr. 20, 42119 Wuppertal. Tel: (0202) 43 93 295

English department: FB 4: Anglistik/Amerikanistik, Gaußstr. 20, 42119 Wuppertal.

German department: FB 4: Germanistik, Gaußstr. 20, 42119 Wuppertal. *Vacation courses:* Not available.

Würzburg

Verkehrsverein: Congress- und Tourismuszentrale, Am Congresszentrum, 97070 Würzburg. Tel: (0931) 37 24 36 Fax: (0931) 37 36 52

Jugendherberge: DJH-Jugendgästehaus, Burkarderstr. 44, 97082 Würzburg. Tel: (0931) 42 590 Fax: (0931) 41 68 62

Industrie- und Handelskammer: IHK Würzburg-Schweinfurt, Mainaustr. 33, 97082 Würzburg. Tel: (0931) 41 940 Fax: (0931) 41 94 100 Email: info@wuerzburg.ihk.de

AOK: Kardinal-Faulhaber-Platz 1, 97070 Würzburg. Tel: (0931) 38 80 Fax: (0931) 38 82 99

Local newspaper: Mainpost: www.mainpost.de/nl2view/?ressort=ws. If you write *Mainpost* into *AltaVista*, you should find it at the fourth or fifth 'hit'.

Town, area and industry

Würzburg: It is first mentioned as *in castello Virteburch* in 704 CE. By 741 it is written as *Wirzaburg* from Old High German *wirz* (herb) and *burg* (castle), so it means 'hill or castle (where) herbs (grow)'. Würzburg is the capital of Lower Franconia (*Unterfranken*). It is the centre of the Franconian wine-growing district. 85 per cent of it was destroyed in the Second World War, but has been largely rebuilt and restored so that it retains much of its medieval appearance.

Population: c. 130,000; there are c. 20,000 students at the university, with a further 6,500 students at other HE institutions.

Position: NW Bavaria, close to the Spessart area on the River Main.

Sights: Residenz, cathedral, famous bridge over the Main, much Baroque architecture.

Culture: Museums, galleries, theatre, music.

Industry: Steel, paper, printing, electronics, leather, wood, wine, tourism.

Twinning: GB: Dundee; US: Rochester, New York

Bayrische Julius-Maximilians-Universität

Sanderring 2, 97070 Würzburg. Tel: (0931) 31–0 Fax: (0931) 31 26 00 Web site: www.uni-wuerzburg.de

Akademisches Auslandsamt: Ottostr. 16, 97070 Würzburg. Tel: (0931) 31 28 06 Fax: (0931) 31 26 03 Email: auslandsamt@zv.uni-wuerzburg.de

Studentenwerk: Am Studentenhaus, 97072 Würzburg. Tel: (0931) 80 050 Fax: (0931) 80 05 214 Email: claudia.geyer@mail.uni-wuerzburg.de

AStA: Studentenvertretung, Mensagebäude, Am Hubland, 97074 Würzburg. Tel: (0931) 88 85 818/819 Fax: (0931) 88 84 612 Email: sprecherrat@mail.uni-wuerzburg

Frauenbeauftragte: Prof. Dr Ursula Brechtgen-Manderscheid, Mathematisches Institut, Am Hubland, 97074 Würzburg. Tel: (0931) 88 85 019 Fax: (0931) 88 85 599 Email: brechtgen@mathematik.uni-wuerzburg.de

Behindertenbeauftragte(r): Martin Kroker, Zimmer 223, Sanderring, 97070 Würzburg. Tel: (0931) 31 23 71 Email: rechtsamt@zv.uni-wuerzburg.de

Computer/email access via: Rechenzentrum der Universität, Am Hubland, 97074 Würzburg. Tel: (0931) 88 85 076 Fax: (0931) 70 70 12 Email: leitung@rz.uni-wuerzburg.de

English department: Institut für englische Philologie, Am Hubland, 97074 Würzburg. Tel: (0931) 88 85 671 Fax: (0931) 88 84 615 Email: i-anglistik @mail.uni-wuerzburg.de

German department: Institut für deutsche Philologie, Am Hubland, 97074 Würzburg. Tel: (0931) 88 85 611 Fax: (0931) 88 84 616 Email: heidrun. patterson@mail.uni-wuerzburg.de

Vacation courses: Not available.

8.4 *Fachhochschulen*

Aachen

Verkehrsverein: Atrium Elisenbrunnen, Friedrich-Wilhelm-Platz, 52062
Aachen. Tel: (0241) 18 02 960
Jugendherberge: Maria-Theresia-Allee 260, 52074 Aachen. Tel: (0241) 71
101
Industrie- und Handelskammer: IHK Aachen, Theaterstr. 6–10, Postfach
650, 52007 Aachen. Tel: (0241) 44 60 0 Fax: (0241) 44 60 259 Email:
info@aachen.ihk.de
AOK: Karlshof am Markt, 52062 Aachen. Tel: (0241) 46 40 Fax: (0241)
40 36 27
Local newspapers: Aachener Nachrichten: www.an-online.de/; *Aachener
Zeitung*: www.aachener-zeitung.de/

Town, area and industry

Aachen: The name is derived from the Latin *Aquisgrani*, 'Granus's
Waters/Spa', Granus being a Celtic god. By 972 CE, the name had
been translated into a more Germanic form as *Ahha* (waters). The
town thus dates back to pre-Roman times. This was Charlemagne's
capital and the place where the Holy Roman emperors were crowned
until the Reformation. Despite much destruction in the Second
World War, much remains or was reconstructed after the war. There
is a great deal in the way of Charlemagne memorabilia. Aachen,
incidentally, has the warmest springs in Germany and is an important
Carnival centre.

Population: c. 254,000; there are *c.* 32,000 students at RWTHA, with a
further 10,200 at the FH.

Position: SE North Rhine-Westphalia. It is at the so-called *Dreiländereck*
(three country corner) – the town is on the border of both Holland
and Belgium, and it is possible to find a place just outside the town
where you can walk round in a small circle and be in three countries
in as many seconds.

Sights: Altstadt, cathedral has many treasures, many historical sites.

Culture: Museums, theatres, orchestra, galleries.

Industry: Iron, steel, machinery, foodstuffs, textiles, engineering, chemicals, glass, electronics, cosmetics, needles and pins, computers,
insurance.

Twinning: GB: Halifax; USA: Arlington

Fachhochschule Aachen

Kalverbenden 6, 52066 Aachen. Tel: (0241) 60 09 0 Fax: (0241) 6009 10
   90 Web site: www.fh-aachen.de
Akademisches Auslandsamt: Kalverbenden 6, 52066 Aachen. Tel: (0241) 60
   09 10 18/10 19/10 43 Fax: (0241) 60 09 10 90 Email: lex@fh-aachen.de
Studentenwerk: Goethestr. 3, 52072 Aachen. Tel: (0241) 88840
AStA: ASTA der FH Aachen, 52064 Aachen. Tel: (0241) 710 91
Frauenbeauftragte: Stefanstr. 58/62, 52064 Aachen. Tel: (0241) 60 09 18 09
Behindertenbeauftragte(r): Frau Birgit Malinowski, Boxgraben 100, 52064
   Aachen. Tel: (0241) 60 09 17 03 Fax: (0241) 60 09 17 30 Email:
   malinowski@fh-aachen.de
Computer/email access via: Remote Operating Center der Datenver-
   arbeitungszentrale, Goethestraße 1, 52064 Aachen. Email: kutscher
   @fh-aachen.de
English & German departments: Fachbereich Wirtschaft, Eupener Str.
   70, 52066 Aachen. Tel: 0241/60 09 19 01 Fax: 0241/60 09 22 81
   Email: ifo@fh
Vacation courses: Not available.

Flensburg

Verkehrsverein: Norderstr. 6, 24939 Flensburg. Tel: (0461) 23 090
Jugendherberge: Fichtestr. 16, 24943 Flensburg. Tel. (0461) 37 742
Industrie- und Handelskammer: IHK zu Flensburg, Heinrichstr. 28–34.
   Postfach 1942, 24909 Flensburg. Tel. (0461) 80 60 Fax: (0461) 80 61
   71 Email: ihk@flensburg.ihk.de
AOK: Helenenallee 4, 24937 Flensburg. Tel: (0461) 86 70 Fax: (0461)
   86 73 82
Local newspaper: Flensburger Tagblatt: www.shz.de/

Town, area and industry

Flensburg: The name is first mentioned in 1196 as *Flensborgh*. The first
   part of the name will be derived from an Old Danish word *flen*, the
   apex of a gable, and *aa* from Old High German *aha*, water, so that
   Flensburg means 'castle on the stretch of water with a pointy bit',
   which probably refers to a local coastal inlet of that shape. Flensburg
   is Germany's most northern port and an important naval base. The
   capital of Danish-occupied Schleswig from 1848, it became Prussian
   from 1864, and the citizens voted to remain part of Germany in 1920.

The town, which for the last days of the Third Reich harboured the government of Hitler's successor Doenitz, sustained little damage in the Second World War.

Population: c. 90,000; there are *c.* 1,700 students at the university, and a further 2,500 at the FH.

Position: Northern Schleswig-Holstein, close to the Danish border, by the Flensburger Förde, a sort of fjord.

Sights: Gabled houses, *Nikolai-Kirche* with huge Renaissance organ, *Südermarkt, Nordermarkt* (South Market, North Market).

Culture: Galleries, museums.

Industry: Shipbuilding, metalworking, paper, rum production, smoked eels, services.

Twinning: GB: Carlisle

Fachhochschule Flensburg

Kanzleistr. 91–93, 24943 Flensburg. Tel: (0461) 80 51 Fax: (0461) 80 53 00 Web site: www.fh-flensburg.de

Akademisches Auslandsamt: Kanzleistr. 91–93, 24943 Flensburg. Tel. (0461) 80 53 13 Fax: (0461) 80 55 31 Email: sachau@verw.fh-flensburg.de

Studentenwerk: Studentenwerk Schleswig-Holstein, Westring 385, 24118 Kiel. Tel. (0431) 80 54 16 Fax: (0431) 40 00 81 09 Email: studentenwerk.s-h@t-online.de

AStA: Kanzleistr. 91–93, 24943 Flensburg. Tel: (0461) 80 51 Fax: (0461) 80 53 00 Email: asta@fh-flensburg.de

Frauenbeauftragte: Jutta Gügel, Kanzleistr. 91–93, 24943 Flensburg. Tel: (0461) 80 53 83 Email: frauenbeauftragte@fh-flensburg.de

Behindertenbeauftragte(r): Reinhold Ewald, Kanzleistr. 91–93, 24943 Flensburg. Tel: (0461) 80 52 15 Email: ewald@fh-flensburg.de

Computer/email access via: Raum A 106, Kanzleistr. 91–93, 24943 Flensburg. Tel: (0461) 80 51 290 Email: support@fh-flensburg.de

English & German departments: Technikübersetzen, Kanzleistr. 91–93, 24943 Flensburg. Tel: (0461) 80 56 38 Fax: (0461) 80 57 50 Email: rammelt@fh-flensburg.de

Vacation courses: Not available.

Heilbronn

Verkehrsverein: Marktplatz (beim Rathaus), 74072 Heilbronn. Tel: (07131) 19 433 Fax: (07131) 56 33 49

Jugendherberge: Schierrmannstr. 9, 74074 Heilbronn. Tel: (07131) 17 29 61 Fax: (07131) 16 43 45

Industrie- und Handelskammer: Rosenbergstr. 8, 74072 Heilbronn. Tel: (07131) 96 770 Fax: (07131) 96 77 199 Email: info@heilbronn.ihk.de

AOK: Allee 72, 74072 Heilbronn. Tel: (07131) 63 92 66 Fax: (07131) 63 93 32

Local newspapers: Heilbronner Stimme: www.stimme.de/

Town, area and industry

Name: The derivation is an easy one, having scarcely changed since 889 CE, when it was called *Heiligbrunno*: 'holy spring'. Heilbronn has a long history, since it was built around the site of a Roman settlement. Badly damaged in the Second World War, the town has been rebuilt, with many of the historic buildings reconstructed. Of literary note: this is the Heilbronn in Kleist's *Käthchen von Heilbronn*.

Population: c. 122,000; there are *c.* 3,500 students at the *Fachhochschule*.

Position: In Baden-Württemberg, between Stuttgart and Heidelberg.

Sights: Gothic *Kilianskirche* (also original site of the *Heiligbrunno*), *Rathaus* with interesting clock, various spurious monuments to the above-mentioned *Käthchen*.

Culture: Museums, theatres, orchestra.

Industry: Electronics, foodstuffs (Knorr, Pfanni), car components, paper, printing, chemicals, salt (Südwestdeutsche Salzwerke), service industries.

Twinning: GB: Stockport, Port Talbot

Fachhochschule Heilbronn

Max-Planck-Str. 39, 74081 Heilbronn. Tel: (07131) 50 40 Fax: (07131) 25 24 70 Web site: www.fh-heilbronn.de

Akademisches Auslandsamt: Max-Planck-Str. 39, 74081 Heilbronn. Tel: (07131) 50 42 62 Fax: (07131) 57 22 98 Email: heller@fh-heilbronn.de

Studentenwerk: Studentenwerk Heidelberg, Marstallhof 1–5, 69117 Heidelberg. Tel: (06221) 54 26 40 Fax: (06221) 54 27 41 Email: gf.stw @urz.uni-heidelberg.de

AStA: Max-Planck-Str. 39, 74081 Heilbronn. Tel: (07131) 25 14 60 Email: asta@fh-heilbronn.de

Behindertenbeauftragte(r): Dr O. Grandi, Max-Planck-Str. 39, 74081 Heilbronn. Tel: (07131) 50 42 62 Fax: (07131) 25 24 70
Computer/email access via: Raum FO19, 39 Max-Planck-Str. 39, 74081 Heilbronn. Tel: (07131) 50 43 33 Fax: (07131) 25 24 70 Email: knobloch@fh-heilbronn.de
English & German departments: Professor Richard Hill, Max-Planck-Str. 39, 74081 Heilbronn. Tel: (07131) 50 42 63
Vacation courses: Not available.

Köln

Verkehrsverein: Unter Fettenhennen 19 (am Dom). Tel: (0221) 33 45
Jugendherberge: Jugendherberge Köln-Deutz, Siegesstr. 5A, 50679 Köln Tel: (0221) 81 47 11
Industrie- und Handelskammer: IHK zu Köln, Unter Sachsenhausen 10–26, 50448 Köln. Tel: (0221) 16 400 Fax: (0221) 16 40 123 Email: webmaster @ihk-koeln.de
AOK: Machabäerstr. 19–27, 50668 Köln. Tel: (0221) 94 15 760 Fax: (0221) 16 18 580
Local newspaper: *Kölner Stadt-Anzeiger*: www.ksta.de/; *Kölnische Rundschau*: www.rundschau-online.de/

Town, area and industry

Köln (Cologne): The name was originally *Colonia Claudia Ara Agrippinensium* (Settlement of Claudius Altar of Agrippa). Agrippa was the wife of Claudius and she was born here. The name was clearly felt to be a bit of a mouthful by the fourth century and was reduced to *Colonia Agrippina* and in the fifth century to *Colonia*, whence eventually *Köln*. Cologne is a major economic centre, filled with monuments to the city's Roman history. Despite the horrific devastation in the Second World War, much of the town has been restored, the bomb damage and consequent excavations revealing more and more of its Roman origins. The town is the seat of the *Bundesverfassungsschutz* (Federal Office for the Protection of the Constitution).
Population: c. 1 million; there are *c.* 63,000 students at the university, 17,000 at the FH, with a further 12,300 at five other HE institutions.
Position: On the Rhine, south of Düsseldorf, north of and very close to Bonn.
Sights: Cathedral, *Praetorium* (preserved underneath the *Rathaus*), all the

museums, mediaeval *mikvah* (Jewish ritual bath), *Altstadt*, *Gestapo* cells with preserved graffitti drawn by victims.

Culture: All the museums and galleries, philharmonic orchestra, opera, theatres. Although it is unfair to pick anything out, it has to be said that the *Römisch-Germanisches Museum* is an astonishing experience.

Industry: Banking, insurance, engineering, motor vehicles (Ford), technology, textiles, foodstuffs, brewing, printing, publishing, trade fairs, inland port, television and radio stations (*Westdeutscher Rundfunk*, *Deutschlandfunk*, *Deutsche Welle*).

Twinning: GB: Liverpool, London, Portsmouth; US: Indianopolis

Fachhochschule Köln

Mainzer Str. 5, 50678 Köln. Tel: (0221) 82 75 32 91 Fax: (0221) 82 75 33 12 Web site: www.fh-koeln.de

Akademisches Auslandsamt: Claudiusstr. 1, 50678 Köln. Tel: (0221) 82 75 31 93 Fax: (0221) 82 75 31 31 Email: reitze@hp715.zv.fh-koeln.de

Studentenwerk: Universitätsstr. 16, 50678 Köln. Tel: (0221) 94 26 50 Fax: (0221) 94 26 51 15 Email: arst1@uni-koeln.de

AStA: Betzdorfer Straße 2, 50679 Köln-Deutz. Tel: (02 21) 98 16 70 Fax: (02 21) 98 16 799 Email: bya01@mail.dvz.fh-koeln.de

Frauenbeauftragte: Frauenbüro, Raum 406, Claudiusstr. 1, 50678 Köln. Tel: (0221) 82 75 34 55 Fax: (0221) 82 75 34 55

Behindertenbeauftragte(r): Herr Olthoff, Claudiusstr. 1, 50678 Köln. Tel: (0221) 82 75 31 10 Fax: (0221) 82 75 31 85 Email: olthoff@zv.fh-koeln.de

Computer/email access via: Datenverarbeitungszentrale der FH Köln, Mainzerstr. 5, 50678 Köln. Tel: (0221) 82 75 27 32 Fax: (0221) 82 75 28 36 Email: heiser@dvz.fh-koeln.de

English & German departments: Fachbereich Sprachen, Mainzerstr. 5, 50678 Köln. Tel: (0221) 82 75 33 04 Fax: (0221) 82 75 33 12 Email: lothar.cerny@fh-koeln.de

Vacation courses: August. Language and culture.

Reutlingen

Verkehrsverein: Fremdenverkehrsamt Reutlingen, Listplatz 1, 72764 Reutlingen. Tel: (07121) 30 32 622 Fax: (07121) 33 95 90

Jugendherberge: Contact Fremdenverkehrsamt for cheap accommodation.

Industrie- und Handelskammer: IHK Reutlingen, Hindenburgstr. 54, Post-

fach 1944, 72709 Reutlingen. Tel: (07121) 20 10 Fax: (07121) 20 11
81 Email: ihk@reutlingen.ihk.de
AOK: Konrad-Adenauer-Str. 23, 72762 Reutlingen. Tel: (07121) 20 90
Fax: (07121) 20 92 15
Local newspaper: Reutlinger General-Anzeiger: www.gea.de/

Town, area and industry

Reutlingen: The name, mentioned as *Rutelingin* in 1089, means 'the
people of (someone called) Riutilo'. Reutlingen is a very important
and prosperous economic centre. Despite much destruction in the
Second World War, much has been preserved or restored.
Population: c. 100,000; there are *c.* 3,000 students at the FH, and a
further 400 at another HE institution.
Position: Central Baden-Württemberg, below *Schwäbische Alb* (Swabian
Mountains), and close to Tübingen, Stuttgart, Ulm, Black Forest.
Sights: Ancient churches, gates of old fortifications, *Fachwerkhäuser*
(half-timbered houses).
Culture: Museums, theatre.
Industry: Textiles, leather, engineering, electronics, steel.
Twinning: GB: Ellesmere Port and Neston

Hochschule für Technik und Wirtschaft

Alteburgstr. 150, 72762 Reutlingen. Tel: (07121) 27 14 56 Fax: (07121)
27 12 24 Web site: www.fh-reutlingen.de
Akademisches Auslandsamt: Alteburgstr. 150, 72762 Reutlingen. Tel: (07121)
27 14 93 Fax: (07121) 27 14 98 Email: baldur.veit@fh-reutlingen.de
Studentenwerk: Studentenwerk Tübingen, Wilhelmstr. 15, 72074 Tübingen.
Tel: (07071) 29 73 830 Fax: (07071) 29 38 36 Email: studentenwerk
@studentenwerk.uni-tuebingen.de
AStA: Alteburgstr. 150, 72762 Reutlingen. Tel: (07121) 27 14 47 Email:
dagmar.haug@fh-reutlingen.de
Frauenbeauftragte: Prof. Brigitte Scheufele, Alteburgstr. 150, 72762
Reutlingen. Tel: (07121) 27 16 69 Email: brigitte.scheufele@fh-
reutlingen.de
Behindertenbeauftragte(r): Dieter Weible, Alteburgstr. 150, 72762 Reut-
lingen. Tel: (07121) 27 14 67
Computer/email access via: Rechenzentrum der FH Reutlingen, Alteburgsstr. 150, 72762 Reutlingen. Tel: (07121) 27 13 86 Email: anton.
frick@fh-reutlingen.de
English & German departments: Prof. Dr Jens-Mogens Holm, Studien-

gangsleiter, Deutsch-englischer Studiengang, Alteburgsstr. 150, 72762
Reutlingen. Tel: (07121) 27 14 410 Fax: ()7121) 24 09 71 Email: esb
@fh-reutlingen.de
Vacation courses: Not available.

Zittau

Verkehrsverein: Rathaus, Markt 1, 02763 Zittau. Tel: (03583) 75 21 37
Jugendherberge: JH Görlitz, Goethestr. 17, 02826 Görlitz. Tel: (03581)
40 65 01
Industrie- und Handelskammer: IHK Dresden (Geschäftsstelle Zitau),
Bahnhofstr. 30, 02763 Zittau. Tel: (03583) 50 22 30 Fax: (03583) 50
22 40 Email: service@dresden.ihk.de
AOK: Hochwaldstr. 4, Postfach 122, 02753 Zittau. Tel: (03583) 774 30
Fax: (03583) 774 388
Local newspaper: Sächsische Zeitung: www.sz-online.de/news/news.
pl?ausgabe=417. When you reach the site, click on Zittau in *Regional-*
ausgaben.

Town, area and industry

Zittau: The name is probably derived from an Old Sorbian word, *zito*:
'the place of the cereals/corn'. Zittau is an industrial and cultural
centre, which survived the Second World War very much unscathed,
and is in a setting which has remained picturesque, despite the failure of
the GDR to maintain the town's fabric.
Population: c. 38,000; there are c. 2,500 students at the *Hochschule*, which
has a further campus at Görlitz with a school of engineering.
Position: Just about as east in Saxony as you can get, right on the borders
with Poland and the Czech Republic, so especially interesting for
students doing Eastern European studies.
Sights: Old churches, Rococo and Baroque architecture, *Rathaus*, observatory.
Culture: Theatres, museums, music.
Industry: Textiles, lignite (i.e. brown coal, presumably now in decline
owing to its polluting effect), machinery, chemicals, vehicles.
Twinning: US: Portsmouth

Hochschule Zittau/Görlitz

Th.-Körner-Allee 16, 02763 Zittau. Tel: (03583) 61 14 45 Fax: (03583) 61 15 24 Web site: www.htw-zittau.de

Akademisches Auslandsamt: Frau Evelyn Prinke, Haus Z III, Raum 404, 406, Theodor-Körner-Allee 16, 02763 Zittau. Tel: (03583) 61 14 45 Fax: (03583) 61 15 24 Email: prinke@htw-zittau.de

Studentenwerk: via Studentenwerk Dresden, 3. Geschoss, Zi.304, Fritz-Löffler-Str. 18, 01069 Dresden. Tel: (0351) 46 97 50 Fax: (0351) 47 18 154 Email: studwerk.dd@t-online.de

AStA: Studentenrat der HTWS, Zittau/Görlitz FH, Theodor-Körner-Allee, 02763 Zittau. Tel: (03583) 61 13 91 Email: stura@htw-zittau.de

Frauenbeauftragte: Frau Prof. Dr Drews, Goethestr. 5–8, 02763 Zittau.

Computer/email access via: Hochschulrechenzentrum, Theodor-Körner-Allee 16, 02763 Zittau. Tel: (03583) 61 13 77 Fax: (03583) 61 13 29 Email: postmaster@htw-zittau.de

English & German departments: Fachbereich Sprachen, Schwenninger Weg 1, Haus Z VII, 02763 Zittau. Tel: (03583) 61 18 41 Email: fb-sprachen@htw-zittau.de

Vacation courses: Not available.

Zwickau

Verkehrsverein: Hauptstr. 6, 08056 Zwickau. Tel: (0375) 29 37 13

Jugendherberge: Nearest: JH Chemnitz, Augustusburger Str. 369, 09127 Chemnitz. Tel: (0371) 71 331

Industrie- und Handelskammer: Regionalkammer Zwickau, Äußere Schnee-berger Str. 34, 08056 Zwickau. Tel: (0375) 81 40 Fax: (0375) 81 41 27 Email: zwickau@z.chemnitz.ihk.de

AOK: AOK Zwickau, Franz-Mehring-Str. 3–7, 08010 Zwickau. Tel: (0375) 34 90 Fax: (0375) 34 91 89

Local newspaper: Freie Presse: www.freiepresse.de/texte/region/west.html

Town, area and industry

Zwickau: The name is thought to have an Old Sorbian/Middle High German derivation: *zwic*, meaning 'a nail- or bolt- or wedge- (shaped place)'. Zwickau was the birthplace of the composer Robert Schumann, and the home of the famously non-biodegradable *Trabi* car (no longer in production since the fall of the Wall). Despite destruction during the Second World War, much of the town has been rebuilt or restored.

Population: c.110,000; there are c. 2,400 students at the FH.

Position: Western Saxony on the River Mulde, gateway to the Erz mountains.

Sights: Cathedral, *Schloss*, churches, Schumann's house, fifteenth- and sixteenth-century architecture.

Culture: Theatre, ballet, concerts, museums.

Industry: Cars (Audi, VW), coal-mining, machinery, cloth.

Twinning: No formal links.

Westsächsische Hochschule Zwickau (FH)

Dr.-Friedrichs-Ring 2A, 08056 Zwickau. Tel: (0375) 53 60 Fax: (0375) 53 61 127 Web site: www.th-zwickau.de

Akademisches Auslandsamt: Dr.-Friedrichs-Ring 2A, 08056 Zwickau. Tel: (0375) 53 61 060 Fax: (0375) 53 61 033 Email: lothar.wolf@fh-zwickau.de

Studentenwerk: Studentenwerk Chemnitz-Zwickau, Innere Schneebergstr. 23, 08056 Zwickau. Tel: (0375) 27 100 Fax: (0375) 27 10 100 Email: stuwe@fh-zwickau.de

AStA: Studentenrat der FH Zwickau, Dr.-Friedrichs-Ring 2A, 08056 Zwickau. Tel: (0375) 53 61 650 Email: studentenrat@fh-zwickau.de

Frauenbeauftragte: Prof. Dr Brigitte Mack, Dr.-Friedrichs-Ring 2A, 08056 Zwickau. Tel: (0375) 53 61 775 Fax: (0375) 53 61 749 Email: brigitte.mack@fh-zwickau.de

Behindertenbeauftragte(r): Prof. Dr Werner Stanek, Dr.-Friedrichs-Ring 2A, 08056 Zwickau. Tel: (0375) 53 61 728 Fax: (0375) 53 61 754 Email: werner.stanek@fh-zwickau.de

Computer/email access via: Hochschulrechenzentrum, Dr.-Friedrichs-Ring 2A, 08056 Zwickau. Tel: (0375) 536 12 00 Fax: (0375) 536 12 02 Email: hochschulrechenzentrum@fh-zwickau.de

English & German departments: Studiengang Languages and Business Administration (with German as a Foreign language), Dr.-Friedrichs-Ring 2A, 08056 Zwickau. Tel: (0375) 53 63 501 Fax: (0375) 53 63 56 61 Email: susanne.bleich@fh-zwickau.de

Vacation courses: At Chemnitz: September. Language and communication.

8.5 *Pädagogische Hochschulen*

Freiburg

Verkehrsverein: Rotteckring 14, 79098 Freiburg i/B. Tel: (0761) 38 81 880

Jugendherberge: Karthäuserstraße 151, 79104 Freiburg i/B. Tel: (0761) 67 656

Industrie- und Handelskammer: IHK Freiburg, Schnewlinstr. 11–13, Postfach 86079008, 79098 Freiburg im Breisgau. Tel: (0761) 38 580 Fax: (0761) 38 58 222 Email: ihk@freiburg.ihk.de

AOK: Fahnenbergplatz 6, 79089 Freiburg im Breisgau. Tel: (0761) 21 03 207 Fax: (0761) 23 281

Local newspaper: Badische Zeitung: www.badische-zeitung.de/

Town, area and industry

Freiburg im Breisgau: The name is formed from Middle High German *vri*, 'free', and *burg*, 'fortified place'. Freiburg's inhabitants were granted unusual freedoms, being allowed to elect their own vicars and sheriffs. The words *Burg* (castle) and *Berg* (hill/mountain) are related to each other, and will originally have meant 'high place' (since a high place would give a castle a commanding position). The people of Freiburg live in the *Gau* (a medieval word for 'region', a name which, incidentally, the Nazis resuscitated to indicate an administrative district in the Third Reich) where the Brisgavi (Roman auxiliary troops) had been stationed. Freiburg is a traditional old university town, founded in 1120. The medieval town centre was destroyed in the Second World War, but the cathedral was spared and there has been much reconstruction.

Population: c. 200,000; there are 23,000 students at the university, with a further 5,000+ students at other HE institutions in the city.

Position: Southern Baden-Württemberg, in the western part of the Black Forest, close to France and Switzerland.

Sights: Altstadt, Gothic Freiburger Münster, many medieval churches, towers, gateways.

Culture: Theatres, museums, art galleries.

Industry: Wine growing, timber, tourism, publishing, electronics, pharmaceuticals, banking, insurance.

Twinning: GB: Guildford; US: Madison

Pädagogische Hochschule Freiburg

Kunzenweg 21, 79117 Freiburg. Tel: (0761) 68 20 Fax: (0761) 68 24 02
Web site: www.ph-freiburg.de/
Akademisches Auslandsamt: Kunzenweg 21, 79117 Freiburg. Tel: (0761)
68 25 78 Fax: (0761) 68 25 75 Email: aaa-ph@ruf.uni-freiburg.de
Studentenwerk: Schreiberstr. 12–16, 79098 Freiburg. Tel: (0761) 21 011
Fax: (0761) 38 39 30 Email: swfr@studentenwerk.uni-freiburg.de
AStA: Kunzenweg 21, 79117 Freiburg. Tel: (0761) 68 23 70 Fax: (0761)
68 24 72 Email: asta@ph-freiburg.de
Frauenbeauftragte: Waltraut Günnel, Kunzenweg 21, 79117 Freiburg.
Tel: (0761) 68 24 17 Fax: (0761) 68 24 64
Behindertenbeauftragte(r): Olaf Kühn, Kunzenweg 21, 79117 Freiburg.
Tel: (0761) 68 23 33 Email: kuehn@ph-freiburg.de
Computer/email access via: Zentrum für Informations-und Kommuni-
kationstechnologie, Kunzenweg 21, 79117 Freiburg. Tel: (0761) 68 23
39 Fax: (0761) 68 24 86 Email: zik@ph-freiburg.de
English department: Institut für Fremdsprachen FB Englisch, Kunzen-
weg 21, 79117 Freiburg. Tel: (0761) 68 23 18 Fax: (0761) 68 24 75
Email: kfehse@t-online.de
German department: Institut für deutsche Sprache und Literatur,
Kunzenweg 21, 79117 Freiburg. Tel: (0761) 68 23 19 Fax: (0761) 68
24 75 Email: deutsch-sekretariat@ph-freiburg.de
Vacation courses: See Universität Freiburg.

Heidelberg

Verkehrsverein: Bahnhofsplatz, 69115 Heidelberg. Tel: (06221) 21 341
Jugendherberge: Tiergartenstr. 5, 69120 Heidelberg, Tel: (06221) 41 20 66
Industrie- und Handelskammer: IHK Hauptgeschäftsstelle Heidelberg,
Hans-Böckler-Str. 4, 69115 Heidelberg. Tel: (06221) 90 17 0 Fax: (06221)
90 17
AOK: Friedrich-Ebert-Platz 3, 69117 Heidelberg. Tel: (06221) 52 96 00
Fax: (06221) 52 96 99
Local newspaper: Rhein Neckar Zeitung: www.rnz.de/

Town, area and industry

Heidelberg: The name, first mentioned as *Heidelberch* in 1196, probably
refers to the bilberries (*Heidelbeeren*) growing on the hills surrounding

the town. This is the oldest university town in Germany, with many renowned scientific institutes. The university was founded in 1386 at the instigation of a Palatinate count, Ruprecht I; owing to various religious–political problems, it kept being closed down and then reopened. In 1803 it was reopened (presumably permanently now) under Grand Duke Karl-Friedrich of Baden, hence the hybrid name *Ruprecht-Karl Universität*. Heidelberg is as picturesque as its reputation suggests, thus attracting (literally) millions of tourists every year.

Population: c. 140,000; there are *c.* 28,000 students at the university, with a further 5,000+ students at other HE institutions in the city.

Position: In Baden-Württemberg, SW Germany, in the Neckar valley close to Mannheim and the Odenwald.

Sights: Altstadt, Schloss, in which there is a huge wine cask with a capacity of 185,000 litres, *Alte Brücke* (Old Bridge), *Heiliggeistkirche* (Church of the Holy Ghost), Baroque *Rathaus,* above the town the *Thingstätte,* an eerie amphitheatre built by the Nazis to hold mystical gatherings.

Culture: Theatres, museums, including the house where Ebert was born, much music.

Industry: Tourism, electronics, steel, machinery, surgical instruments, leather, tobacco, wood, building materials (*Heidelberger Zement*), pens (*Lamy*), publishing (*Springer Verlag*).

Twinning: GB: Cambridge

Pädagogische Hochschule Heidelberg

Keplerstr. 87, 69120 Heidelberg. Web site: www.ph-heidelberg.de
Akademisches Auslandsamt: Keplerstr. 87, 69120 Heidelberg. Tel: (06621) 47 75 43 Fax: (06621) 47 74 32 Email: aaa@ph-heidelberg.de
Studentenwerk: Marstallhof 1–5, 69117 Heidelberg. Tel: (06221) 54 26 40 Fax: (06221) 54 27 41 Email: gf.stw@urz.uni-heidelberg.de
AStA: Keplerstr. 87, 69120 Heidelberg. Tel: (06221) 47 71 27 Fax: (06221) 47 71 40 Email: asta@ph-heidelberg.de
Frauenbeauftragte: Margit Berg, Zimmer Z.3/203, Keplerstr. 87, 69120 Heidelberg. Tel: (06221) 47 74 51
Behindertenbeauftragte(r): Senatsbeauftragter für Behindertenfragen, Prof. Dr Günther Clörkes, Zi.Z3/008, Keplerstr. 87, 69120 Heidelberg. Tel: (06221) 47 74 34
Computer/email access via: Institut für Datenverarbeitung/Informatik, Im Neuenheimer Feld 561, 69120 Heidelberg. Tel: (06221) 47 72 82 Fax: (06221) 47 74 33 Email: ifdi@ph-heidelberg.de

English department: FB II Englisch, Im Neuenheimer Feld 561, 69120
  Heidelberg. Tel: (06221) 47 73 18 Fax: (06221) 47 74 32 Email: holweck
  @ph-heidelberg.de
German department: FB II Deutsch, Im Neuenheimer Feld 561, 69120
  Heidelberg. Tel: (06221) 47 73 10 Fax: (06221) 47 74 33 Email: deutsch
  @ph-heidelberg.de
Vacation courses: See Ruprecht-Karls-Universität.

Karlsruhe

Verkehrsverein: Verkehrsverein Karlsruhe e.V., Bahnhofplatz 6, 76137
  Karlsruhe. Tel: (0721) 35 530 Fax: (0721) 35 5343
Jugendherberge: Moltkestr. 24, 76133 Karlsruhe. Tel: (0721) 28 248
  Fax: (0721) 27 647
Industrie- und Handelskammer: IHK Karlsruhe, Lammstr. 13–17, 76133
  Karlsruhe. Tel: (0721) 17 40 Fax: (0721) 17 42 90 Email: info@karlsruhe.
  ihk.de
AOK: Kriegsstr. 41, 76133 Karlsruhe. Tel: (0721) 37 11 255 Fax: (0721)
  37 11 550
Local newspaper: Badische Neueste Nachrichten: At the time of writing,
  this newspaper does not have an online news site.

Town, area and industry

Karlsruhe: The name means exactly what it looks like: Karl-Wilhelm,
  Margrave of Baden-Durlach, made his royal residence here, so they
  called it *Carols-Ruhe* (1715), then *Carlsruhe*, finally replacing the 'C'
  with a 'K': 'Karl's Repose'. Karlsruhe is the seat of the *Bundes-
  verfassungsgericht* (Federal Constitutional Court), of the *Bundesgerichtshof*
  (Federal Supreme Court), the *Bundesanwaltschaft* (Federal Supreme
  Court Prosecutors) and the *Bundesanstalt für Wasserbau* (Federal
  Institute of Hydraulic Engineering). There was much destruction in
  the Second World War, but many buildings have been restored.
Population: c. 270,000; there are 18,000 students at the university, with a
  further 7,000+ at other HE institutions.
Position: Baden-Württemberg, on the Rhine, situated between the
  Vosges Mountains (*Vogesen*) and the Black Forest (*Schwarzwald*).
  Close to Alsace and the Palatinate.
Sights: Baroque *Schloss* with street layout fanning out from it, churches,
  orangery, architecture in general.

Culture: Many museums, galleries, theatres, music.

Industry: High-tech (Siemens), electrical products, oil refineries, machinery, bicycles, perfumes, pharmaceuticals, foodstuffs, clothing, local nuclear reactor, paper (Holtzmann), steel.

Twinning: GB: Nottingham

Pädagogische Hochschule Karlsruhe

Bismarckstr. 10, 76133 Karlsruhe. Tel: (0721) 92 5 3 Fax: (0721) 92 54 000 Web site: www.ph-karlsruhe.de

Akademisches Auslandsamt: Bismarckstr. 10, Raum I/205, 76133 Karlsruhe. Tel: (0721) 92 54 221

Studentenwerk: Adenauerring 7, 76131 Karlsruhe. Tel: (0721) 69 090 Fax: (0721) 69 09 292 Email: studentenwerk@stud.uni-karlsruhe.de

AStA: Bau I, Raum 005, Bismarckstr. 10, 76133 Karlsruhe. Tel: (0721) 92 540 75 Fax: (0721) 92 54 000 Email: asta@ph-karlsruhe.de

Frauenbeauftragte: Organisation des Frauenbüros, Gebäude II, Raum 126, Bismarckstr. 10, 76133 Karlsruhe. Tel: (0721) 92 54 100 Email: behrens @ph-karlsruhe.de

Computer/email access via: Zentrum für Informationstechnologie und Medien, Bismarckstr. 10, Gebäude II im Kellergeschoss. Tel: (0721) 92 54 400 Fax: (0721) 92 54 402 Email: behrens@ph-karlsruhe.de

English department: FB English, Bismarckstr. 10, 76133 Karlsruhe.

German department: Institut für deutsche Sprache und Literatur und ihre Didaktik (und Deutsch als Fremdsprache), Bismarckstr. 10, 76133 Karlsruhe

Vacation courses: Not available.

Ludwigsburg

Verkehrsverein: Verkehrsverein Ludwigsburg, Marktplatz 5, 71634 Ludwigsburg. Tel: (07141) 90 099

Jugendherberge: JH Ludwigsburg, Gemsenbergstr. 21, 71640 Ludwigsburg-Oststadt/Schlösslesfeld. Tel: (07141) 515

Industrie- und Handelskammer: IHK Region Stuttgart, Jägerstr. 30, Postfach 102444, 70020 Stuttgart. Tel: (0711) 20 050 Fax: (0711) 20 05 354 Email: info@stuttgart.ihk.de

AOK: AOK Ludwigsburg-Bietigheim, Gottlob-Molt-Str. 1, 71636 Ludwigsburg. Tel: (07141) 13 60 Fax: (07141) 13 63 20

Local newspaper: Stuttgarter Zeitung: www.stuttgarter-zeitung.de/news/
Click on *Region Stuttgart* to reach the Ludwigsburg local edition.

Town, area and industry

Ludwigsburg: Duke Eberhard Ludwig of Württemberg built a castle here
(1705) and the town that grew up around it was named after him:
'Ludwig's Castle'. The town is especially notable for the Baroque
castle, the largest in the country with 450+ rooms. The *Zentrale Stelle
zur Aufklärung nationalsozialistischer Gewaltverbrechen* (Central Office
for the Investigation of National Socialist Crimes of Violence) is
based here.

Population: c. 86,000; there are *c.* 4,000 students at the PH.

Position: Baden-Württemberg, on River Neckar, north of and close to
Stuttgart.

Sights: Eponymous castle with enormous gardens, palace, churches,
parks, other castles.

Culture: Museums, theatre, concerts, garden show.

Industry: Machinery, iron, organs, china, textiles.

Twinning: GB: Caerphilly; US: St Charles

Pädagogische Hochschule Ludwigsburg

Reuteallee 46, 71634 Ludwigsburg. Tel: (07141) 14 00 Fax: (07141) 14
04 34 Web site: www.ph-ludwigsburg.de

Akademisches Auslandsamt: Raum LSB 240, Reuteallee 46, 71634 Ludwigsburg. Tel: (07141) 14 03 71 Fax: (07141) 14 04 45 Email: strauch
@ph-ludwigsburg.de

Studentenwerk: 3. Obergeschoss, Zi.304, Höhenstr. 10, 70710 Fellbach.
Tel: (0711) 95 74 410 Fax: (0711) 95 74 400 Email: studentenwerk.
sws@t-online.de

AStA: Raum L013, Reuteallee 46, 71634 Ludwigsburg. Tel: (07141) 14
04 25

Frauenbeauftragte: Hauptgebäude L236, Reuteallee 46, 71634 Ludwigsburg.
Tel: (07141) 14 02 89 Email: frauenbeauftragte@ph-ludwigsburg.de

Behindertenbeauftragte(r): Dr Marie-Jose Schneider-Ballouhey, Raum
LSB 301, Reuteallee 46, 71634 Ludwigsburg. Tel: (07141) 14 03 73

Computer/email access via: Rechenzentrum der PH Ludwigsburg,
Reuteallee 46, 71634 Ludwigsburg

English department: Abteilung Englisch, LSB 304, Reuteallee 46, 71634
Ludwigsburg. Tel: (07141) 14 03 55 Email: elm.karin@ph-ludwigsburg.de

German department: Abteilung Deutsch, LSB 239, Reuteallee 46, 71634 Ludwigsburg. Tel: (07141) 14 03 55 Email: bullinger.britta@ph-ludwigsburg.de

Vacation courses: Not available.

Schwäbisch Gmünd

Verkehrsverein: Kornhausstr. 14, 73525 Schwäbisch Gmünd. Tel: (07171) 60 34 55

Jugendherberge: 14 Gartenstr. 22/2, 73525 Schwäbisch Gmünd. Tel: (07171) 23 002

Industrie- und Handelskammer: IHK Region Stuttgart, Jägerstr. 30, Postfach 10 24 44, 70020 Stuttgart. Tel: (0711) 20 050 Fax: (0711) 20 05 354 Email: info@stuttgart.ihk.de

AOK: Pfeifergäßle 21, 73525 Schwäbisch Gmünd. Tel: (07171) 60 10 Fax: (07171) 37 394

Local newspaper: Rems-Zeitung: www.rems-zeitung.de/

Town, area and industry

Schwäbisch Gmünd: The name was originally *Gamundias*, a plural form referring to the fact that in the area lie the mouths of various riverways. The adjective *Schwäbisch* (Swabian) was not added until 1934. This very old town dates back to a settlement that grew up around a monastery in the eighth century; by the twelfth century it was an administrative centre for the Hohenstaufen dynasty in Swabia. The Roman line of fortifications (*limes*) passes the northern part of the town.

Population: c. 64,000; there are *c.* 1,600 students at the PH, which is the oldest in existence (founded 1825).

Position: Eastern Baden-Württemberg, on the River Rems (hence the name of the local newspaper), east of and close to Stuttgart.

Sights: Churches, medieval fortifications, Roman baths.

Culture: Museums, music, theatre. Proximity to Stuttgart means that there is much more on offer.

Industry: Jewellery, goldsmiths, silversmiths, glassware.

Twinning: GB: Barnsley; US: Bethlehem.

Pädagogische Hochschule Schwäbisch Gmünd

Oberbettringer Str. 200, 73525 Schwäbisch Gmünd. Tel: (07171) 98 30
Fax: (07171) 98 32 12 Web site: www.ph-gmuend.de
Akademisches Auslandsamt: Oberbettringer Str. 200, 73525 Schwäbisch
Gmünd. Tel: (07171) 98 32 09 Fax: (07171) 98 33 87 Email: dagmar.
schuster@ph-gmuend.de
Studentenwerk: Studentenwerk Ulm, James-Franck-Ring 8, 89081 Ulm.
Tel: (0731) 50 23 810 Email: stw-ulm@uni-ulm.de
AStA: Sekretariat: Zimmer A017 (EG), Oberbettringer Str. 200, 73525
Schwäbisch Gmünd. Tel: (07171) 98 33 13 Fax: (07171) 98 32 12
Frauenbeauftragte: Brunhilde Kanzler, Oberbettringer Str. 200, 73525
Schwäbisch Gmünd. Tel: (07171) 98 32 28 Fax: (07171) 98 33 70
Email: brunhilde.kanzler@ph-gmuend.de
Computer/email access via: Medien- und Informationstechnisches
Zentrum, Arbeitsbereich Datenverarbeitung (DV), Oberbettringer Str.
200, 73525 Schwäbisch Gmünd. Tel: (07171) 98 33 10 Fax: (07171)
98 32 12 Email: volker.hole@ph-gmuend.de
English & German departments: Institut für Sprache und Literatur, Ober-
bettringer Str. 200, 73525 Schwäbisch Gmünd. Tel: (07171) 98 32 17
Fax: (07171) 98 33 70 Email: fb2@ph-gmuend.de
Vacation courses: Not available.

Weingarten

Verkehrsverein: Ravensburger Verkehrsverein, Kirchstr. 16, 88212
Ravensburg. Tel: (0751) 82 324
Jugendherberge: Veitsburg, 88212 Ravensburg. Tel: (0751) 25 363
Industrie- und Handelskammer: IHK Bodensee-Oberschwaben, Lindenstr.
2, Postfach 1364, 88242 Weingarten. Tel: (0751) 40 90 Fax: (0751) 40
91 59 Email: ihk@weingarten.ihk.de
AOK: Liebfrauenstr. 17, 88250 Weingarten. Tel: (0751) 56 13 50 Fax:
(0751) 56 13 599
Local newspaper: Schwäbische Zeitung: www.schwaebische-zeitung.de/

Town, area and industry

Weingarten: There is nothing esoteric about this name: it means 'vine-
yard'. This is a small town which was built round a convent, and it
has been known as Weingarten since 1053. The PH has grown out of

an institute of education, which was founded in 1949 as part of a new monastery.

Population: c. 23,000; there are c. 2,100 students at the PH.

Position: Southern Baden-Württemberg, close to Ravensburg.

Sights: Baroque convent church, medieval architecture.

Industry: Machinery, textiles, metalwork.

Twinning: No official links.

Pädagogische Hochschule Weingarten

Kirchplatz 2, 88250 Weingarten. Tel: (0751) 50 10 Fax: (0751) 50 12 00
   Web site: www.ph-weingarten.de

Akademisches Auslandsamt: Kirchplatz 2, 88250 Weingarten. Tel: (0751)
   50 18 222

Studentenwerk: Universitätsstr. 10, 78464 Konstanz. Tel: (07531) 881
   Fax: (07531) 88 39 99

AStA: AStA-Büro, St.-Longinus-Str. 1, 88250 Weingarten. Tel: (0751)
   50 12 30 Fax: (0751) 45 366

Frauenbeauftragte: Frau Zitlspelger, Kirchplatz 2, 88250 Weingarten.
   Tel: (0751) 50 10 83 09

Computer/email access via: Institut für Bildungsinformatik

English department: Fach Englisch, Fakultät II, Kirchplatz 2, 88250
   Weingarten. Tel: (0751) 50 12 11

German department: Seminar für Deutsche Sprache und Literatur,
   Fakultät II, Kirchplatz 2, 88250 Weingarten. Tel: (0751) 50 12 11

Vacation courses: Not available.

Filling in the application form
Antrag auf Zulassung zum Studium

Before you make use of the following guidelines, read through the form, and see how much you can fill in without help. It has been our experience over years that many reasons for the failure to understand things have more to do with phobic reactions to forms than with an inability to comprehend them.

The large box on the left marked with an 'x' is telling you to fill in the form properly, to enclose certain papers, which we will point out to you at the appropriate section, and points out that the form should be returned before 15 July for the winter semester and by 15 January for the summer semester – earlier than that if possible.

Have a look at the boxes on the first page of the form:

The box in the middle marked *Eingang* is for office use only, so ignore it.

The box on the right marked *Lichtbild* is for you to attach a passport photograph (it has to be stuck on properly with glue, not stapled).

The long, narrow box on the right marked *Nicht vom Bewerber auszufüllen* is for office use only.

The rest of these instructions follow the numbering system on the application form:

Antragauf Zulassung zum Studium

zum Wintersemester `--` **Sommersemester** `--`
(Nichtzutreffendes streichen!)

an der TU Muenchen
(Name der Hochschule)

Eingang

Bitte Antrag vollständig ausfüllen!   Siehe Merkblatt „Zulassungsinformationen"
Folgende Bewerbungsunterlagen beifügen:
- alle erworbenen Studienzeugnisse und Immatrikulationsbescheinigungen und Übersetzungen in amtlich beglaubigter Kopie
- Nachweise der Deutschkenntnisse

Bewerbungsfristen: 15.7. für das Wintersemester   (Anträge wenn möglich   **X**
                15.1. für das Sommersemester   früher einsenden)

Matrikel-/
Registrier-Nr.

Lichtbild

Diplom = 1 Fach   Staatsexamen = 1 Fach   Magister = 2 oder 3 Fächer – in 1.1 + 1.2 eintragen

1 Angaben zum beabsichtigten Studium

1.1 Studiengang 1. Wahl

Hauptfach
2. Hauptfach bzw. 1.
Nebenfach
2. Nebenfach

1.1.1 Für welches Fachsemester bewerben Sie sich?
Nur eintragen, wenn Anrechnungsbescheid vorliegt

1.1.2 Angestrebter Studienabschluß:
☐ Diplom   ☐ Staatsexamen   ☐ Sonstiger Studienabschluß
☐ Magister   ☐ Promotion   ☐ Kein Studienabschluß in der
                                   Bundesrepublik beabsichtigt

Falls Sie in dem von Ihnen gewünschten Studiengang nicht zugelassen werden können, für welchen anderen Studiengang bewerben Sie sich? (Möglichst nur freie Fächer)

1.2 Studiengang 2. Wahl

Hauptfach
2. Hauptfach bzw. 1.
Nebenfach
2. Nebenfach

1.2.1 Für welches Fachsemester bewerben Sie sich?
Nur eintragen, wenn Anrechnungsbescheid vorliegt

1.2.2 Angestrebter Studienabschluß:
☐ Diplom   ☐ Staatsexamen   ☐ Sonstiger Studienabschluß
☐ Magister   ☐ Promotion   ☐ Kein Studienabschluß in der
                                   Bundesrepublik beabsichtigt

2 Angaben zur Person (bitte genau wie im Paß angeben!)

Familienname

Vorname plus Namenszusätze   Geschlecht: Geburtsort:
Geburtsdatum: **männlich**
     Tag   Monat   Jahr   Staatsangehörigkeit(en)
z.B. 251156

3 Korrespondenzadresse

c/o

Straße, Hausnummer

Postleitzahl   Ort und Zustellbezirk

Telefon-Nr.   Staat

4 Heimatadresse

Straße, Hausnummer   Staat

Postleitzahl   Ort und Zustellbezirk

Nicht vom Bewerber auszufüllen!

Studiengang 1.W   FS

Studiengang 2.W   FS

Bew.Gruppe   Note

Zulassungsbesonderheit
(§ 45 Vergabe VO)

Qualifikation

Weitere Verarbeitungsvermerke

1 Title: Application for a university place.

    1.1 Your preferred course (as you almost certainly will not be wanting to take a course that restricts numbers, preference will not be a problem for you).

    If you are studying German at your home institution, then the obvious choice for *Hauptfach* will be *Deutsch*. If you are taking any subsidiary or minor subjects, you can enter those under *Nebenfach*.

    1.1.1 Which semester are you applying for – winter (WS) or summer (SS)? This is not applicable to you unless you are intending to complete your studies in Germany, which is unlikely for most students from English-speaking countries, so you can leave this box empty.

    1.1.2 Unless you are intending to complete your studies in Germany, place your cross in the box *Kein Studienabschluss in der Bundesrepublik beabsichtigt*.

    1.2 As an exchange student or one who is intending to spend just one or two semesters at a German university, you are unlikely to be applying for a course where there are restrictions on the numbers entering it. You can safely leave boxes 1.2.1 and 1.2.2 empty.

2 Personal details (to be entered as they appear in your passport). These are completely straightforward enquiries as to your name, date and place of birth, sex and nationality.

3 *Korrespondenzadresse* is the one where you can **always** be reached. Therefore, if at the time of application you are in the process of moving or are thinking of moving in the next two or three months, then give your home address and make sure that your family are aware that any correspondence from Germany might be *very* important, so that they will let you know of its arrival or forward it to you at once. This might be a little awkward, but it is far better than having a letter arrive at an address where you are no longer to be found.

4 Your home address need not be entered if it is the same as the *Korrespondenzadresse*.

5 Angabenzur Schulbildung

Alle Angaben zur Vorbildung müssen Sie belegen durch Nachweise, die diesem Antrag beizufügen sind. Keine Originale beifügen, sondern amtlich beglaubigte Kopien und amtlich beglaubigte Übersetzungen.

5.1 Angaben zur Schulbildung

Welche Berechtigung zum Universitäts-(Hochschul-)Studium haben Sie erworben?
[G.C.E. (O+A-Level), baccalaureat, Lise Diplomasi, Apolyterion, Maturität etc.?]
Genaue Originalbezeichnung des Zeugnisses:

Ort und Datum des Erwerbs:

5.2 Hochschulaufnahmeprüfung im Heimatland ☐ ja ☐ nein

bei ja: z.B.1985
Datum:
+Bezeichnung:
Bitte alle für die Aufnahme des Studiums im Heimatland erforderlichen Dokumente beifügen!

6 Angabenzum Studienkolleg und zur Feststellungsprüfung

6.1 Beantragen Sie zum kommenden Semester die Aufnahme in ein Studienkolleg für ausländische Studierende zur Vorbereitung auf die Feststellungsprüfung? ☐ ja ☐ nein

6.2 Haben Sie bereits an einer Aufnahmeprüfung zum Studienkolleg teilgenommen? ☐ ja ☐ nein

6.3 Besuchen oder besuchten Sie in der Bundesrepublik Deutschland ein **Studienkolleg?** Falls ja: Ort und Zeitraum angeben. Nachweis beifügen! ☐ ja ☐ nein

6.4 Wünschen Sie die Zulassung zur externen Feststellungsprüfung zum nächstmöglichen Termin (ohne Besuch des Studienkollegs)? ☐ ja ☐ nein

6.5 Haben Sie bereits in der Bundesrepublik Deutschland an der Feststellungsprüfung teilgenommen? Falls ja: Ergebnis, Ort und Datum der Prüfung angeben. Nachweis beifügen! Bitte unbedingt **Einzelnoten** beifügen! ☐ ja ☐ nein

7 Angabenüber bisheriges Studium

An welchen Hochschulen haben Sie bisher studiert?

Abgelegte Hochschulprüfungen – auch nicht bestandene angeben.

Staat	Name der Hochschule	Fach	Zeit-Dauer von bis	Prüfung? Welche?	Wann?	Ergebnis/ Note
1.						
2.						
3.						
4.						
5.						
6.						

Bitte alle erworben Studienzeugnisse, Immatrikulationsbescheinigungen und Übersetzungen in amtlich beglaubigter Kopie beifügen.
Wenn Sie die Anrechnung bisher erbrachter Studien-, Prüfungsleistungen bzw. Studienzeiten beantragen wollen, wenden Sie sich bitte an das zuständige Prüfungsamt.

5 Details of educational background.
   5.1 You have to be able to prove that you are qualified for entrance into a German university, so that you have to provide copies of your educational certificates, e.g. if you are from the UK, then GCSE and 'A' Level.
   You should not submit originals, but photocopies. The request for *amtlich beglaubigte Kopien* (notarised copies) does not normally apply to certificates from English-speaking countries, and you do *not* have to provide translations of certificates which are in English.
   Genaue Originalbezeichnung des Zeugnisses: Give the precise title of the certificate, e.g. General Certificate of Education, Advanced Level, or High School Diploma.
   Ort und Datum des Erwerbs: Look at your certificates, and it will tell you on them when and where you obtained the qualification.
   5.2 Answer for UK student is: *Nicht notwendig in Großbritannien - 'A' Level reicht für Zulassung aus.*

6 If you do not fulfil the requirements for entry into a German university, you can still go to a preparatory institution for a year, which would fill the holes in your educational background sufficiently for you to enter German HE thereafter. If you are already in HE, it is likely that you are going to a German university to build on the knowledge of German that you have already acquired and that you will therefore fulfil the requirements of the institution you will be visiting. In this case you can answer *nein* to all the questions in this section, which really is intended for people who are intending to come to Germany in order to do a complete course of study.

7 Details of studies thus far: simply enter the name of any HE institution at which you have studied, with subjects and dates of attendance, e.g. *University of Northumbria, GB, Deutsch, Französisch, BWL (Betriebswirtschafts-lehre), vom September 2000 bis dato.*
   The request to enclose a further sheet in case the space available for this section is insufficient is directed at anyone who might have attended more than two universities already. Unless you are a serial attender of universities, you can safely ignore this.
   You will almost certainly have already completed at least one level or year at your home institution. A suitable reply to *Prüfung? Welche?* would be, for example, *Zwischenprüfung* (intermediate examination - vague, but adequate for our purposes here), *Wann: Juni 2000, Ergebnis/Note* (result/mark): *bestanden* (passed).
   You are then reminded to enclose certificates pertaining to your studies hitherto, including a transcript of your university results. It is *not* necessary to provide translations from English.
   Anrechnung bisher erbrachter Studienleistungen: You will not need to have marks from your home institution credited to you at the German university unless you intend to remain and complete your studies in Germany. You can safely ignore this instruction.

8 Deutschkenntnisse

8.1 Haben Sie Deutsch gelernt? ☐ ja ☐ nein

Wo [   ]

Wie lange [   ]   Wie viele Stunden [   ]

Genaue Bezeichnung der Institution, genaue Bezeichnung erworbener Sprachzeugnisse, Ort und Datum des Erwerbs angeben! Nachweise beifügen! [   ]

Befinden Sie sich zur Zeit in einem Deutschkursus? ☐ ja ☐ nein
Falls ja: Genaue Bezeichnung der Institution angeben! Nachweise beifügen!

[   ]

8.2 Beantragen Sie zum kommenden Semester die Aufnahme in einen Deutschkursus der Hochschule? ☐ ja ☐ nein

(siehe Zulassungsinformationen Ziffer 8.2!)

9 Sonstige Fragen

9.1 Studienfinanzierung
Erhalten Sie ein Stipendium? Von welcher Institution? ☐ ja ☐ nein
(Nachweis beifügen!)
Andere Finanzierungsquellen (Angaben freiwillig) [   ]

9.2 Ist Ihnen in der Bundesrepublik Deutschland Asylrecht gewährt worden? ☐ ja ☐ nein
Falls ja: Nachweis beifügen!

9.3 Kann der beantragte Studiengang im Heimatland studiert werden? ☐ ja ☐ nein

9.4 Gehören Sie einer deutschsprachigen Minderheit im Ausland an? ☐ ja ☐ nein
Welcher? [   ]   Nachweis beifügen

9.5 Nehmen Sie an einem Austauschprogramm teil? ☐ ja ☐ nein
An welchem? [   ]   seit: [   ]

10 Lebenslauf (Curriculum vitae)

Tabellarische Übersicht über Ihren bisherigen Ausbildungsgang bis zum Datum der Antragstellung

Zeitangaben von – bis	

8   Knowledge of German.
     8.1 You know where you learnt your German better than we do. Your
     answer here will probably be *Schule*, unless you have learnt your German
     from scratch at your university, in which case the answer will be *Hochschule*.
        You are asked to calculate the number of classes you have had. This
     might be a little difficult to work out if you have been studying German for
     a few years: allow five per week per academic year for school and however
     many sessions you have had at university. This should be an interesting
     little test of your maths.
        Sufficient evidence of your knowledge of German should be provided by
     your school certificates and/or transcripts of your marks from your home
     university.
     8.2 You are likely to take part in a German course for foreign students if
     there is a suitable one on offer. Put your cross in the *ja* box.

9   Other questions
     9.1 Few people nowadays receive a grant. This question is really to
     ascertain that you can afford to study in Germany: usually the German
     institution will want to know how you are financing yourself. Although the
     answer to the question about other sources of income is voluntary, unless
     you have any axes to grind about your privacy, you could write here:
     Selbstfinanzierung or *Finanzierung durch die Eltern*.
     9.2 You are unlikely to be an asylum seeker, but if you **have** been seeking
     political asylum in Germany and have been granted it, you should answer *ja*
     here, otherwise clearly *nein*.
     9.3 Obviously you could study the same course in your home country, but
     language students need residence in the country of their language(s). The
     object of this question is clearly to exclude students from oversubscribed
     courses. Write *nicht zutreffend*.
     9.4 Well, are you from a German-speaking minority? If you are, you need
     to say which.
     9.5 If you are taking part in an exchange programme between your
     institution and the German one to which you are applying, this is where
     you point it out.

10   See Appendix 3 for an example of how you might write a CV.

11 Nennen Sie bitte alle deutschen Hochschulen, an denen Sie sich ebenfalls bewerben/beworben haben.

Haben Sie sich bereits in früheren Semestern an der Hochschule beworben, für die dieser   ☐ ja ☐ nein
Antrag auf Zulassung zum Studium gilt?

Wenn ja, in welchem Semester?

Für welchen Studiengang?

12 Besondere Gründe für die Wahl des Hochschulstandortes

Sollten besondere Gründe dafür sprechen, daß Sie Ihr Studium an einer bestimmten Hochschule aufnehmen, so geben Sie diese Hochschule an und nennen Sie die Gründe!

Ich versichere, daß ich alle Angaben nach bestem Wissen und Gewissen vollständig und richtig gemacht habe. Die geforderten Unterlagen (Nachweise, Belege) sind beigefügt. Mir ist bekannt, daß fahrlässig oder vorsätzlich falsche Angaben ordnungswidrig sind und zum Ausschluß vom Zulassungsverfahren oder – bei späterer Feststellung – zum Widerruf der Zulassung bzw. Einschreibung führen können.
Ich erkläre, daß ich die Zulassungsinformationen zur Kenntnis genommen habe.

Ort   Datum   Unterschrift

Die vorstehenden Angaben werden von den Hochschulen gespeichert und ausgewertet. Sie unterliegen in vollem Umfang den derzeitig geltenden Datenschutzbestimmungen.

Bearbeitungsvermerke der Hochschule.

11 You are asked to list all other German universities to which you have applied. This question is directed at students who want to do a full course at a German university. You probably want to go to this university but if you are applying to more than one, then you should indicate this here. Otherwise strike this question out. If you should have applied to this university before, then tick the *ja* box. It is highly unlikely that these questions will apply to you.

12 Particular reasons for choosing this university.

You could be sycophantic and say you want to go to this institution because you have heard the professors are so wonderful, but as no one will believe you, you should provide an answer on lines such as these:

Wegen des bestehenden Austauschprogrammes zwischen der Fachhochschule Köln und der Universität Northumbria (because of the existing exchange programme between FHK and UNN). Insert the name of your home university and the institution you intend to visit – FH Köln and University of Northumbria are meant to be examples and should not be entered if you are intending to go to Heidelberg and are from the University of Birmingham.

Keine besonderen Gründe, außer dass ich die Stadt schon kenne/ Freunde hier habe/ mein tutor mir diese Universität empfohlen hat (no particular reasons except that I know the town/have friends here/my tutor recommended this university to me).

After the twelfth section you have to swear that you have told the truth, the whole truth, and nothing but the truth. If you have provided false information and this is discovered, you can be thrown out of the university.

You then name the place of signing, date, and add your signature.

The last huge rectangle is for office use only.

You can now send off your form.

Bewerbung für einen Studentenwohnplatz

An das
Studentenwerk Heidelberg
- Anstalt des öffentlichen Rechts -
Marstallhof 1- 5
69117 Heidelberg

Druckschrift oder Schreibmaschine benutzen!
Die dem Antrag folgenden Erläuterungen beachten!

Ich bewerbe mich um ein: (Zutreffendes bitten ankreuzen) 1) ☐möbliertes ☐unmöbliertes
☐Einzelzimmer☐Zimmer im Doppelappartement☐Einzelappartement
in folgendem Wohnheim: _____
Bei Bewerbung für Wohnheime mit Internetanschluss angeben: Ich benötige einen Internet-
Anschluß ☐ nein ☐ ja (falls ja, Angabe zu PC-Besitz und studienbedingter Internet-Nutzung erforderlich)

Ich akzeptiere auch☐anderes Wohnheim☐anderen Zimmertyp2)   Ich bin Nichtraucher   ja   nein

---

gewünschter Vertragsbeginn: _____3) PKW-Besitzer☐nein☐ja - Kennz.: _____

Ich habe schon in einem Studentenwohnheim/-haus gewohnt:☐ja☐nein
wenn ja: Name des Heims:_____ Ort:_____ Wohndauer:_____

Familienname: _____Vorname(n): _____
geboren am: _____☐männlich☐weiblich   Nationalität: _____

Student(in) an☐Universität Heidelberg☐Pädagog. Hochschule   Matrikel-Nr.: _____
Studienfächer: _____ Semesterzahl: _____

Filling in the accommodation form
Bewerbung um einen Studentenwohnheimplatz

These instructions follow the numbering system on the application form:

1   Place a cross in the appropriate circle to indicate whether you would prefer a single room/apartment, a double room/apartment or a flat.

The latter is unusual. It is often best to opt for a double room, since this increases your chances of being accepted. The system in many German halls of residence means that you will still have your own bedroom, simply sharing toilet and shower facilities, even with a *Doppelzimmer*. This arrangement is likely to be cheaper and also have the advantage that you are more likely to meet other students and speak more German straight away. If you know the name of a particular hall of residence, which you may be given by your home institution, then fill that in under *Wohnheim/-haus*.

2   You are required to say whether you are prepared (*bereit*) to accept a place in another hall (*ein anderes Heim/Haus*). Placing a cross in this circle will obviously increase your chances of being allocated a place. You are usually asked nowadays, as in the sample, to say whether you are a non-smoker (*Nichtraucher*).

3   Fill in the date when you want to take up a place in hall (*gewünschter Vertragsbeginn*), which should be the first of the month in which your period of residence starts. Places in hall are usually from 1 April for the summer semester and from 1 October for the winter semester. By way of exception – this sometimes applies to *Fachhochschulen* – you could ask for a place from 1 March or 1 September.

Since it is not unusual for German students to have a car (*PKW*), you are asked to cross the circle if you have a car or leave it blank if not.

The next two lines of the form ask, first, if you have already lived in a hall of residence. You answer either *ja* or *nein*, and if this is the case, then the name of the hall, place and length of stay (*Wohndauer*).

On the next four lines you simply complete the usual details: surname, first

Heimatanschrift: 4) Straße: _____Tel.: 5) _____
Wohnort: _____(Bundes-) Land _____

Jetzige Anschrift, Straße: _____Tel.: 5) _____
Wohnort: _____ (Bundes-) Land _____ ☐
E-Mail: _____

Angaben zu den wirtschaftlichen Verhältnissen 6) - Einkommensnachweise der Eltern beifügen!
Vater: Beruf: _____Nettoeinkommen DM _____ ☐
Mutter: Beruf: _____Nettoeinkommen DM _____ ☐
Zahl der von den Eltern wirtschaftlich abhängigen Kinder: _____ ☐
Monatlich verfügbare Mittel des Bewerbers: DM _____ ☐
Herkunft: Eltern DM _____, eigene Einkünfte DM _____BAföG DM _____ ☐
Stipendien DM _____, wenn ja, welche _____

name(s), date of birth; put a cross against male (*männlich*) or female (*weiblich*) and write in your nationality (e.g. *amerikanisch*, *britisch*).

Then fill in the name of the institution at which you will be studying in Germany, a registration number (*Matrikel-Nr*), if you have one (if not, leave blank) the subject(s) (*Fächer*) you will be studying – perhaps *Deutsch als Fremdsprache* – and what semester you are in. If you have studied for two years at home before going to Germany, then write in *4*, to show that you have completed two years, or whatever is appropriate.

4   *Heimatanschrift* asks for your home address and telephone number. *Land* on the form really means which federal state (*Bundesland*) for German students, so you can either leave it blank or write in the name of the country where you normally reside. *Jetzige Anschrift* asks for your current address. It is best to give your home address, which you have already entered, so there is no need to repeat it. We suggest that you put an email address or fax number there, if you have one.

5   Here you must give a telephone number where you can be reached most easily. We suggest your home number. Just fill it in once, under the first number 5.

6   This is really aimed at German students. It is intended to gain information about your parents' income, and therefore your personal financial circumstances, as German students from a well-to-do background are less likely to be allocated a place in hall. You are also expected to indicate the source of your income. You may feel that this is nobody's business but yours. Since both you, and presumably your parents too, come from a different culture, we suggest that you look up the job title in German for each of your parents, but omit their salary (*Nettoeinkommen* DM). Make your own decision here.

Indicate the number of brothers and sisters, if you have any, who are financially dependent on your parents.

Next you are asked how much money (in DM) you normally have at your disposal (*monatlich verfügbare Mittel*). It would be sensible to fill in a figure of between DM 1,300 and 1,600 per month; less than that (at the time of writing) might suggest to the German authorities that you will not have enough money to support yourself (and you will *not* get any financial support from them); a lot more than that will give them the impression that you have sufficient funds to afford private accommodation. If you write in an amount as high as DM 5,000, for example, you are unlikely to be offered a place in hall! Under source of income (*Herkunft*), which can be parental (*Eltern*), your own earned income (*eigene Einkünfte*), *BaFöG* (state grant for German students, so definitely not applicable) and *Stipendien* (grants) you should enter amounts which in total correspond with what you have entered under *monatlich verfügbare Mittel*.

Mitwohnen soll 7) Familienname: _____ Vorname: _____
geboren am: _____ Nationalität: _____

Besondere Begründung des Antrags: 8) _____

_____ ☐

_____

Die Speicherung und Verarbeitung der grau unterlegten Daten erfolgt gem § 12 LDSG.
Unvollständige Anträge führen zur Ablehnung! Bitte Ziff. 6 und 9 der Erläuterungen beachten.

Ich versichere, alle Angaben wahrheitsgemäß nach bestem Wissen und Gewissen gemacht zu haben. (Bei wissentlich falschen Angaben erfolgt keine Aufnahme bzw. fristlose Kündigung!)

Ort/Datum: _____ Unterschrift _____ ☐

Bitte fügen Sie Ihrer Bewerbung einen mit DM 1,10 sowie einen weiteren mit DM 3,-- (DIN A 5) frankierten Rückumschlag bei!

7   *Mitwohnen soll* (the following person will be sharing the accommodation with me) is a reference to a partner/spouse, which most likely will not apply to you, but if you do intend to bring a partner, then that should be indicated here.

8   Special reason for your application. Enter *Austauschprogramm* (exchange programme), if that is the case – otherwise leave blank.

Finally you are informed (the words underlined at the bottom) that the form will not be processed without proof of your right to study in Germany, a curriculum vitae and a photograph.

Finally you have to sign at the bottom to say that you have completed the form to the best of your knowledge and with a clear conscience. On the bottom left you write the place where and the date when you are signing, e.g. *Nottingham, den 5. Mai 2001*, and sign on the bottom right.

Curriculum vitae

A fictitious name, address and details have been used to give an example of a typical CV (curriculum vitae).

Lebenslauf

Persönliche Daten

Familienname:	Jones
Vorname(n):	Helen Sarah
Adresse:	16 Linfield Close
	Coventry
	CV3 7FB
Tel:	01203 641 203
Email:	helenjones@hotmail.com
Geburtsdatum:	den 15. April 1979
Ort:	Stockport, Cheshire, GB
Staatsangehörigkeit:	britisch
Familienstand:	ledig

Schulbildung: 1984–1990: North Felton Primary School
1990–1997: Heatonside High School
A levels (Abitur): 06/1997: Deutsch, Geschichte, Business (BWL)

Studium (bis dato): 1997– : University of Northumbria at Newcastle
07/1998: BA erstes Jahr: Deutsch, Französisch mit Nebenfach Wirtschaftswissenschaften – bestanden
07/1999: BA zweites Jahr: Deutsch, Französisch mit Nebenfach Marketing – bestanden

Berufspraxis: Fremdsprachensekretärin bei Eckart u. Sohn GmbH, 50670 Köln, Sommer 1996. EDV Textverarbeitung

Sprachkenntnisse:	Englisch (Muttersprache) Deutsch (sehr gut: fließend in Wort und Schrift) Französisch (sehr gut: fließend in Wort und Schrift) Spanisch (Grundkenntnisse)
Sonstige Fähigkeiten:	Führerschein. Vier Auslandsaufenthalte in Deutschland u. Frankreich
Hobbys:	Sport (Schwimmen, Tischtennis, Turnen), Kino, Kochen

Appendix IV
Letter of application

Helen Jones

16 Linfield Close
Coventry
CV3 7FB

den 10. April 2001

Personalabteilung
Schulz und Hartmann AG
Hauptstr. 35
D- 41225 Düsseldorf
Germany

Betr.: Bewerbung um ein Praktikum

Sehr geehrte Damen/Herren,

ich bin Sprachstudentin an einer englischen Hochschule und möchte mich um eine Stelle in Ihrem Haus bewerben. Wäre es möglich, bei Ihrer Firma entweder ein sechsmonatiges oder ein zwölfmonatiges Praktikum zu absolvieren? Ich möchte gern meine Sprachkenntnisse als Übersetzerin (Deutsch–Englisch oder Französisch–Englisch) anwenden oder auf einem anderen relevanten Gebiet arbeiten und ein halbes oder ganzes Jahr Berufserfahrung in der BRD sammeln. Wie Sie aus meinem beigefügten Lebenslauf entnehmen können, ist meine Muttersprache Englisch. Seit zwei Jahren studiere ich moderne Sprachen mit Schwerpunkt Wirtschaft auf der Universität Northumbria in Newcastle in Nordostengland.

Falls es eine Möglichkeit für mich gibt, wäre ich ab September oder Oktober einsetzbar.

Ich freue mich auf eine Antwort von Ihnen.

Mit freundlichen Grüßen,

Helen Jones

Anlagen:
Lebenslauf
3 Zeugnisabschriften

Appendix V
Useful addresses

General

Botschaft der Bundesrepublik Deutschland/Embassy of the FRG, 23 Belgrave
    Square, London, SW1X 8PZ
    Tel: (0171) 235 5033 Fax: (0171) 235 0609
    Informationszentrum Fax: (0171) 824 1350

Deutsche Zentrale für Tourismus/German National Tourist Office, Nightingale
    House, 65 Curzon Street, London, W1Y 7PE
    Tel: (0171) 495 3990 Fax: (0171) 495 6129

DER Travel Service – Deutsches Reisebüro, 18 Conduit Street, London, W1R 9TD
    Tel: (0207) 290 1111 Fax: (0207) 629 7501
    Email: sales@dertravel.co.uk

German language and culture

Goethe-Institut, 50 Princes Gate, Exhibition Road, London, SW7 2PH
    Tel: (0171) 411 3400 Fax: (0171) 581 0974

Also see 4.1.6 for Goethe-Institut website, which gives details of institutes
worldwide and the language courses they run.

Deutscher Akademischer Austauschdienst e.V. (DAAD), Kennedyallee 50, 53175
    Bonn
    Tel: (0228) 88 20 Fax: (0228) 88 24 44

DAAD (London), 34 Belgrave Square, London, SW1X 8QB
    Tel: (0207) 235 1736 Fax: (0207) 235 9602
    Email: info@daad.org.uk

German Academic Exchange Service, 950 Third Avenue, 19th Floor, New York, NY 10022, USA
Tel: 0212 758 32 23 Fax: 0212 755 57 80
Email: daadny@daad.org

The DAAD publishes a brochure detailing all summer courses run at German HEIs.

Working in Germany

Zentralstelle für Arbeitsvermittlung der Bundesanstalt für Arbeit/Auslandsabteilung, Postfach 17 05 45, Feuerbachstr. 42–46, 60079 Frankfurt am Main
Tel: (069) 71 110 Fax: (069) 71 11 555

Anglo-Continental Au pairs Placement Agency, 21 Amesbury Crescent, Hove, BN3 5RD
Tel: (01273) 705959

Solihull Au Pair and Nanny agency, 1565 Stratford Rd, Hall Green, Birmingham, B28 9JA
Tel: 0121 733 6444 Fax: 0121 733 6555
Email: solihull@100s-aupairs.co.uk

Au Pair International, Dürenstraße 3, 53173 Bonn
Tel: (0228) 36 70 215 Fax: (0228) 36 70 216

The Federation of Recruitment and Employment Services (FRES), 36–38 Mortimer Street, London, W1N 7RB
Tel: (0207) 323 4300 Fax: (0207) 255 2878

Verein für Internationale Jugendarbeit, 39 Craven Road, London. W2 3BX
Tel: (0171) 723 0216

Voluntary work

IBG, Schlosserstraße 28, 70180 Stuttgart
Tel: (0711) 64 91 128 Fax: (0711) 64 09 867.

Internationale Jugendgemeinschaftsdienste, Kaiserstraße 43, 53113 Bonn
Tel: (0228) 22 80 011 Fax: (0228) 22 80 024

Vereinigung Junger Freiwilliger e.V., Hans-Otto-Str. 7, 0407 Berlin
Tel: (030) 42 85 06 03 Fax: (030) 42 85 06 04

Assistantships

Information about teaching assistantships for UK citizens is obtainable from:

Central Bureau for Educational Visits and Exchanges, Seynour Mews House,
  Seymour Mews, London, W1H 9PE
  Tel: (0171) 486 5101 Fax: (0171) 935 5741

Information about teaching assistantships for US citizens is obtainable from:

Institute of International Education

  809 United Nations Plaza, New York, NY 10017-3580

  401 N. Wabash Ave, Chicago, IL 60611-3580

  700 Broadway, Denver, CO 80203-3439

  515 Post Oak Blvd, Houston, TX 77027-9407

  41 Sutter St, San Francisco, CA 94104-4903

Embassies

British and US embassies and consulates in the Federal Republic (you may need
these if your passport expires during your residence, or if, heaven forefend, you
should lose it):

British Embassy, Friedrich-Ebert-Allee 77, 53113 Bonn
  Tel: (0228) 91 670 Fax: (0228) 91 67 331

British Consulate-General, Yorckstr. 19, 40476 Düsseldorf
  Tel: (0211) 94 480 Fax: (0211) 48 81 90

British Consulate-General, Triton House, Bockenheimer Landstr. 42, 60323
  Frankfurt am Main
  Tel: (069) 17 00 020 Fax: (069) 72 95 53

British Consulate-General, Harvesterhude Weg 8a, 20148 Hamburg
  Tel: (040) 44 80 320 Fax: (040) 41 07 259

British Consulate-General, Bürkleinstr. 10, 80538 München
  Tel: (089) 21 10 90 Fax: (089) 21 10 91 44

British Consulate-General, Breite Str. 3, 70173 Stuttgart
  Tel: (0711) 16 26 90 Fax: (0711) 16 26 930

British Consulate-General, Berliner Allee 5, 30175 Hannover
  Tel: (0511) 99 19 100 Fax: (0511) 99 19 115

British Consulate, Herrlichkeiten 6, Postfach 10 38 60, 28199 Bremen
Tel: (0421) 59 090

British Consulate, Buchenstr. 4, 72525 Gundelfingen
Tel: (0761) 58 31 17

British Consulate, Maklerstr. 1, 24159 Kiel
Tel: (0431) 33 19 71 Fax: (0431) 35 395

British Consulate, Maxfeldstr. 3, 90409 Nürnberg
Tel: (0911) 36 09 522 Fax: (0911) 36 09 861

US Embassy, Deichmanns Aue 29, 53179 Bonn
Tel: (0228) 33 91 Fax: (0228) 33 27 12

US Embassy Office, Neustädtische Kirchstrasse 4–5, 10117 Berlin
Tel: (030)   23 85 174

Consular Section: Clayallee 170, 14169 Berlin
Tel: (030) 83 29 233 Fax: (030) 83 14 926

US Consulate, Kennedydamm 15–17, 40476 Düsseldorf
Tel: (0211) 47 06 123 Fax: (0211) 43 14 48

US Consulate, Siesmayerstrasse 21, 60323 Frankfurt
Tel: (069) 75 350 Fax: (069) 75 35 23 04

US Consulate, Alsterufer 27/28, 20354 Hamburg
Tel: (040) 41 17 13 51 Fax: (040) 44 30 04

US Consulate, Wilhelm-Seyfferth-Strasse 4, 04107 Leipzig
Tel: (0341) 21 38 418 Fax: (0341) 21 38 417

US Consulate, Koeniginstrasse 5, 80539 Munich
Tel: (089) 28 88 722 Fax: (089) 28 09 998

Austrian and Swiss contact addresses:

Austrian Embassy, 18 Belgrave Mews West, London, SW1X 8HU
Tel: (0207) 235 3731 Fax: (0207) 344 0292
Email: embassy@austria.org.uk

Austrian Consulate General, 31 East 69th Street, NY 10021
Tel: (0212) 737 64 00 Fax: (0212) 58 51 992
Email: austroko@interport.net

Austrian Embassy, 3524 International Court NW, 20008 Washington
Tel: (0202) 895 6700 Fax: (0202) 895 6750
Email: obwascon@sysnet.net

Swiss Embassy, 16–18 Montagu Place, London, W1H 2BQ
Tel: (0207) 616 6000 Fax: (0207) 724 7001
Email: vertretung@lon.rep.admin.ch

Embassy of Switzerland, 2900 Cathedral Avenue NW, 20008 Washington DC
    Tel: (0202) 745 7900 Fax: (0202) 387 2564
    Email: vertretung@was.rep.admin.ch

Bibliography

AOK-Adressenverzeichnis, (1998), Remagen, AOK Verlag.

Berger, D. (1993), *Geographische Namen in Deutschland*, Mannheim, Duden Verlag.

Bode, Christian, Werner Becker and Rainer Kloat (eds) (1995), *Universitäten in Deutschland Universities in Germany*, Prestel.

Britannica. URL: www.britannica.com/ [April/May 2000].

Collier, I. (1998), *Live and Work in Germany*, 2nd edn., Oxford, Vacation Work.

Court, A. (ed.) (1996), *Baedeker Germany*, 2nd edn. in English, Basingstoke, Automobile Association.

Cousins, R., R. Hallmark and I. Pickup (1994), *Studying and Working in France*, Manchester University Press.

Der Brockhaus multimedial CD-ROM (1998), Mannheim, F. A. Brockhaus AG.

Herrmann, D. and A. Verse-Herrmann (1998), *Studieren, aber wo?*, Frankfurt am Main, Eichborn.

James, P. (ed.) (1998), *Modern Germany*, London, Routledge.

Klippel, Friederike (1993), *Keep Talking*, 11th edn., Cambridge, Cambridge University Press.

McDougal, Rosamund (2000), *The Gap-year Guidebook 2001: 2001/2002*, London, Peridot Press.

McLachlan, Gordon (1998), *Germany, The Rough Guide*, London, Rough Guides/ Penguin.

Mudra, S. (1996), *Leben und Studieren in Deutschland*, Bonn, Deutscher Akademischer Austauschdienst (DAAD).

Sekretariat der Ständigen Konferenz der Kultusminister der Länder der BRD (herausgegeben) (1997), *Das Bildungswesen in der BRD. Kompetenzen – Strukturen – Bildungswege*, Luchterhand Verlag.

Theato, G. (1997), *Adressbuch Deutschland*, 4th edn., München, Wilhelm Heyne Verlag.

Further reading

Aktuell 2001 (2000), Dortmund, Harenberg Lekikon Verlag.

Fischer Weltalmanach (2000), Frankfurt am Main, Fischer Taschenbuch Verlag.

Gros, J. and M. Glaub (1999), *Faktenlexikon Deutschland*, München, Wilhelm Heyne Verlag.

Harenberg (2000), Dortmund, Lexikon Verlag.

Jeffrey, C. and R. Whittle (eds) (1997), *Germany Today: A Student's Dictionary*, London, Arnold.

Sandford, J (ed.) (1999), *Encyclopedia of Contemporary German Culture*, London, Routledge.

Tatsachen über Deutschland (2001), Frankfurt am Main, Societäts-Verlag.

Index